CIRQUE

A Literary Journal for the North Pacific Rim

Volume 12, No. 1

Anchorage, Alaska

Cover Photo Credit: Tami Phelps, "Grounded"
Table of Contents Photo Credit: Daniela Naomi Molnar, "Web 4"

Design and composition: Signe Nichols

ISBN: 9798793424530
Independently Published
ISSN 2152-4610 (online)

Published by

CIRQUE PRESS

Anchorage, Alaska

www.cirquejournal.com

cirquejournal@gmail.com

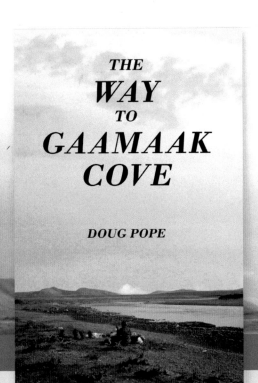

THE WAY TO GAAMAAK COVE
DOUG POPE
Available on Amazon.com

CIRQUE PRESS

—— PRAISE FOR THE WAY TO GAAMAAK COVE ——

Doug Pope writes about the Alaskan backcountry better than any writer I've ever read. **The Way to Gaamaak Cove** is more than just a great adventure, it is coming-of-middle-age in which one man confronts life's big questions, reevaluates his priorities, and discovers the biggest adventure of all—love.

—Jonathan Evison, author of *All About Lulu, West of Here,* and *The Revised Fundamentals of Caregiving*

In **The Way to Gaamaak Cove,** Doug Pope asks himself, "Is love your greatest risk or is risk your greatest love?" The answer emerges as he chronicles the exhilaration, tribulations, and serenity of wilderness travel. What makes this book so distinctive is how beautifully Pope ranges beyond the usual tales of Alaska adventure to reveal the story of a man who discovers his truest self with the woman who shares so many of these journeys. In language spare and affecting, these accounts overlap and braid and eddy out, illuminated by a rare vulnerability and a keep attentiveness to the moments that add up to a life filled with meaning.

—Sherry Simpson, author of *Dominion of Bears: Living With Wildlife in Alaska, The Accidental Explorer: Wayfinding in Alaska,* and *The Way Winter Comes: Alaska Series*

—— ABOUT THE AUTHOR ——

Doug Pope was born and raised in Interior Alaska. When he was twelve, after spending a winter night on a bed of spruce boughs in an army surplus sleeping bag, he read Jack London's *To Build A Fire*. His first non-fiction story, published when he was in high school, was set in a drafty trapper's shelter while four friends struggled to feed a fire at forty-five below. His writings have appeared in *Alpinist, American Alpine Journal, Alaska Dispatch, Cirque, A Literary Journal of the Pacific North Rim,* and the *Fairbanks Daily News-Miner,* and his writings and photos have appeared in the *Anchorage Daily News* and the *Anchorage Press*.

He lives in Hope, Alaska with his wife Beth.

CIRQUE PRESS

FORTHCOMING FROM CIRQUE PRESS

"This memoir is like no other book I have read. It will entertain you as it crushes you." – MARTHA AMORE

Matt Caprioli was born in California and raised in Alaska. He holds an MFA in creative writing from Hunter College, where he was a Hertog Fellow. His fiction and essays have appeared in *Newtown Literary*, *Opossum*, *Best Gay Stories 2017*, and *Chicken Soup for the Soul*. His story on moving to New York is featured in the Netflix docuseries Worn Stories. He teaches English literature and writing at Lehman College in New York City.

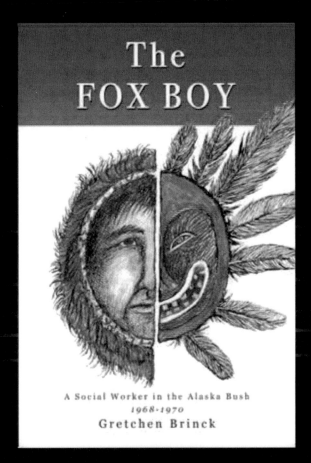
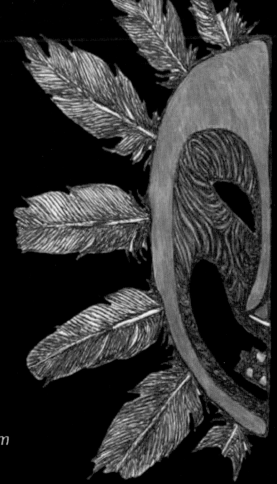

MY LIFE IN POEMS SO FAR
"STICKS AND STONES"
by Hamish Todd

~~~

Fall Frivolities

A low wind has picked up
A group of leaves...
They are brown
And purple and yellow
And orange
Spade-shaped and
Kinda round too
They skip and bounce
And roll along
Like a group of teenage
Girls coming from hearing
Or going towards
Some good news
Or maybe just girls
Together, having fun
Unencumbered
Unmolested
Unobserved
Making their way home
On a clear fall day
After school.

Warm words and breath in my ears and on my neck, your delicate tongue and lips at play. My senses are full of nothing but Woman.
From "Androgyny"

The wind blew and his olive skin smelled of rosemary and the sea
And I tried to speak but he bade me to shhhhhh, "Be still.'
In the morning
I woke refreshed
School girl blue in a Catholic dress
Knowing I'd had God in my mouth
I'd had God in my mouth
I'd had God in my mouth, like bread
From "Strange Salvation"

APPORTIONING THE LIGHT

BY ALASKAN POET KAREN TSCHANNEN

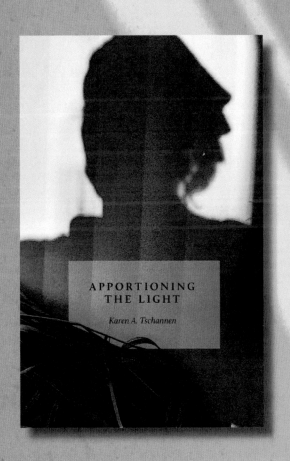

Poems so compressed the page itself trembles. So brave, in dark places, the reader clutches the poet's sure hand. *Apportioning the Light* shines. It shines.

AVAILABLE AT AMAZON OR BY EMAIL:
cirquejournal@gmail.com, $16 - CIRQUE PRESS
Sandra Kleven & Michael Burwell, CIRQUE Publishers

"A life lived to its fullest, a craft perfected so that it seems seamless, the highest compliment I can give to any writer. I read it from its beginning to its end without putting it down. Kudos to Cirque for publishing *Apportioning the Light.*"

– TOM SEXTON, ALASKA POET LAUREATE

CIRQUE PRESS

Karen Tschannen has been published in *Alaska Quarterly Review, Ice-Floe, PNW Poets and Artists Calendar(s), North of Eden* (Loose Affiliation Press), *The Sky's Own Light* (Minotaur Press), *Crosscurrents North, Cirque,* and other publications. Tschannen was nominated for a Pushcart Prize in 2016. Her perceptive verse is notable for the care taken with language in both the sound of a phrase and the appearance on the page.

THE COLLECTION

CIRQUE PRESS

ALASKA'S #1
LITERARY PUBLISHER
Established in 2018
to promote fine writing from
Alaska **and** the Northwest

Dan Branch, "ignorant but lucky," turned what began as a one-year lawyering commitment in Bethel, Alaska into a lifetime of learning, adventure, compassion, and reflection upon what makes a "good" life. — *Nancy Lord*
$15

Fish the Dead Water Hard
by Eric Heyne
These poems appear for us like cairns in a dark wood and we read them with delight and curiosity.
— *Emily Wall* $15

Dale Champlin

The magic of Dale Champlin's exuberant narrative, like Callie herself, is impossible to tie down. Beyond a braided story that will buckle you, the cascade of poems reveals a sensuous and hard, lonely and austere landscape. —*John Morrison*
$15

Out There in the Out There
McDonnell's stories are forceful, tender, violent, funny, and thought-provoking.
— *Monica Devine*
$15

One Headlight,
by Matt Caprioli
Like no other book...it will entertain you as it crushes you .
— *Martha Amore* $18

November Reconsidered
Marc Janssen's satire takes a lyric yet steely look at a market's cereal aisle, an eighth grade English class, a Toyota dealership, a California mall on Black Friday, a Happy Hour at Charlie Browns. Although he never flinches from the dark realities of life, Janssen also gives us moments of assuaging respite.
-- *Paulann Peterson*
$15

In their innocence, young children are at once naïve and brilliantly perceptive.

Miss Tami, Is Today Tomorrow? Kindergarten in Alaska: Stories for Grown-Ups.
By Tami Phelps
Illustrated by Tammy Murray $20

Baby Abe: A Lullably
These verses from Ann Chandonnes, imagine scenes from Abraham Lincoln's life, from his 1809 winter arrival in the world to his third birthday (1812). $15

CIRQUE PRESS
More Poetry

THE LURE OF IMPERMANENCE
Poems
Carey Taylor

The Lure of Impermanence by Carey Taylor. These poems, firmly rooted in the Pacific Northwest, flow with clearly defined imagistic lines and understatement.
— *Christianne Balk*
$15

Silty Water People, by Vivian Faith Prescott, is a collection of poems exploring the effects of assimilation on contemporary Tlingit/Scandinavian families in Wrangell, a small island community in Southeast Alaska.
$15

Silty Water People
Poems by Vivian Faith Prescott

Echolocation by Kristin Berger. In a time of diminishing truth and light, this book locates beauty and holds space for its returning.
— *Annie Lighthart* $15

ECHOLOCATION
POEMS
Kristin Berger

APPORTIONING THE LIGHT
Karen A. Tschannen

Karen Tschannen

Apportioning the Light, Karen Tschannen
A life lived to its fullest, a craft perfected so that it seems seamless, the highest compliment I can give to any writer.
— *Tom Sexton*

Wassilie's poems are a wellspring of keen observations, written purely from the heart, with a sense of deep time and connection to place.
— *Kathleen Tarr*
$15

The Dream That Is Childhood
A Memoir in Verse
SANDRA WASSILIE

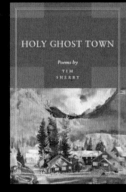

HOLY GHOST TOWN
Poems by TIM SHERRY

Holy Ghost Town is a remarkable book-length evocation of a very special place. In the genre of place writing, it compares to "Paterson" by William Carlos Williams. —*Derek Sheffield*
$15

Lily is Leaving
Poems by Leslie A. Fried

Poet, Leslie Fried is an archeologist of the soul, digging through the fractured histories of ancestors, and her own past
— *Tonja Woelber*
$15

Athabaskan Fractal
POEMS OF THE FAR NORTH
KARLA LINN MERRIFIELD

Athabaskan Fractal: Poems of the Far North, by Karla Linn Merrifield
In poems of intimacy and celebration, elegy and generous mythologizing, Karla Linn Merrifield's new book is teeming with the 'minute particulars' of her Alaskan travels.
—*Ralph Black* $25

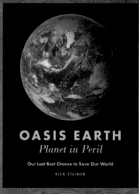

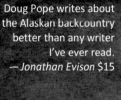
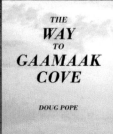

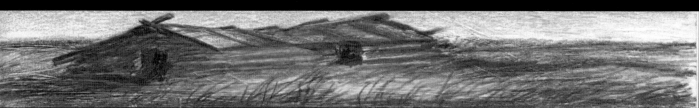

Cirque
A Literary Journal for the North Pacific Rim

CIRQUE PRESS

Michael Burwell

CIRQUE was stablished in 2008 by Michael Burwell to give writers and artists of the region more opportunities to publish their work. Issue #23 was published in December of 2021.

Sandra Kleven joined *Cirque*, in 2011, and seven years later, they founded Cirque Press.

Karen Tschannen's *Apportioning the Light* was the first book published by Cirque Press.

Cynthia Steele serves as Associate Editor and Paul Haeder is a regular contributor and collaborator.

Cynthia Steele

Sandra Kleven

Karen Tschannen

Paul Haeder

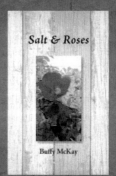

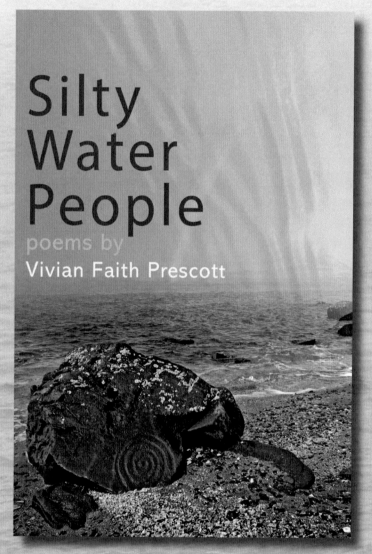

49 Writers

Creativity | Craft | Culture | Community | Catalyst

Our Vision:
A vibrant community of diverse Alaskan writers of all levels
and ages, coming together to find and share our voices.

Our Core Purpose:
Engaging, empowering, inspiring and expanding
a statewide community of Alaskan writers.

We rely on member support to offer dynamic
programming statewide:
Free Public Readings with Acclaimed Authors
Classes & Workshops to Hone Your Skills
Generative Retreats in Beautiful Places to Foster Your Work
A Weekly Newsletter & Blog to Help You Stay Connected
A Community of Shared Support

49 Writers

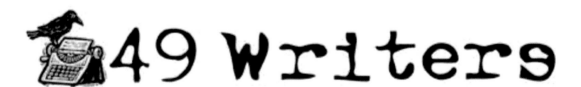

Please Join or Renew Today!
www.49writers.org/join

Reverberations from Fukushima

50 JAPANESE POETS SPEAK OUT

SECOND EDITION

EDITED BY LEAH STENSON

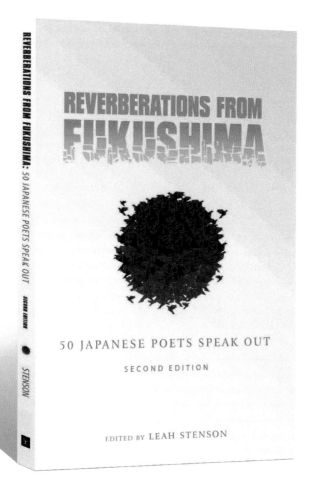

FUKUSHIMA: Ten Years After

This anthology conveys the enormity of Fukushima, the first nuclear disaster of the 21 st Century, on both the environmental and human scale. Contributions by Nobel Peace Prize nominee Dr. Helen Caldicott, Fairewinds Energy Education founder Maggie Gundersen, and professor emerita Dr. Norma Field discuss the Fukushima nuclear disaster in the context of social, political, and environmental concerns. Poems by 50 Japanese poets portray the disaster from a personal perspective, including prophetic visions of a nuclear future, the plight of nuclear refugees, the relationship of exploiters and the exploited in Japan's nuclear power industry, and the deception by which nuclear power was sold to an anti-nuclear Japan. Truly an eye-opening read.

This collection of poems is essential reading, as are the essays. I wept reading this book and you will too.

> —**Melissa Tuckey**, editor of *Ghost Fishing: An Eco-Justice Poetry Anthology*

Poetry speaks the language of the heart, and this is the language of peace and justice. One cannot read these poems without feeling the very real threat posed by the so-called "peaceful" uses of nuclear power.

> —**David Krieger**, President Emeritus, Nuclear Age Peace Foundation

The poems and essays featured in the book help us fathom the unfathomable and understand the injustice inherent in nuclear power from a deeply human perspective.

> —**Kelly Campbell**, Executive Director, Oregon Physicians for Social Responsibility

The human health toll of environmental radiation exposure extends far beyond thyroid damage. Obfuscation of this truth constitutes an unforgiveable wrong against those irretrievably harmed by these exposures.

> —**Trisha T. Pritikin**, *The Hanford Plaintiffs: Voices from the Fight for Atomic Justice*

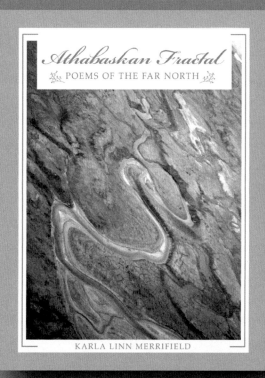

Brenda Jaeger Art Studio

PRIVATE LESSONS   ART SALES   CONSULTATIONS

brendajaegerartstudio.com | Instagram.com/brendajaegerartstudio |
brendajaegerartstudio@startmail.com

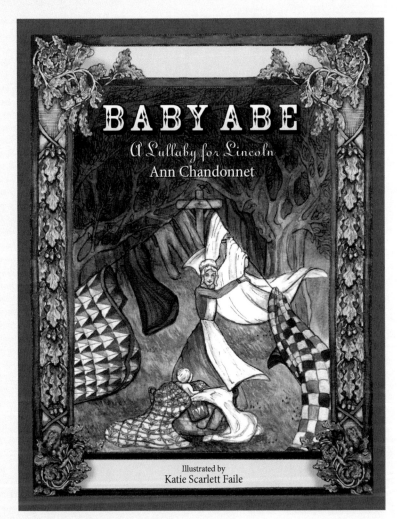

Illustrated by
Katie Scarlett Faile

Lullaby for Baby Abe

This lullaby imagines scenes from Abraham Lincoln's life, from his 1809 winter arrival in the world to his third birthday (1812). Period objects, foods, verbal expressions and manners are twined into the text. Scenes described are typical of life on the Kaintuck (Kentucky) and Indiana frontiers. Research began with Carl Sandburg's two-volume biography; and, some years later, embraced the details of Sidney Blumenthal's *A Self-Made Man: The Political Life of Abraham Lincoln*, 1809-1849 (2016).

Characters are generally true to history with the exception of the preacher, the tinsmith, the shoemaker, the Yarb Woman and the Widder. Although fictional, these characters are typical of individuals who would regularly visit remote homesteads.

Cousin Dennis Hanks is one of the few family members whose pronouncements about the future of baby Abraham were recorded.

Ann Chandonnet

Raised on a colonial land grant, author Ann Chandonnet swallowed a deep sense of history as present. A former college English instructor and police reporter, Chandonnet intends her lullaby to reinvigorate interest in Abraham Lincoln's formative years. Abe was a country boy, just three generations from the Linkhorns of Britain. How did an obscure frontier lawyer and government representative rise to become America's greatest leader?

Chandonnet has won a national prize for wilderness poetry as well as national and state awards for educational writing. She has been nominated three times for the Pushcart Prize. She is also the author of the "Alaska Food" article in the *Encyclopedia of American Food and Drink* (Oxford University Press).

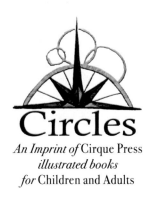

Circles

An Imprint of Cirque Press
illustrated books
for Children and Adults

Sandra Kleven
Michael Burwell
Editors & Publishers

With precise, poetic language, Chandonnet evokes the early years of America's 16th President. Young readers interested in history will enjoy the glimpses of Abraham Lincoln as a baby, as well as the accompanying notes explaining historical and regional terms as well as culinary delights. The book encourages a vivid imagining of early childhood in Kentucky, presenting readers with the cultural and societal influences that shaped *Baby Abe*.

—Emily J. Madsen, Assistant Professor of English, University of Alaska Anchorage

Callie Comes of Age

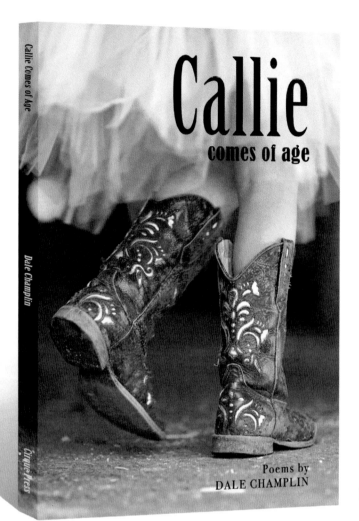

Callie's indomitable spirit corrals everything she does. Self-reliant, quirky, intelligent, sensual and untamed, she throws herself wholeheartedly into every new experience.

For full effect, read *Callie Comes of Age* as you would a novel. The overall trajectory is best considered as a single narrative. In Callie's search, each poem leads to the next discovery, her voice and personality irresistible as we follow her from childhood loss to adult resolution.

Callie doesn't question the grit required to get through her daily chores on the cattle ranch. An arid landscape dictates her hardscrabble existence.

Ultimately, there's a mystery for Callie to unravel.

—George Champlin

Sandra Kleven
Michael Burwell
Editors & Publishers

Callie Comes of Age is pretty darn masterful. The magic of Dale Champlin's exuberant narrative, like Callie herself, is impossible to tie down. Beyond a braided story that will buckle you, the cascade of poems reveals a sensuous and hard, lonely and austere landscape. The sharp characters and sure-handed narrative pull us, while in a rhythm that alternates between shuffle, gallop, and gusty breeze, the poems with their details of *snake belly*, *scar*, and *bone* won't let us go.

—John Morrison, author of *Monkey Island*

Ringing with an exquisite lyricism, Dale Champlin's amazing *Callie Comes of Age*—a novel in the form of poetry—holds me in thrall. Set in the harsh ranch country of the American West, which shapes her life, Callie's story evolves from an early childhood filled with tenderness and a strong sense of belonging into a grim tale of a sexually precocious and fiercely independent adolescence, in which glimmers of a dark secret begin to emerge. The deftly nuanced narrative kept me on the edge of my seat all the way to the end, throbbed by wonder.

—Ingrid Wendt, Oregon Book Award winner in poetry, author of *Evensong*

ABOUT THE AUTHOR

Dale Champlin, an Oregon poet with an MFA in fine art, has poems published in *Willawaw*, *Visions International*, *San Pedro River Review*, *catheXis*, *The Opiate*, *Pif*, *Timberline Review* and elsewhere. Her first collection *The Barbie Diaries* was published in 2019. Three collections, *Leda*, *Isadora*, and *Andromina, A Stranger in America* are forthcoming.

Ever since her daughter married a bull rider, Dale's been writing cowboy poems. Memories of her early days hiking in the Black Hills of South Dakota, the bleachers at Pendleton Roundup, and summers camping at Lake Billie Chinook imbue her poetry with the scents of juniper and sage.

EMPTY BOWL 14172 Madrona Drive Anacortes, WA 98221 www.emptybowl.org emptybowl1976@gmail.com

NEW & RECENT TITLES

VIRGA BY SHIN YU PAI

Empty Bowl is honored to publish VIRGA, Shin Yu Pai's elegant eleventh collection of poems, a crisp and intelligent response to recent and ancient history. VIRGA portrays Buddhist thought from lived experience and demonstrates the everyday life of a poet who can see for herself in the "shafts of rain going sublime" the reality of being an Asian American woman in America today. This collection rediscovers who we are in an age when hate-crimes and terrorization destroy the lives of Asians and all people of color. Shin Yu Pai rises in and through the wearying atmosphere of the "dominant caste," as historian Isabel Wilkerson calls white culture, to hold herself, her child, her community, in that sublime state that, within the Zen mind, arises "before touching the ground." 106 PAGES   PAPERBACK 5"X 7" $16.00   ISBN978-1-73704-080-4

RAIN VIOLENT BY ANN SPIERS

Earth and its creatures in crisis. Each page holds one short poem paired with a weather symbol. The symbols inject poems with a link to specific climate phenomena. Sixty poems about climate crisis: political, mythical, surrealistic, scientific, personal. Animals, humans, and natural and built landscapes create the content. Point of view and narrator shift from poem to poem, migrating through past, present and future scenarios. Tone also shifts from lyrical to strident, objective to personal, humor to tragedy. Weather symbols create tensions within poems such as "Drizzle Slight," "Drizzle Heavy," "Drizzle Heavy Freezing." Citizen scientists and aeronautical professionals use these International Weather Symbols to denote conditions at local weather stations. Artist Bolinas Frank hand painted the symbols to emulate those at weather stations worldwide. 100 PAGES PAPERBACK 5"X7" $16.00   ISBN978-1-73418-739-7

The Madrona Project II, 1: Keep a Green Bough, Ed by Holly J. Hughes ISBN978-1-73418-738-0 $16 146 pp Paper 8.5x11

Forthcoming in Dec, 2021: The Madrona Project II, 2: Human Communities in Wild places, ed by Michael Daley $16 130 pp

Waymaking by Moonlight by Bill Yake ISBN978-1-7341873-4-2 $20.00   Paperback 204 pages
"An astonishing feat of language and human imagination, these poems don't just evoke the living systems and manifold interconnections of this, our only Earth, and all her creatures, but ARE these things as much as language can accomplish."
                                                            -- Derek Sheffield

Zen Roots: The First Thousand Years tr. Red Pine ISBN 978-1-73418-736-6 $35   Hardback 250 pages
Red Pine has gathered nine texts from the first thousand years of Zen, dating from the middle of the second century BC to the middle of the ninth century.

The Straits by Michael Daley 5.5" X 9" ISBN 9780912887043 $30   Hardback 72 PAGES
Originally published in 1983, in a paperback edition, this first collection of poems has been bound in cloth in a limited edition, with a dust jacket designed by Lauren Grosskopf.

FISH THE DEAD WATER HARD

Poems

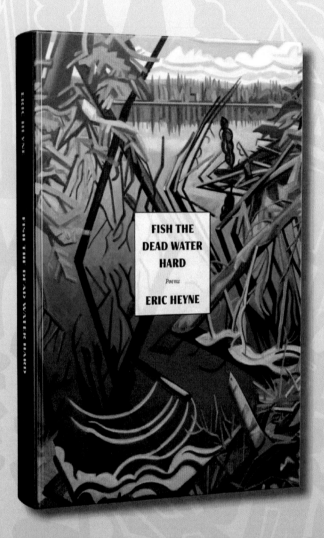

Though centered in Alaska, Eric Heyne's poems travel the world. Brilliantly observed and buttressed by a strong poetic craft, they take us to the spot and open our eyes. Whether set in the Brooks Range or at the Acropolis, a steady thoughtful voice holds the book together, while intimate poems of family life embody Heyne's core emotions. This collection resonates with life.

> **John Morgan**, author of *The Moving Out: Collected Early Poems, Archives of the Air,* and *River of Light: A Conversation with Kabir*

In *Fish the Dead Water Hard*, Eric Heyne shares Alaska in summer, when hieroglyphic lichens "spell out their slow story in a dead language." During brutal, long winters, ice fog fossilizes all trace of life. He mourns a young one gone too soon who leaves us "to mourn the impossible lives of the living." He honors a beloved stepmother who "talked to us like we were worth listening to." These poems are dispatches from above ground, where the poet asks "What else can't I be?" He advises those of us not quite ready to go yet to "just assume you're still in love." Eric Heyne shows us, with delicacy and grace, the quality of light in a forest half eaten by leaf miners, then wonders about what forest his daughter will see. That succession-in-progress, like a five-armed sea star, is "balanced and incomplete, like poetry, like life."

> **Peggy Shumaker**, author of *Gnawed Bones, Just Breathe Normally,* and *Cairn*

These poems appear for us like cairns in a dark wood and we read them with delight and curiosity. Each word of Eric Heyne's poems is stacked with intention and meant to show us something about the complex and layered woods we are walking through. Heyne doesn't shy from the darker moments—the fear of a biopsy, the loss of sexual desire, the warming of our world. But these poems are also markers, built to help us find our way. "And someone, awaiting migration, finds/this stack of stones on the horizon and is no longer alone."

> **Emily Wall**, Professor of English at the University of Alaska, and author of *Flame* and *Breaking Into Air*

Eric Heyne is a Professor of English at the University of Alaska Fairbanks. He has published scholarship on American literature and critical theory in a number of journals, and is the editor of *Desert, Garden, Margin, Range: Literature on the American Frontier* and the University of Alaska Press edition of Jack London's *Burning Daylight*.

CIRQUE PRESS

AVAILABLE ON
amazon

$15

November Reconsidered
poems by Marc Janssen

November Reconsidered
poems by Marc Janssen

"There are adjustments now
To the November rain
To the November expectation
To the November settlement
Schedules and scoldings
Homework and housework
They adjust to me and I adjust to them."

Part rant, part meditation, part acerbic commentary, *November Reconsidered* is a gritty and darkly funny collection of November poems that transports us from site to site, back and forth through time. Marc Janssen's satire takes a lyric yet steely look at a market's cereal aisle, an eighth grade English class, a Toyota dealership, a California mall on Black Friday, a Happy Hour at Charlie Browns. Although he never flinches from the dark realities of life, Janssen also gives us moments of assuaging respite. On a solitary walk taken to escape the family hubbub of Thanksgiving Day, he notes this: *The cold damp air made exhalation look full and white and alive, / White breath in a reverent day.*

–Paulann Petersen, Oregon Poet Laureate Emerita, author of *One Small Sun* and *Understory*

Sandra Kleven
Michael Burwell
Editors & Publishers

CIRQUE PRESS

About the Author

It would be easy to say that Marc Janssen lives in a house with a wife who likes him and a cat who loathes him. It is more complicated than that. Marc:

- was born in Ventura, California and grew up in the State of Jefferson
- has a bachelor's degree in Communication Arts from California Lutheran University
- is a veteran of the Ventura poetry scene
- has worked as a copywriter, a marketer, a salesman, an employee of the state, and was also hopelessly unemployed
- has been published by journals in the US and around the world
- Coordinates the Salem Poetry Project and the Salem Poetry Festival

His wife is fun, smart and beautiful. His kids are brilliant and good looking. The cat—the cat absolutely loathes him.

New from Cirque Press

OUT THERE IN THE OUT THERE

Tales from the midst of very big somewheres

Jerry Dale McDonnell

Out There in the Out There takes us deep into the wilderness of the "real" American west at the end of the last century, and it's one helluva rollicking ride! Jerry McDonnell knows this time, this country, these characters. You can smell the wood smoke, the horseshit, and the bears. His yarns and fish stories are infectious, but it's his navigation of the human heart that will haunt you sweetly down the trail. This is a no-bullshit collection from an old bullshitter of the first order. Take a joy-ride into the out-there—let the tail go with the hide!

—Mark Gibbons, Montana Poet Laureate, 2021-2023, author of In The Weeds, Connemara Moonshine, blue horizon, Forgotten Dreams and other collections

McDonnell's stories are forceful, tender, violent, funny, and thought-provoking. You wouldn't want to be "out there" with anyone else for this author is a man who sees, smells, and feels the rhythm of the earth and just plain knows how to live and thrive in the wildest of places.

—Monica Devine, author of Water Mask and five children's books including Iditarod: The Greatest Win Ever and Kayak Girl

Jerry Dale McDonnell

A writer and actor, Jerry Dale McDonnell's, prose spans from fiction and nonfiction to plays to journalism. His experiences as a retired Alaskan bush teacher in Native villages and hunting guide in Montana and Idaho and bear-viewing guide in Alaska were a source for the writings in this collection. His play, *Engines of Time*, was a finalist in the Tennessee Williams Literary Conference. His other plays have had readings at the Last Frontier Theater Conference in Valdez, Alaska and other theater companies nationally. His play, *The Lone Ranger Rides*, was performed in Homer, Alaska at the Pier One Theater. In his fifty plus years as an actor, he has played roles in stage productions from California to Montana to Alaska and has had bit parts in several films. His prose and poetry have appeared in *Catamaran, South Dakota Review, Over the Transom, MungBeing, Alaska Sampler 2015, Cirque, Dead Snakes, Explorations, Dan River Anthology, Northwood's Journal,* and *Driftwood*. As a freelance photo-journalist, he has appeared in *Anchorage Daily News, Alaska Journal of Commerce, Peninsula Clarion, Calaveras Enterprise,* and *The Dispatch*.

Both retired, Jerry Dale writes and Judi Ann creates her magical, visual art. Allowing time, of course, for a saunter . . . out there in the out there.

CIRQUE PRESS

Sandra Kleven
Michael Burwell
Editors & Publishers

Someday I'll Miss This Place Too

DAN BRANCH

Dan Branch, "ignorant but lucky," turned what began as a one-year lawyering commitment in Bethel, Alaska into a lifetime of learning, adventure, compassion, and reflection upon what makes a "good" life. His memoir in essays provides a fascinating personal and historical record of western Alaska in the 1970s and '80s. While much of what he experienced as lawyer and magistrate is heart-breaking, Branch balances his account with admiration for those he learned from, humility for his own missteps, and a big-hearted sense of humor.

Nancy Lord, former Alaska writer laureate and author of *Fishcamp, Beluga Days*, and *pH: A Novel*

From the frozen sloughs and tundra of the Kuskokwim River country to the deep forests of Ketchikan, Branch takes us on a "stranger in a strange land" journey with the boundless empathy of a perpetual outsider wanting only to understand what it means to be an Alaskan.

Richard Chiappone, author of *The Hunger of Crows, Water of an Undetermined Depth*, and *Liar's Code*

In the tradition of Heather Lende and Seth Kantner, these dispatches from the Kuskokwim are insightful and funny and fully human. Dan Branch has written a heart-breaking book that is also filled with wit and wonder. A true joy to read.

Brian Castner, author of *Stampede*

Dan Branch lives in Juneau, Alaska. His essays and poems have been published in *Kestrel, Cardiff Review, Gravel, Metonym, Tahoma Literary Review, Punctuate, Stoneboat, Swamp Ape, Windmill*, and *Portland Magazine*. He received an MFA in creative nonfiction from the University of Alaska Anchorage.

CIRQUE PRESS

Available on

$15

Miss Tami, Is Today Tomorrow?

Kindergarten in Alaska:
Stories for Grown-Ups

TAMI PHELPS
Montessori Teacher

Illustrated by
TAMMY MURRAY
a former student from Miss Tami's kindergarten class

with
Kerry Dean Feldman

In their innocence, young children are at once naïve and brilliantly perceptive.

Dear Miss Tami,
Thank you for teaching me to think and read. I hope you never die.

Love, Alexander

Author Tami Phelps

This heartwarming book maps the humor and curiosity of kids as they learn the meaning of words and the logic that underpins their experiences. In these vignettes for grown-ups, Tami Phelps, a Montessori teacher for 20 years, describes encounters with her students as they process the world around them.

~ *Monica Devine, author,* Water Mask

Circles
An Imprint Of Cirque Press

Miss Tami, Is Today Tomorrow?
Kindergarten in Alaska: Stories for Grown-Ups
By Tami Phelps
Illustrated by Tammy Murray $20
Find on Amazon.

"The story-telling is magical, lyrical, top-notch."
—Gordon Aalborg,
    Canadian Spur Award winner

Coming January 19 2022

From Five Star/Cengage

Kerry Dean Feldman's long-awaited historical frontier novel, *ALICE'S TRADING POST: A NOVEL OF THE WEST* arrives in January. *Alice's Trading Post* is about an unforgettable woman who faces all the west could throw at a mixed-blood woman, 1870s- 1900s, and survives 103 years with courage, wit, and an untamable spirit.

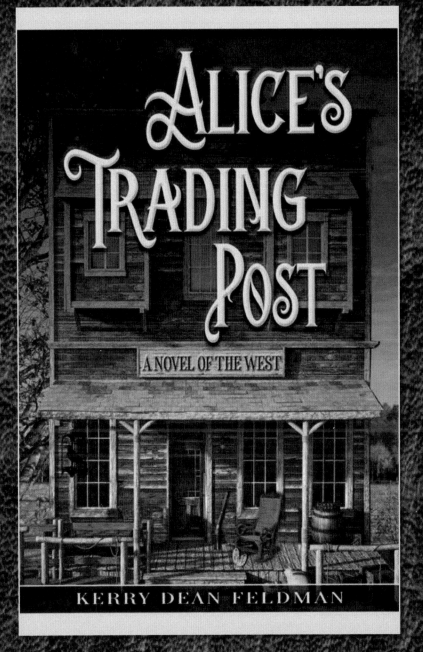

Treat her with respect, you walk away; if you don't, there are consequences. This novel is dedicated to Native American mothers, daughters and grandmothers, whose courage inspires the author. This is the author's debut novel, three decades in the making. He grew up on the eastern Montana prairie where much of this story occurs. Kerry Dean Feldman is also a Cirque Press author (*Drunk On Love: Twelve Stories to Savor Responsibly*, 2019).

Published by Five Star/Cengage

WATER MASK

by Monica Devine

University of Alaska Press

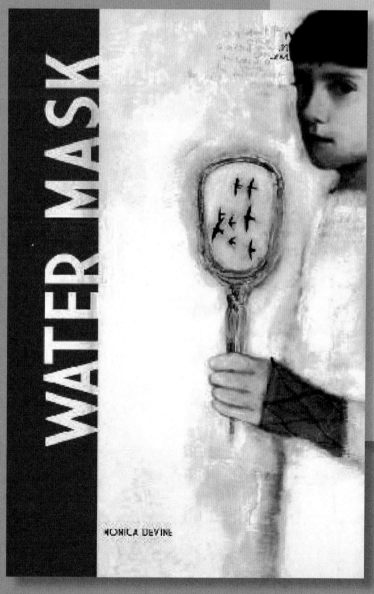

Picture Alaska--her braided rivers and Arctic tundra, her tidal shorelines and thrashing salmon. *Water Mask* reflectively captures these Alaska experiences alongside stories of New Mexico deserts, Wyoming horses and family ties both near and far...making accessible through lyrical essays this remarkable American landscape.

—Page Lambert, author of *In Search of Kinship and Shifting Stars*

In *Water Mask*, Monica Devine explores the unmapped edges of the human spirit with the same poet's eye that she describes her raw encounters with the natural world. This is a book to be savored, the way one might sip the first rays of sunshine cresting the peaks of the Chugach Range.

—Kaylene Johnson Sullivan, author of *Canyons and Ice and Our Perfect World*

Amazon, Amazon Kindle, Barnes & Noble, or your favorite bookstore

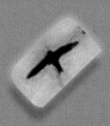

New from Cirque Press

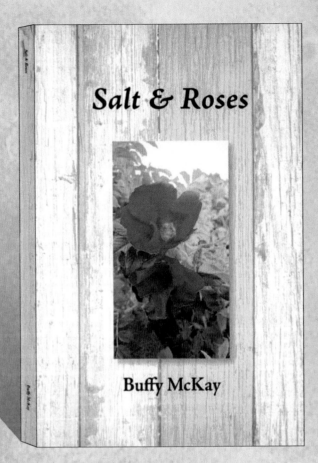

Buffy McKay is a poet of power. In *Salt & Roses*, she looks hard at life across a range of free verse, villanelles, and haikus, and leaves us with poignant and glimmering lines that can stop you dead in your tracks. When she captures the ethereal essence of inner and outer landscapes, you can imagine her with the likes of Mary Oliver and Elizabeth Bishop, sipping tea and swapping lines about fish.

—Doug Pope, author of *The Way to Gaamaak Cove*

The gorgeous poems in Buffy McKay's *Salt & Roses* traverse the wilds of Alaska and comb the watery landscapes of Rhode Island and Scotland. McKay's connection to each place runs deep, and these roots she shares in a generous and loving way. In one poem, she illustrates how ancestry lives in a smoked fish and her mother's word for it: *dunghnak*. This collection sensually explores the lands dear to McKay, family homelands which nourish her body as well as her soul. She captures life's beauty with a wide-angle lens. Yes, there are salt and roses within these pages, but also cancer, death, loss, and regret. More than a book of poems, *Salt and Roses* is a book of prayers.

—Martha Amore, author of *In the Quiet Season and Other Stories*

Buffy McKay

Roberta "Buffy" McKay is of Scottish and Inupiat descent. She enjoys writing about memory, time, and place, and has written poems since age 3. First published in the *We Alaskans* section of the Pulitzer Prize-winning *Anchorage Daily News* in 1993, her work has appeared in various literary journals including *Cirque*. She has won scholarships to the Community of Writers, Olympic Valley, CA and Billy Collins' master class at The Key West (FL) Literary Seminar, and remains grateful for their value and life lessons.

"I'm inspired by my environment and geography and their effects on me. I've lived in some incredible places and had some amazing adventures so far in this life, and that seems to turn into poems."

Currently, Buffy can be found beachcombing with a new dog, Benji, in New England and writing her autobiography, *To Sir Sean Connery, With Love*.

CIRQUE PRESS

Sandra Kleven
Michael Burwell
Editors & Publishers

Our mission: to build a literary community and memorialize writers, poets and artists of the region.

From the Editors

As this issue of *Cirque* was completed, we were saddened by the news that Dan Branch had passed away. When we agreed to publish *Someday I'll Miss this Place Too*, Dan told us he was not well and if the book wasn't published by fall, it would be too late for him to take part in events and readings. We met Dan's date and last month, friends and family joined on Zoom to celebrate the launch of this remarkable memoir — the story of a young lawyer who heads to remote Bethel, Alaska, with plans to stay for a year or so. Twelve years later, Dan was still there, racing sled dogs, lawyering and eventually serving as magistrate in a nearby river village. Word came to us early last week that Dan died peacefully in his sleep. In Bethel, Juneau, Aniak, Anchorage and Ketchikan, we will be missing Dan.

David Wagoner, the esteemed master of poetry in our region since the early 1950s, passed away in December 2021. *Cirque 2.2* (found in back issues at cirquejournal.com), carries an interview with Wagoner conducted by Michael Kleven. In *Cirque, 4.2,* we published Wagoner's, "In Memory of Closing Time." The poem begins like this.

*There comes a time in the night when all young singers
and scribblers and dabblers and sketchers and storytellers
and revisionaries disunited have to accept
the closing of tavern doors in front of their faces
in the form of going home…*

Sandra Kleven with David Wagoner in 2013

Condolences to the families of these two amazing writers.

Pushcart Awards

The Pushcart Prize is an American literary prize published by Pushcart Press that honors the best "poetry, short fiction, essays or literary whatnot" published in the small presses over the previous year. Cirque Press is pleased to announce our Pushcart nominees from *Cirque 11.2* and *12.1*.

Poetry
"Fukushima — Elegy for the North Pacific," by Michael Burwell
"The Arctic Refuge Coastal Plain: Fifteen Motets, 1999-2021," by Carolyn Kremers
"Palace at Fish Creek," by Leslie Fried
"New Hampshire 1957-1975," by Anne Ward-Masterson

Fiction
"Johnny Boy (JT) and Black Kettle," by Paul Haeder

Nonfiction
"The Cuban Brown Rabbit," by Jennifer Fernandez

Andy Hope Award

The Andy Hope Award is the brainchild of writer Vivian Faith Prescott. Andy Hope, an influential Alaska Native political activist and writer of prose and poetry, died after a brief battle with cancer in 2008 at the age of 58. The $100 annual award goes to an author of prose or poetry published in *Cirque*. This year the award was given to Carolyn Kremers, for the poem, "The Arctic Refuge Coastal Plain: Fifteen Motets, 1999-2021." Kremers' opus was also nominated for the Pushcart Prize, as indicated above.

~~~

Cirque Press

Cirque Press continues to produce beautiful books. Since our start, in 2018, we have published twenty-five books. Most recently, we've published *Callie Comes of Age* by Dale Champlin, *November Reconsidered* by Marc Janssen, *Fish the Dead Water Hard* by Eric Heyne, *Baby Abe: A Lullaby for Lincoln* by Ann Chandonnet, *Miss Tami, Is Today Tomorrow?* by Tami Phelps, *Someday I'll Miss this Place Too* by Dan Branch, and *Out There In The Out There* by Jerry McDonnell. Pages found in the front of this volume will introduce you to these titles.

In January 2022, Cirque Press will publish *Salt & Roses* by Buffy McKay, *Growing Older in This Place* by Margo Waring, *Kettle Dance* by Kerry Dean Feldman, *Nothing Got Broke* by Larry Slonaker, *Yosemite Dawning* by Shauna Potocky, and *Sky Changes on the Kuskokwim* by Clifton Bates.

Cirque Press has been selected to publish Joanne Townsend's *Between Promise and Sadness*. This former Alaska Laureate and her husband, Dan, had been living in New Mexico up to her passing in January of 2021.

~~~

If you have been published in *Cirque* and have a book manuscript, please send a quick email and we will give you detailed information about publishing with us.

Thank you so much for supporting *Cirque* with your submissions, contributions, and donations. You have sustained this journal since 2008, paying our bills without institutional support. You provide the foundation on which we build.

—Sandra L. Kleven - Michael Burwell, editors

Letter from Guest Editor—Cynthia Steele

I first got to know Mike Burwell in a poetry course at UAA that I'd taken to explore form at a time when my life was losing shape; my other half through divorce, and my right arm through having a son go to long-term treatment. I'd just gained full custody of my daughter. Gratefully, I returned to writing. Through poetry we escape, encapsulate, make essential, the meaning of the elemental moments, situations, and ideas of our time and other times. Mike encouraged me to submit *Tremolo*—a poem of a friend's drowning.

> When I close my eyes, murky, tepid lake water
> and you stand frozen in time. For ten years I could
> never go anywhere near that foreboding lake.

He'll never *know* what it meant to me, but then, poetry classes transform so many of us. My own creative writing began in earnest at Sheldon Jackson College when I was 18, in the 90's. I learned to write "in the style of" while reading a poem called "Reflections on a Gift of Watermelon Pickle Received from a Friend called Felicity" by John Tobias, which reads:

> When shiny horse chestnuts
>   (Hollowed out
>   Fitted with straws
>   Crammed with tobacco
>   Stolen from butts
>   In family ashtrays)
> Were puffed in green lizard silence
> While straddling thick branches
> Far above and away
> From the softening effects
> Of civilization…

Cynthia Steele

I didn't know that plays by John Tobias would later be produced at leading theatres in 15 countries, as well as Off Broadway, but neither did he. I just knew he could take me to that moment in time, and that's what I needed to learn. *Cirque* submissions continue to take my mind places and teach me. We never know what will become of our writing, but we birth it and hope.

The next year lead me to Women's Literature, where I would embrace the challenges of life:

> The bird that would soar above the level plain of tradition and prejudice must
> have strong wings. It is a sad spectacle to see the weaklings bruised, exhausted,
> fluttering back to earth.
>   —Kate Chopin, *The Awakening*

Clearly, what I wanted from UAA, before my English MA, was a Creative Writing and English Literature degree, but these departments were, at that time, in a sort of war. So, I continued to learn on the side, as it were, through literature courses and Saturday writing groups, and later, Poetry Parley.

Under the true gift of tutelage by Mike and Sandy, many writers' fiction, nonfiction, and poetry creations submitted to *Cirque Journal* became for me an offering of life. Many selections cross these categories, genre bend. I've consumed them, and they've kept me intrigued, fascinated, and sustained. Your submissions are my very lifeblood. But, it is from Mike that I learned the great value of the offering—the written word and the connection to the human being, their world, and experiences. Nowadays, I only experience Burwell through email, as well as in my memories of the classroom and the times we have met online due to geographic differences. He shares his heart on his sleeve, publishing those works he feels need to rise and be read. During the editing of his issue, I've worked with Mike, who reviewed my delicate, if difficult, and certainly subjective, choices.

I must say that as a lover of the theater and a reader for the Valdez Theatre Conference (a new title), I'm a bit saddened by the fact that there were no play submissions for this issue. Still, I was encouraged by the fact that the fiction submissions for this issue were particularly plentiful, and the writing significantly elevated my spirit. And, the places they took me tickled me, broadened, and stretched my mind. The nonfiction and poetry are likewise superb. Still, the play's the thing, so be encouraged to submit plays. The natural dialogue that I hear in plays helps me to provide voices in my own writing. This dialogue increases the pace of my stories as well as the audience's understanding of particular characters.

In my mind, plays, fiction, nonfiction, and poetry are all read with reverence for their origination and authorship but also their culture, forms, and ability to transcend the place from which they originate—their ability to form new shapes in the minds and times in which they are read. Of course, my English MA and literary criticism courses developed that perspective.

The images for this issue stun me as well. The potential cover images thrill me.

I see the writing that comes in "through a glass darkly," knowing I have obscure or imperfect vision. I reread the submissions many times, seeing where they take me, if they take me, and grow more and more willing to see things differently. The most difficult part is the pruning of the pages, and, if the purple of the coleus tells us anything, it is that life requires choices. I can only hope many of those not placed in *Cirque* find a home.

I, too, submit and wait at the door to many journals. And, to plug one of my own pieces, "Too Dark for Father's Day" comes out this year, this month, in the important book *When Home is Not Safe*, Judith Skillman—whose work has appeared in many issues of *Cirque*—and Linera Lucas, editors.

The reality of the current state of the world has hit many of us repeatedly over the past couple years—financially and through deaths. I've traveled to three states in the past month and a half: Oregon (where Sandra and myself did a live event), Ohio, and Kentucky. Oregon's homeless population and their problems with solving it continue to haunt me. The tiny place we went in Kentucky delivers 14 Narcan doses a day to save the lives of people who live there. People in those places are truly living life on its edge.

Many thought we were survivors of a post-COVID world. I was, I believed, fairly untouched until a close friend's mother, who had COVID early on, had her blood continue to coagulate. My friend got her mother to a hospital quickly, and she survived. Some don't. Some adults and children experience multisystem inflammatory syndrome after they have had COVID-19. The results of the virus and its mutations are only now becoming clear. We live in a pseudo-sci-fi world where the best we can do is, first, all we can, and second, all we can write.

The editors of *Cirque* cannot wait to read your work.

—Cynthia Steele

Cirque: A Literary Journal for the North Pacific Rims
Sandra Kleven and Mike Burwell, Editors
Cynthia Steele, Associate Editor
Paul Haeder, Projects Editor
Signe Nichols, Designer
Published twice yearly near the Winter and Summer Solstice
Anchorage, Alaska

Paul Haeder

A Sturdy Tree Brings Forth the Light of Creation (Art)

*The tree of life is growing where the spirit never dies, and
the bright light of salvation shines in dark and empty skies*
　　　—Bob Dylan

Oh, how a picture is worth a thousand words. Just that cover ("Grounded" by Tami Phelps) of this collection—roots and sturdy trunk of tree spreading out from base to top—speaks of the rootedness of the journal. This is where we are in this next decade—people of all ages seeking solace, some sense of shelter from the storm, some sense of home and permanency. Roots! A sheltering sky.

Those roots and soil, the air and water, the sun and the electromagnetic waves, many times forgotten, disabused. Oh those trees, the masters of synergy, orchestration, and community building. This issue, emblazoned with that prominent piece of art on the cover, is the true taproot of what the writers in this volume are shooting for: A home, a community, transcendence from the mundane, and a forum for their form.

I've read the proof of this issue, and there are weighty poems and deep essays fixed in time. The fiction is grounded in writers' lives, as stories should be.

Using the term, *literature*, broadly, I see this volume emblematic of what all writers work their magic and their wares into—art. The work is an existential form of guiding reader into a process of how we live, how they live, how the world lives.

Much work in literary rags do have an undergrowth of writers expressing in various literary forms how people emerge from distress. The poems, nonfiction and fiction herein generate ebb and flow of getting through trauma. Surviving… Or almost surviving. This synthesis of these works remits an overall engagement of reader, writer and editor like myself on many planes of consciousness. Yet, the total effort of getting through the volume brings delight.

Yes, songs of lament can bring delight to a reader. These are lived, learned and celebrated experiences, caught in a Sargasso Sea of each writer's mat, snag and swirl of words. That rootedness reflected prominently on the cover transforms into a synergy of works put together as a whole, and this is synergy of forces of good: art.

A pile of submissions grows, and most of the pieces come from people who do not know each other. Blind submissions. A hope imbued in each work that it will find light under the tree of collective literary knowledge.

Like a deciduous tree, or a perennial, the works shed their glory, add to the rootedness of literature, and bring a tree into dormancy above ground but so dynamically active below ground. Art shedding to create rich loamy topsoil from which to grow anew.

Are we the microbes, the symphony players navigating between solar and photosynthesis and all the tricks and bio-webbing of capillaries and roots with the harmonies of fungi, bacteria, mineral and liquid?

Is it strange that this frontispiece is energized by botanical allusions? That I as editor see the work not as separate but part of the whole. We now call the action and dynamism of a tree, roots, leaves and transpiration, and all the actors below ground, as part of a *wood-wide web*. A literary journal, to me, is that web, and while a frontispiece is a façade, I do not play with decorative things much.

Let me get deeper into this analogy of *writers as fungi*. Newer science allows us to understand some common fungi exist in subtle symbiosis with plants. Repeat—these artists, fungi, bring not infection but a connection.

These writers/fungi push out gossamer-fine fungal tubes called hyphae. Like that hyphae, which colonize soil and weave into the tips of plant roots at a cellular level, writers set down the roots and fungi combine to form what is called a mycorrhiza: a growing-together of the Greek words for fungus (mykós) and root (riza).

All the submissions I have read are from individuals with vibrant and reflective lives, and each story, poem and essay is joined to one another by—to take this a step further—a hyphal network. This journal's entries are both simple and straightforward as well as intricate—and this analogy came to me around 100 pages into my reading. Alas, this is a profoundly complex and collaborative living thing called *The Literary Arts Journal*.

Art, like the relationship of mycorrhizal fungi and the plants they connect is now known to be ancient (around four hundred and fifty million years old). The relationship of artists to artists and then to their audience is for me a similar mutualism.

I have benefited from writers' work, and it is a symbiosis to be a part of a growing web of hyphae: all these pieces now connected inside my illusory/elusory brain.

The written works are the food audiences siphon off this great tree of creativity, tree of life, tree of knowledge. Some of the narratives and poetic themes maybe a bitter pill, but these writers allow for us, the reader, to savor and absorb until intellectual elixir condenses into a realization: art impacts people, cultures, history.

Truly, I am thinking about this botanical process while reading this issue – the audience obtains the nutrients from these writers/fungi. Words and images are the phosphorus and nitrogen. In concert, photosynthesis assist, and then fungi (writers) break down soil with their unique enzymes to feed the tree.

We, the community, are the tree.

Right from the start, the first piece, Helen Fagan's "Grappling with Edges" sets the tone of the book. Here, lines that make their mark:

> "Yes, that's what we all want, I guess. It's tough, moving toward the end of life," I offered.
> "I'm crawling toward it," she said.

The metaphor is apt. She is moving in increments toward her death. Without her daughters, she would not still be in her own home. Without her daughters, perhaps not even still alive. Now dependent on us as we once were on her, this part of the story is not unusual.

Fagan writes about her mother—a survivor of the Holocaust: three years in the Lodz Ghetto and time in Auschwitz and Bergen-Belsen concentration camps. Here it is, those traumas, direct and generational. The kick off nonfiction piece brings to light that grappling that writers have, really, taking fear and death and torture but bringing it to a point of delight: that life can be written about, cared for, massaged into something an audience will cry about and learn from.

Those sharp and broken edges poke out throughout this volume, and that is what makes the whole so dazzlingly complex and oddly complete. Sandra Kleven and Mike Burwell, editors and publishers, and Cynthia Steele, associate editor are the rays of sun hitting those leaves to bring about this collection, the small and large roots that make up each and every *Cirque* issue, in my humble opinion.

Steele's piece, "A Naked Lady in a Library," is emblematic of her youth, and she utilizes Alberto Rios' words as an epigraph:

> The library is the book of books,
> Its concrete and wood and glass covers
> Keeping within them the very big,
> Very long story of everything.

A piece of fiction, Mark Crimmins' "Spreader," is a workers' story about cutting and sewing large sheets of fabric. One of the characters speaks about his own hands and fingers, symbolic in a way of our own lives with various things cut from our bodies and soul:

> Steve was ten years older than the rest of us. He'd been a cutter for a long time. That's why he lost so many fingers. It was just part of the job. Cutters end up cutting their fingers off one way or the other. Funny thing was, Steve wasn't worried about his mutilated hands. He was always talking about if he cut off that last important finger—the index finger on his right hand that you needed to operate the knife's key switch—he'd get a steel hand up at the hospital. A prosthetic limb. A metal claw.

Other good pieces: Doug Margeson's "The People With Sincere Lips," Russell Thayer's "The Pie Safe," Karen Tschannen's "SF Avenues"—a longer piece about a married couple who have tested the waters of matrimony and survived.

There it is—that many branched tree, all those gnarled roots, the hooked limbs and rough bark and the tree—the journal—lifting into the light. Even the occluded sun.

Then the poems come like forbidden, not-yet-ripened and fully sweet fruit. An avalanche of fruit and seeds and tastes and smells. So many poems about place, or about the vagaries of life, or those remembrances or observances.

John Baalke's "Wrangell Mountains Triptych" gets into a Wallace Stegner sort of milieu, and the long poem tells many stories about people, about the narrator, about Baalke. Here, the ending with visceral vigilance:

> Rounding Fireweed Mountain again, we soon saw the hunter's
> truck, still there, and the hunter himself stepping out of some
> willows. He was bent and wheezing. His heart he said. Had to
> get his nitro pills, said he shot the moose; said we could have it
> if we packed it out. Through an alder thicket, across wet
> hummocky tundra, slippery algal mud, to the far side of the pond
> where the animal, barely gutted, lay in a small grove of poplar.
> Will removed the entrails, accidentally cut my hand when his
> knife slid too quickly between skin and rib. I bled a little and
> he proceeded to quarter the bull. Then I packed as much as I
> could carry, making eight, maybe ten, loads of flesh and bone,
> on a warm, buggy August afternoon.

Then we get a lean look into love of life, and nature, through Christianne Balk's piece, "Snow Lake":

> Take me in your glacial heart
> And hold me
> stunned above silty beds
> of soft, crushed stone—
> shake my limbs numb

rock me
in your breathless clarity—
nudge me through your ice and show me
how to crawl
wide-eyed towards your gravel shore.

There are many many more poems to come that tell the story of the writer's photographer's eye, and their love of place, and the wisdom in simplicity. So many hands and lips and eyes and people populate this volume's poetry. The leaves of that wisdom tree. I could write on and on, holding each poem and long piece in my hands, and scrapping through to come into the writers' respective fields of vision and sense of time and struggle.

Like an entomologist studying each square foot of tree for rare insects, from the top of the canopy to each layer of limb architecture, each inch of soil, magnifying glass in hand and microscope at the ready. This is what a good collection of work will do to the interested reader who shapes each word and line with his or her own creative interpretation through the looking glass.

Kaleidoscopic, we are in our seeing, each of us clutching the written form in our minds and heart like a cross-country skier fits into gloves and holds onto poles, locomotion as a forward and backward motion, each one of us with our own unique movements.

Here, front and center, a son's perspective on that mother, that grandmother, captured so well in Mark Burke's "Stories She Told." The universality of the poem is a safe harbor for any reader, and this tree we are under, the roots holding us firm, allow us to see and feel what Burke holds dear:

She made up stories, what we all do,
invent, sometimes without knowing,
how a stranger would walk the dirt-road,
come to call, singers clapping
when she sprang the sword-dance
across the scraped linoleum, spinning alone
through the kitchen's coal-oil shadows...

...So much turns on the choices,
hard to see past the first steps on the road.

These rooted poems rush at the reader with fractals of images. There are many poems of mountains, glaciers, some footpath, and places remembered as refuges of the heart and mind. A journal that sells itself as something for writers with a connection to the Pacific Northwest, to include Hawaii, we might expect those poems celebrating and dissecting nature. But there are poems that cull the heavy sigh of relationships, friendships aged like manzanita bark, and families splintered by time and disconnect.

Jazzy poems, and style and form that penetrates possibly new realms for each poet attempting to move muse and voice into some form of magic. Tundra and sea, animals and wind. The bare shapes of what it is to call home a place. Where roots are set, maybe fresh roots, or those that uplift dirt and boulders, tripping up the unwary reader through a dark dank pathway into creative disharmony.

Or, the black bird, the crow, again, dive bombing in several poems. Here, some corvid magic, in Jim Hanlen's "Wheat Field with Crows":

The crows are painting too.
Their strokes leave black
spots for wings. Look,
the wheat field is twisting
itself, trying to take flight.
The sun smears its yellow
finger. The wind has bent
the day into afternoon.
What holds this canvas
in place? Some black spots
are cawing off canvas.
The fury would make you
stagger if you didn't stand
and look.

The tree of creativity in this volume's poems is variegated, disparate looking, too: one about a Palestine mother bombed, or another getting deep into the Northwest territories, and yet another contemplating the weight of guilt in homeless people. There is earth, wind, fire, smoke in much of the poetry. Tundra and dredging deep pools of memory about times long past through the tumbling fall of aging and moving on, yes, expect those concepts hitched to amazing observations and wordsmithing.

This volume will enrich you, kind reader. You will fall, you will be tripped up, and the writers will help you steady yourself as they take you into worlds—literal and ephemeral. This is the forest now, all those written down pieces, interspersed with art. The settings and collision of art and white space, the sharp edges of typeface, all of it makes sense as a whole, as that tree.

This is the symbiosis and parallel mutualism of writers who now are in this rootedness, together. We are in a web, galvanized together, making offerings to our muses so readers can find all the realms to enter. The writers will transform you into diggers, or spelunkers, as you find some shelter from your day or hard life, in the comfort of the spreading canopy of an amazing magical tree.

Sandra Yannone's poem, the last one in the poetry section, brings us to a point of reincarnation in a soul, Rachel Corrie—"Let No One Stand Alone." Again, ripped from history, the young activist Corrie is bulldozed into earth for her stand for Palestine. This is what poets do—keep things alive, keep them in play, not frozen by words, but revived by the energy in the very process of planting these seeds called poetry:

The day I reconnected with evil
again, driving south on I-5 to escape my own
mini-series of headlines in Bellingham, the news
from Rafah broke, horrific, like all history
emerging, that she had died, clutching
fistfuls of dirt, that day when she stood

her ground alone, bulldozer and American college girl, a stand
off, March 16th, 2003, and NPR reporting that evil
had prevailed in not so many spoken words. Outside of Everett, I clutched
the story's every word and the steering wheel harder than a car owner
should, my knuckles turning whiter than history
recorded, each mile driven bringing news of worse news

Life extinguished at age 24, Rachel Corrie is a symbol of hope, even while we as readers contemplate the pure evil of murdering a peace protestor. This is what this tree of creativity-knowledge-life brings to us. The mysterious dark arts and magic of soil and fungi. What is the final emotion or feeling after pouring through this volume? Hope and delight. In Kathleen Stancik's poem, "Hope," she quotes Herman Melville: *Hope is the struggle of the soul*. That is all we can do as writers—send out tendrils and roots to bring a reader to a place under our tree where hope can be reconciled and revered. Even in hopeless times.

As you find a place under your own tree, as you read and marvel at words and images, remember you too are part of our rootedness—those of us lucky enough to have found a temporary-but-etched-in-hardwood place from which to live in this literary world wide web.

CIRQUE   A Literary Journal for the North Pacific Rim

Volume 12 No. 1

NONFICTION

Helena Fagan *Grappling with Edges* 45
Jennifer Healey *Roses of Old Oregon* 46
Rebecca Morse *Picking Violets* 50
Ali Shaw *Stardust* 51
Cynthia Steele *A Naked Lady in a Library* 52
Hamish Todd *The God Issue — Part Two* 54

FICTION

Mark Crimmins *Spreader* 59
Paul Haeder *Johnny Boy (JT) and Black Kettle* 64
Doug Margeson *The People With Sincere Lips* 69
Russell Thayer *The Pie Safe* 72

POETRY

John S. Argetsinger *Looking Back* 77
Gabrielle Baalke *Tithe* 77
John Baalke *Wrangell Mountains Triptych* 78
Thomas R. Bacon *Posted From the Northern Province* 82
Christianne Balk *Smoke* 83
                            Snow Lake 83
Gabrielle Barnett *Milepost 107, shortly after fall eqinox* 84
Rachel Barton *The Sky is Falling* 85
Jennifer Bisbing *The Missions* 86
Kristina Boratino *Vintage Bait* 86
Mark Burke *Stories She Told* 87
Dale Champlin *Down on Her Knees* 88
                            A Dove! Callie Said 89
Nancy Christopherson *Sculptor* 90
                            Philips Resevoir, Watching the Cranes Come In 90
Jennifer Dorner *The House on Reedway Street* 92
Gene Ervine *The Juncos Left: Jim Sisk 1943-2021* 92
Amelia Diaz Ettinger *The Seven Poles at Minam, Circled Chief Joseph Dreams* 93
                            Larix laricina not a slag 94
Chase Ferree *The Double* 94
                            Hand-wringing 95
Leslie Fried *Palace at Fish Creek* 95
Brigitte Goetze *How to Get Filthily Rich* 97
Paul Haeder *Seeking Solace behind Writer's Mask* 99
Jim Hanlen *Wheat Field with Crows* 100
Sarah Isto *Post from Peru, March 2021* 101
Brenda Jaeger *Sustain* 101
Marc Janssen *On A Jetty Unnamed* 103
Eric Gordon Johnson *Dog Dish Rock* 104
Penny Johnson *Short Lives of Animals* 105
Marilyn Johnston *The Year That Was (and Still Is)* 106
Carol Levin *Only Got Bones & Joints* 107
Joe McAvoy *World's shortest poem with the longest title* 108
Karla Linn Merrifield *Long Strange Climate Trip* 109
James Merrill *I Went to School Today* 110
Thomas Mitchell *The Old Red Wool Coat* 111
Susan Morse *The Quilter* 112
Anne Carse Nolting *Glimpse Into Eternity* 113
Al Nyhart *To One Experiencing Sentience* 114

Mary Odden *Do you recognize anyone, asks the Capitol Police* 114
Barbara Parchim *A Small Passing* 115
Diane Ray *More Begats* 116
Michael Eden Reynolds *How to Deice your Glacier* 117
Richard Roberts *Hills Above Plains* 118
Zack Rogow *Lord Byron to His Daughter Ada* 118
Joel Savishinsky *Dogs Outnumbered People: Colville Lake, Northwest Territories* 119
Tamara Kaye Sellman *In the Safeway Parking Lot* 120
Tom Sexton *After Reading Hinton's Anthology of Classical Chinese Poetry* 121
             Transfiguration of Our Lord, Ninilchik 121
             April in Ketchikan 122
Merna Dyer Skinner *Secret-Keepers of Easter Island* 122
             She Could Have Lost a Hand 123
Kathleen Stancik *Hope* 124
             Yesterday 124
Richard Stokes *December Storm* 125
Doug Stone *Fog at Yachats* 126
Mark Thalman *The Locomotive in Odell Lake* 126
Lucy Tyrrell *I Dwell in Possibility* 126
John Van Dreal *Crimson to Pink to Gone* 127
Jeanine Walker *To Hold a Cross* 128
             Walking Home in a Drizzle During a Drought 129
Anne Ward-Masterson *New Hampshire 1957-1975* 129
             Heliotropism 131
Patty Ware *Jesus died ~~for our sins~~* 131
Margo Waring *Poplars and Alders* 132
O. Alan Weltzien *Man with Mop* 133
Tonja Woelber *Light* 133
Christian Woodard *Go that way* 134
John McKay *The Skies Wept: Reflections on an "Academic" Discussion* 135
Sandra Yannone *Let No One Stand Alone* 140

REVIEWS

Paul Haeder *A Review of Sean Ulman's* Seward Soundboard 143
Frances McCue *A Review of Leslie Fried's* Lily is Leaving 146
Jean Anderson *A Review of Ann Chandonnet's* Baby Abe: A Lullaby for Lincoln 148

INTERVIEW

Alex J. Tunney *"It's beautiful. It's stupid. It's not practical, but I loved it." An Interview with*
    Matt Caprioli 150

REVIEW

Monica Devine *A Review of Gretchen Brinck's* The Fox Boy: A Social Worker
    in the Alaska Bush 1968-1970 154

FEATURE

Cynthia Steele *An Interview with Poet Karen Tschannen* 155
Karen Tschannen *SF Avenues* 163

REVIEWS

Paul Haeder *A Review of Fred Rosenblum's* Tramping Solo 170
Kerry Dean Feldman *A Review of Monica Devine's* Water Mask 174

CONTRIBUTORS 175

HOW TO SUBMIT TO CIRQUE 181

Inside   Cheryl Stadig

NONFICTION

Helena Fagan

Grappling with Edges

I sit at the white marble counter on the white stool in my mother's white kitchen. She sleeps, her first nap of the day. I will wake her in a few moments to help her get ready for her one o'clock doctor's appointment.

She is such a tiny thing. Always a force of nature, in the best and worst sense, she now takes up less space in all ways. She survived the Holocaust, three years in the Lodz Ghetto and time in Auschwitz and Bergen-Belsen concentration camps, and not surprisingly, carries sharp, broken edges. The toughest of women, always ready to fight, there has often been a storm around her, a mixture of love and anger and fear that can stir even the calmest of waters into a frothing boil. The storm still rages, but the winds are weakened. It is hard to witness. This morning as we made her oatmeal she said, "I thought I'd go out fast with a heart attack."

"Yes, that's what we all want, I guess. It's tough, moving toward the end of life," I offered.

"I'm crawling toward it," she said.

The metaphor is apt. Moving in increments toward her death, without her daughters, she would likely not still be in her own home. Without her daughters, perhaps not even still alive. Now dependent on us as we once were on her, this part of the story is not unusual.

I come to the non-party late. Living over a thousand miles away gives me space, which sometimes saves me and sometimes creates difficulty. My heart breaks with the witnessing of her extreme discomfort, weakness and exhaustion. Her strength has ebbed since my last visit, not long ago. Yet part of me still wants to run. When I am here, I feel I should abandon my own life, completely. Pay my dues for living far away and not being part of the daily care crew. I get that my sisters offer her so much more right now than I, and yet in the midst of her crumbling life, I long for my own. I long for space and stillness and time to process. I long for a bed that doesn't cause sciatica. I long for air not kept at a too warm temperature, air that doesn't stifle and suffocate. The house holds the toxic energy of her years of anger

and need and intense love. Even as I feel compassion and heartache for her suffering, I dream of escape to healthier climes.

I do escape, temporarily, driving away for two nights to my sanctuary, the house on the coast I have owned since the seventies. As I drive through the mountains, I listen to an NPR story about the shift in treatment of primates used for research. For decades they were taken at about the age of two or three from large groups of primates at breeding centers to research facilities and put in cages by themselves. Today there is a trend to keep them in pairs. These highly social animals, one of the caretakers explains, when isolated become so lonely that they go crazy. She says they tear at their skin creating large gashes and rip their hair out to the point of baldness. When they keep them in pairs, this behavior stops, but thousands of chimps remain isolated in facilities, with scientists worried that their research will be compromised by the pairing.

The sun breaks through the clouds as I come around a tight curve. God light streaks through the trees and fog, making it hard to see. I pull over to the side of the road, sit in my rented Toyota and sob, absorbing the beauty of the gold and scarlet leaves punctuated by the deep dusky greens of the fir, hemlock and pine. The swirling light and fog of this late autumn afternoon

Sun Rising Through Frozen Fog   *Matt Witt*

somehow cradle and accentuate the pain of all those primates, the suffering of my mother.

I arrive and haul all my stuff from the car. I bought way too much food for a very short visit and packed too many clothes. It takes several trips to lug it all into the house. A few minutes later my cell chimes and my daughter, Kelsey, tells me she is glad I am here, this day of all days. And then I remember. It is October 17th, the death anniversary of Michael, her father and my first husband. The perfect place to spend this evening by myself, this house that he purchased right out of college and that holds so many memories of him and of our falling from friendship to love and of the three of us as a family. I am brought to tears again and also shamed by my nearly missing the importance of the day. It has been 28 years since he died, but I realize that my body, with its tears and sighs, remembered the date even though my brain was distracted.

I place his photo on my makeshift shrine of agates, shells and candles, pour a glass of port from the bottle I find on the counter, toast him, and then carry the refilled glass to our beach to witness the sunset. When I return to the house, the darkness is nearly complete. I turn on lights, eat a simple dinner and then call my husband. He tells me he is eating pie and I think, that's nice, but it is not until I mention the death anniversary that he wonders at the timing of the pie, a gift of appreciation from Kelsey. The fact that she did this for him, her stepfather, on the anniversary of the death of her father, brings me to tears yet again. I cannot speak for a moment. This time gratitude flows with the sadness. Beauty and pain fold together like origami, sharp edges creating something new. ◪

Jennifer Healey

Roses of Old Oregon

I am searching for sacred spaces in a town that holds nothing sacred. I seek spots worthy of holding some of my friend's ashes. And I've ended up under an old maple tree on east Burnside.

"I'm asking a lot from you" I tell this tree. "I need you to remain here and keep watch. Your exposed roots are cradling the pulverized bone fragments of my best friend. Can you keep them, at least as long as I'm alive?"

It should never have come to this. Trees are not ideal spots to inter human remains for a host of reasons.

Rose Hip in Winter   Matt Witt

For one thing, this particular tree seems unimpressed by my human pain. I get the feeling that it's seen so much already it doesn't want to get involved. Also, its days are numbered, much as ours are. Old trees in Portland stand in the way of progress. But Amanda lived here in the duplex under this tree for almost ten years. Is this not a fitting place to hold some of her?

So many people loved Amanda Bates. Her mother and brother had the unthinkable task of dividing up her ashes to dole out to us. The dark blue bottles sit tucked away on the mantles and dressers of our homes. Some were emptied in backyards in Bellingham. Some were sprinkled on a rocky beach of Camano Island. If I have my way, they will soon land in the freezing waters of Glacier Bay, Alaska and at the edge of a waterfall in the Grand Tetons. It seems right that she will literally be scattered throughout the spaces she lived and loved in her forty-nine years of life on earth. I am only responsible for part of her remains. So it must be done correctly.

In *Underland: A Deep Time Journey*, Robert MacFarlane writes:

In burial, the human body becomes a component of the earth, returned as dust to dust—inhumed, restored to humility, rendered humble. Just as the living need places to inhabit, so it is often in the nature of our memory-making to wish to be able to address our dead at particular sites on the earth's surface. The burial chamber, the gravestone, the hillside on which ashes have been scattered, the cairn: these are places to which the living can return and where loss might be laid to rest. The grief of those who have been unable to locate the bodies of their loved ones can be especially corrosive—acid and unhealing.

One problem is real estate. The list of sacred spaces in Portland shrinks almost daily as our beloved haunts are closed, sold, demolished, repurposed. The 1201 and Satyricon are no more. The Church of Elvis and Berbati's Pan are long gone. Sylvia's Class Act Dinner Theater, site of a surprising amount of revelry, has become a kid-friendly brew-pub. Amanda's beloved restaurant, La Catalana, is now the bar for a pizza joint. Montage and The Space Room still stand, but seem like a gamble. I can live with the idea of some of her remains scattered throughout a man-made landscape, as long as it was sacred to us. But I'll be goddamned if I let her bone fragments end up under a Dutch Bros.

There is also the matter of the unspeakable pact we made. Sometime in the mid-90s, when death was a wisecrack, Amanda said,

"Okay. Whoever dies first gets their ashes entombed inside the troll doll for all eternity." We both cracked up.

"No! No! And… the survivor… has to traipse around the globe with the fucking thing, taking pictures the whole way!" My laughter made it hard to get the words out. We thought we were so funny in 1995. Before her rare blood cancer and bone marrow transplant, and before the ten years of prednisone that probably prolonged her life, but also ended it. Before my marriage and children and appreciation of my mortality, it was easy to say. "Agreed!"

The troll doll is named King Winkie. He is small and only fits a few tablespoons of ashes. And he's so delicate, having barely come through the surgery required to encase the ashes. He's held together with Shoe Goo and sometimes travels in a plastic bag just in case. It's unconventional, but I have kept my word to my best friend.

Amanda's mother Jackie does not give a shit about conventions. She is done with traditional too. She embodies the corrosive, bitter strength reserved for atheists who outlive an only daughter. And yet, the troll

doll was a bridge too far.

"I know about your pact because Amanda told me. I will give you some ashes. But what you do with them, I don't ever want to know."

Fair enough. Too much irreverence, even for her. But then I learned that when she and Amanda's brother Jonathan were dividing up the ashes, they mixed in the remains of her beloved cat, Kasi. A cat who hated me, hated every friend of hers as far as I know. So these precious remains in the blue bottle and the troll doll are possibly mostly the cat. As far as I know.

Because Amanda would laugh at this, me treating her angry cat's ashes as a sacred object, I'm allowing it.

Today I seek a slightly more traditional internment. But not too traditional. Cemeteries seem so…pedestrian. Besides, there is no headstone, so at best I would be depositing her remains in someone else's space. She'd be a stowaway for eternity. No, that's a terrible idea.

My husband and I used to live across from an old park in SE Portland. Locals called it "Goosepoop Park" and rarely went in, as its feathered residents had rendered it unfit for human use. Our elderly neighbor Glenn once shared with me that his wife's last wish was to be cremated and have her ashes sprinkled in the pond. They lived directly across the street, and she had loved the ducks and geese enough to make that her final resting place. So I thought of her when the city trucks pulled up with drainage and dredging equipment. Over the next 18 months, city workers trapped and relocated the non-native waterfowl to "local agencies." Giant plastic tubes sucked the pond dry. Native grasses were planted in the sludge, and people came from all over the city with buckets to scoop up crawfish by the dozens. The smell was horrendous. A banner hung on the fence across from Glenn's house. "Park Closed. We're making your green spaces better!" Through all this, he sat on his front porch and stared at the ongoing "improvement." We never spoke again, but his slumped silhouette and hardened profile return to me in this moment.

The Pioneer Rose Garden occupies a small section of Lone Fir Cemetery in SE Portland. The rose bushes are sown from plants brought along the Oregon Trail by various women. Many of the roses were named and planted in memory of the children who died on the trail. Their bodies were left along the way.

I stare down at the gray powder under the tree in front of her old apartment from the 1990s. It takes so much trust to inter them here, on this dirty street, this tiny brown space harboring cigarette butts and an empty beer can. There is always the possibility of seeing this block razed to build modern condos and a new Salt and Straw. Because we need more lavender-infused ice cream in this fucking town.

Am I too bitter? Could it be that I have to step back and consider my place in the universe in order to understand that my life is not more important than anyone else's? Isn't progress inevitable and even necessary? Our lives are so short, so meaningless, when measured up against the scale of deep time.

MacFarlane writes about air bubbles trapped in ancient ice—in cores stored in an arctic lab. *Ice is memory*, he says. That air is from an earth that is no more. So what exactly is contained in the molecules and perhaps even atoms of those air bubbles?

I think of Amanda's hand on the iceberg near our campsite in Glacier Bay. I took a picture of her posing with it like a supermodel with a Ferrari. Her long red hair is pulled back in a ponytail. She wears Levis and a flannel shirt. That iceberg was already trapped on the rocky beach, mid-July of 1990, so it probably melted

before September. But her hand was there once. Her skin touched the ancient melting ice of an old glacier that's now long gone. And then it happened. Some ice age air bubble escaped into our world, in 1990, released by the warmth of my best friend's hand.

The young pioneer women left their children's bodies in a place they knew they'd never return to.

What if the iceberg refroze? Somehow, it's still there on that beach at our campsite. And one of the little air bubbles inside is her breath. Knowing this isn't likely, I start to cry again. I want deep time to be a comfort. Why isn't it?

When did we humans develop the luxury of mourning? Surely this is a recent invention. Our early ancestors couldn't possibly have felt the same feelings as me. Doesn't a nasty, brutish and short life mean you don't have time to sweat the small stuff? So I may conclude that we suffer more than they did because we modern humans have longing and angst and disappointment and ennui and celebrity envy and unfulfilled potential. All they had to do was live and die.

Yet the earth is teeming with archeological evidence proving how early people mourned and honored their dead. A baby's grave along the coast of Northwest Canada. A female shaman interred upright on a pile of antlers. The mummified Egyptian pharaohs. My own ancestors pulled from the bogs of Ireland. MacFarlane understands my struggle. "Burial often aspires to preservation –of memory, of matter—for time behaves differently in the underland, where it might be slowed or stayed." Exactly what I thought. I tried to figure out how to stop time for the rest of us because it had stopped for Amanda. And when that didn't work, I tried switching over to deep time. It comforts me to know that while I live in sadness, the Juan de Fuca plate is smashing into and under the North American plate, about an inch a year, 300 miles west of Long Beach, Washington—one of Amanda's favorite coastal destinations and home of Jake the Alligator Man.

Icebergs and trees and duck ponds should live on forever; and they must remember us, honor us, and keep a record of our short but important lives.

The roots of this tree cling deep under the sidewalk. And below, the tunnels. And the layer of native people's artifacts. And the water. And the bedrock. And I don't even know what's down there, but I do know that everything up here on Burnside Street is temporary.

A burst of color catches my eye through burning tears. For the first time, I notice the telephone pole that rises up next to our tree. More evidence of man's attempt to shape the earth to his will.

Band posters, once glued to the wood, now stapled on in an ever-expanding coating. Like counting rings in a giant sequoia, the paper fragments can be peeled back to reveal the rich history of the Pacific Northwest music scene. Deep time is visible in the heart of the city after all. It is measured in the telephone poles.

There, beneath Sea Caves and Cool Nutz, it's Blitzen Trapper and the Decemberists, and then Elliott Smith, Everclear, Dead Moon, Heatmiser? Does no one ever take these things down?

Figure 1. Carbon dating of the innermost layers of paper found under the staples date back to the Grunge era.

Every day, when Amanda left her apartment from 1993 to 2001, this pole was blanketed in different posters. Which ones were here when she moved in? Did she ever read them? Did I ever notice, when I parked right here and stepped between this tree and pole, which shows were advertised that month? I don't think so. But now I want to know. I desperately want to see back in time.

I press my hand into the pole, over the Bitches in the Beehive poster, trying to absorb the past into myself. What can you tell me, pole? Do you know something, anything, about her?

We are blips on the radar of deep time.

Amanda deserves to be in a rose garden dedicated to pioneering women, and so she is. I sprinkled her ashes among the neatly pruned stems and near the headstones of the dozen or so women who are buried there. A nearby plaque calls them the Roses of Old Oregon.

Back on Burnside, a vision appears: two girls, laughing and singing. Stumbling home from Holman's in the wee hours. Loud enough to wake the neighbors. I had forgotten what song we sang, but the telephone pole remembered.

> *And love*
> *Life's sweetest reward*
> *Let it flow*
> *It flows back to you*
> *The Love Boat*
> *Soon will be making another run…*

We were young, drunk, invincible. We sang right here, in this place, in a moment that exists somewhere forever.

The telephone pole remembers. The tree keeps secrets. They will be our witnesses. The keepers of this story and all the others that took place here. ◪

Rebecca Morse

Picking Violets

The plate of spaghetti hit the wall directly under the *Prayer Changes Things* plaque. I watched spaghetti worm its way to the floor, some strands collecting on the cold air vent while others traveled right on through to nest in the ductwork. A red circle remained on the yellow wall. I sat glued to my chair, staring. Mom left the house immediately, toting the shotgun to the car, all the while threatening to kill herself. She drove off in the black Nash at the beginning of what was otherwise a fine afternoon. Dad told me to stay in the house with my younger brother and clean up the mess. He was going to the woods, just as he had planned. "She'll be back when she cools off," he said, the screen door slamming behind him.

I chose a rag from the drawer, wet it under the faucet and took it over to the wall together with a can of BAB-O. With a slight dusting of powder on the wet rag, I began wiping the tomato sauce and flecks of ground beef from the wall at arm's reach above my head. Streaks of white replaced the stain. Going back to the sink, I rinsed out the rag and came back at it, this time leaving a clean yellow wall. Then I tackled the floor, sweeping the plate shards and the spaghetti debris into the dustpan and emptying it into the trash. The china plate had shattered, but the scalloped rim was intact in many places, so I played a game of arranging all the violets that edged the plate in a circular fashion before sweeping them up into the pan. The dainty edges of the plate held a delicacy for me that was dear. I chose a shard covered with small lavender faces and put it in my pocket, then went back to my task. My brother had disappeared to play with Tonka toys in his room. Kneeling under *Prayer Changes Things*, I removed the register vent from the floor. Picking off the spaghetti, a residue of slime remained. I washed it off in the sink and began cleaning the debris from the ductwork with my rag. The elbow was full of food and shards, and I cleaned up the mess the best I could.

The afternoon wore on. I tried to read but kept rereading the same sentences over and over. Mom hadn't returned. I worried about the gun she took. Maybe she'd find a woodchuck to shoot instead of shooting herself. When Dad came back to the house, I ran to him and hugged his waist. It was suppertime; he fixed some eggs and toast which we all ate heartily. I helped Dad clean up the counter and dried the dishes after he washed them.

By then, it was dusk, and Mom still wasn't back. The three of us stood at the bathroom window, my brother on the stool, and me peering over the sill, just barely tall enough to see the driveway from inside the room.

The air was static as we watched. Will she come back? What can we do? Should we try to go find her? My father stood behind us and tried to reassure us she would return. My brother started to cry as the light waned. Finally, the Nash pulled into the drive. The first thing I saw when the door opened was not her foot but the barrel of the gun. She was home. ◰

Birdshot, Buckshot   *Jill Johnson*

Ali Shaw

Stardust

I hurry off the bus and onto the light-rail platform, my mind flat but for the workday ahead, until I see that the woman is there again. Our morning commutes have started to coincide most days, but not all. The sun is glaring slantwise on the woman as she turns, tall, stout, her chin jutted forward. Her short brown hair is almost black, almost boyish, exactly like Elissa's.

And just like that, I am back at the timed writing contest, listening to Elissa read her monthly entry, her words smooshing together again as she rushes. Her stories are always twice as long as what other people can write in thirty-six minutes. I remember Elissa's excitement at gifting me a copy of her zine, carefully copied and folded and stapled by hand—priceless.

My mind takes me to the afternoon visit on her porch a few years later, though I try not to follow. The sun was intense that day too. Her brain tumor wouldn't stop growing. The chemo wouldn't keep working. Awkwardly, I asked how she felt.

"I'm on fucking hospice. That's how I feel."

The sun bore down on us both, and our eyes watered.

The woman on the platform adjusts her backpack to pull out a book. I want to ask her if she's read *The Hundred Most Influential Writers in My Life to Date, As Best I Can Remember and Mostly Not Including Zines*. I'd offer it to her, but I have only one copy, stored safely in my hope chest at home. I entertain the idea that the woman is a writer, that her stories are long, long and she's self-conscious about taking people's time. I hope she's funny too. Maybe she has a novel in progress.

No, I scold myself. She is not Elissa, not my friend who named a character after me, who taught high schoolers how to love reading and writing, whose brain worked perfectly until it didn't, whose life left her three years ago.

How can it be that this woman not only looks like Elissa but also moves like her, turning her head incrementally as her eyes travel across the page? I worry that I'm staring, so I shift my focus to the tracks. She's nearly the same age as Elissa, so reincarnation can't explain it. And Elissa told me all her relatives lived in the Midwest, except a sister who has since moved back. Not family. And yet, the woman is deeply familiar.

A shadowy spot crosses the tracks and swoops across the platform. I look up to follow the crow's path across the sun.

We came from stardust, Joni Mitchell said. NASA confirmed.

What if, when we go, our souls disperse into the fine powder of stars again, mixing with other cosmic particles in the creation of countless new souls? What if, when we see a stranger who feels like home, we're recognizing their stardust of the same origin?

When the train arrives, the woman and I board different cars.

I send a prayer into the cosmos and hope some of Elissa's stardust is floating above to receive it. "It's good to see you." ◧

Move   *Sheary Clough Suiter*

Cynthia Steele

A Naked Lady in a Library

The library is the book of books,
Its concrete and wood and glass covers

Keeping within them the very big,
Very long story of everything.

—Alberto Ríos

The stories: S. E. Hinton's *The Outsiders*, Beatrice Sparks' *Go Ask Alice*, as well as the authors Roald Dahl, Judy Blume and Shel Silverstein. Libraries wherever we lived provided a place to get lost as much as possible. Much like, in the '60s, the Spenard Sunrise Bakery provided the yeasty, white flour smells and day-old treats my sister and mother picked through. Beverly Cleary. *The Boxcar Children*. I read primarily to fuel my fantasy of running away and living in a boxcar with some other kids. But I knew Caldecott Award winners like Maurice Sendak's *Where the Wild Things Are*, were way better at stealing my attention. I pull them out to look for the gold seals, read a bit, click my tongue, then push them back. They make a shushing noise. I look around.

The paint lay thick on the walls, dulled with the touch of children's fingerprints. Children, like me, will occasionally not bring back the borrowed book, doled out with stern warnings. "But, I intend to keep it," I wanted to say, just to see their expressions. "Okay," I'd say, instead, instantly forgetting her words, just knowing my intentions. The olive green, mustard yellow, and basic primer brown of woodblock stamped bears cover this library. Posters announcing upcoming novels or reading clubs in white backgrounds spot the once-white brick walls, yellowed by the fluorescent lighting that twitched occasionally. The books, crisp, often with fold-out pages of artwork, cackled at the silence-revering librarian.

I borrowed so many books. I was collecting them. I'd touch the card pocket in the back, the one where a middle-aged lady would long to replace the card. I took a secret pleasure in the book having found its permanent dwelling place in my pile. I'd thwart her. Before long, we'd be forced to move, over and over. The pile of books I'd accumulated always went back.

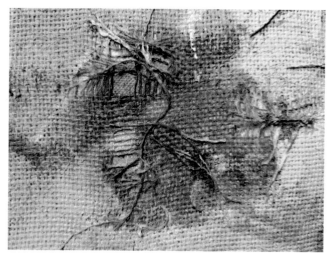

Tentative   *Nard Claar*

A few kids, sixth graders like myself, found nudity in book images made with paint, sketches from charcoal. They may have been Pre-Raphaelite Brotherhood nudes, but, to us, they might as well be photos tucked away in the drawer at a Kodak photo shop to amuse shopkeepers who'd printed doubles, having seen the sort of stuff Marge develops.

In this moment, free to laugh at it all, there it is: nakedness. The world is stripped bare, pretend. It is new and there are no forged, hazy remembrances of wrongfulness. I'm invited to share the weirdness of open displays of nudity, of acting as if it were new and I'd never really seen a body. It makes me feel, if only for a moment, as if I were an innocent at 10.

As if I had not been shown photos in dirty magazines, as if I had not been touched "there" by a grown man. I pull this blanket of childhood over me and feel enveloped by the camaraderie of oneness. Yes, we are all at the same stage: pre-menses, pre-kisses, pre-touches in that way. David Meese would stick his tongue down my throat the same year, but I'd throw my books down and scream at the top of my lungs. It's important for them to know I'm innocent, even if I'm not.

I wonder if they notice, in that one frozen moment, that my eyes flick up to the rectangular windows where daylight reminds me of the outside world. If they can see the pall that pulls my face downward in a suspended animation. I am suddenly, in that speckled, laminate-tile world, struck with a pain in my chest. The difference. I see in all their small faces an accusation—unintended—that I am that naked, drawn sketch of a woman. I have no curves, yet I am the painted lady, grown, unawkward, and a sexual object for children to gawk at. No, I'm imagining it.

Titters. Fingers point, flip crackling, thick pages in another large art book with the librarian peering over her cat-eyes. We all stood shoulder to shoulder around one another, within a foot, anyway. Titters at the body's slopes and curves and ridges, in our words the "titties" and "butts." We are shushed in our clothed bodies, in our wonder of the world ahead of us, in our untied tennies, strings hanging loose and short or knotted.

I deny my life in that moment. I lie about my closeted instances where I mutely push away my stepfather, his mouth, his hot air, his probing fingers, and I revel in this space where he is far away. I'm among other children my age. In this moment, there are only spines, pages of books big as my core. And I know that I will stay here, looking at books and reading long after these children have gone.

Like the custody with my dad, this is only temporary. Like safety, like pretending we kids are all one. I stay until the thick, rectangular glass no longer bleeds sunset through.

Then, I trudge those two long, dusty blocks home to a father who barely knows me. My stepmother is in the kitchen. "Go wash up," she says, in a singsong voice. I absentmindedly belt out the words of "Hey Jude" because I am in love with the Beatles. My father slams his fist down on the kitchen table. "No singing at dinner." I can't get that stuck good in my brain. I shrug, roll my eyes, and, on the way by my room, throw my books on my bed.

Catching my eye, above my headboard, is the set of Laura Ingalls Wilder's boxed volumes of *Little House on the Prairie*, with its scrawled images and light-yellow tone. The only thing besides clothes I'd taken from my mother's place. And, for a moment, quickly shrugged off, I allow my mind to go far away, across town, to think of her. The book of poetry she'd given me—pale blue covered *Poems for a Little Girl* by Anne Farrell, talked about violets, birds, hair ribbons, mud pies, and dressing up. Mama had starred and commented on specific ones. My mother, who could not see danger, could not avoid it for her children or herself, was like me, at least a little.

Feeling fragmented as I lay on my bed awaiting

the "Dinner" call, I read Go Ask Alice's diary "I wouldn't say this to anyone but you, Diary, but I'm not too sure I'm going to make it in a new town. I barely made it in our old town…Oh dear God, help me adjust, help me be accepted, help me belong…" I felt the same way, moving here.

"I'd have died without them [books]. Even now I'm not really sure which parts of myself are real and which parts are things I've gotten from books." Boy, she said it.

"Dinner! Wash up!" Interrupts my refuge. I throw water over my hands, let the water drip to the sink and floor in muddy grey-brown blobs, and wipe my hands on my jeans. I enter the kitchen, belting out:

> Elementary penguin singing Hare Krishna
> Man, you should have seen them kicking Edgar
>   Allen Poe
> I am the egg man
> They are the egg men
> I am the walrus
> koo kook achoo

Dependably, his fist slams on the table, and in a moment, I am mute. Staring. With blank eyes and shirked shoulders, I sit and pick at my food, which is not the kind I'm used to. Back in the library of my mind, I leaf through drawings of naked ladies with the other kids. I laugh out loud, which draws a stern look.

"How was school? Learn anything?" My father booms.

"Leo smashed his finger. Some kids brought Kool-Aid from home in a bag with sugar."

My father shakes his head, releases a slight smile from above his square chin, and excuses me from the table. ◪

Leaves Over Steps, Seattle

Cynthia Steele

Hamish Todd

The God Issue—Part Two
Getting Redwing

Even though I'd met and read with Ginsberg, I'd never read any more than the first few lines of *Howl*. Christ, you didn't have to. David Fewster, my roommate, had read everything. He was quite the fountain of literary knowledge. He'd given me some Bukowski for Christmas: *Women*, this funny, disgusting book about all the women Bukowski had loved and hated and expounded at length about his mad sexual escapades with all sorts of broken-down junky chicks and pretty apartment types and stepping out, fed up housewives, and anyone else he could get his pecker into. David Fewster thought I'd like Bukowski. He seemed to think my writing style was similar. I wasn't so sure, but I loved reading Bukowski. I'd tried reading Kerouac but it never worked for me. I wouldn't read *On the Road* for years to come yet and then it didn't work for me but his short stories, who knew, Kerouac was a real writer!

I had gone to see Vincent Ballestri at the Velvet Elvis, *playing* Kerouac. Vincent Ballestri had lived with Edie Kerouac. She'd told him that he looked a lot like old Jack. And here he was, living with his ex-wife, looking like him and living in the same house that he once wrote and lived in. It inspired him. He thought there must be some reason that all this was happening to him. So, he started to read everything Kerouac had ever written. As an actor, he'd found his calling. And for the next ten years,

he'd tour the country doing his one man show: "Kerouac, The Essence of Jack." Man, he'd been good. He was forty and thick, like an old football player turned to drink. He had a head of black wavy hair, and though I'd never seen Kerouac and the only pictures I'd seen were of him as a young man, I imagined he looked just like he would have looked if he'd still been alive. He had a horn player and a stand-up bassist with him, and they were blasting it out, backing him up like the words and music were meant to go together.

When the Guild had still been running the paper, I'd reviewed the play. I saw it three times, taking every one I could with me, I so wanted to share this wonderful cat. After seeing his show, I felt like I'd met Jack Kerouac, or at least got a real interesting glimpse into that strange soul's particular brand of madness. Once I went with Roland. Another time I went with Jack McMurtry, and once I took this fine blonde girl, who told me she had a boyfriend during intermission. She was a friend of Polly's, worked in some daycare with her, wanted to be a teacher. Good old-fashioned, American as apple pie. We were standing at the bottom of some stairs in the back, crowding around with the rest of the audience, having a glass of wine. I was feeling terribly civilized, standing framed in velvet with this beautiful golden-haired girl, whose gleam I felt surpassed anything I'd ever seen. It came as a big disappointment when she told me she had a boyfriend. I mean, that's just not what a guy wants to hear from his date.

"What are you doing out with me, letting me buy you drinks, seeing this play with me, if you've got a boyfriend?" I wanted to know.

"I don't see what the big deal is. There's no law that says I can't go out with a guy and have a nice time if I've got a boyfriend. Is there?

"You know I was asking you out."

"Well, I'm sorry you misunderstood." Oh, that was the worst, treating me like the dummy I was. It hurt. I had so wanted to get into her trousers, and now it seemed as though that was impossible. I felt used. We'd seen the rest of the play anyway, and I continued to chase her for a little while before I decided she wasn't worth the trouble. Damn but she was fine! I masturbated thinking of her body a couple of times.

I was so impressed with this Vincent Ballestri's knowledge of Kerouac's work, that I thought he must actually dig poetry. Kerouac's spirit must legitimately be speaking through him. He was too good. I took him a poem. One I'd written after reading those first few lines of *Howl*, before Xavier and I went to New York and brought the infamous pischer back to Seattle with us, "To read. One more time." Xavier Cavazos and me, reading with Allen Ginsberg. We were the luckiest sons of bitches in the universe. When I was showing Ballestri my poem, he tried to take the paper from me, to read it, but I said, "No, I've got to read it to you. You've gotta *hear* it." He said he loved it.

"We'll do a thing like we're at a reading," he said. "I've been thinking of recreating a reading by bringing in a couple other poets for a while now. Yeah, this'll be great." And he let me read in the middle of his play, the horn and bass player backing me up. It was the greatest! I loved jazz, loved Ballestri, the spirit of Jack, I absolutely loved everything. I was having the time of my life. Now, we were entering a different chapter. I had no idea what was going to happen, what Redwing would be like, but I felt like it was all destiny, that I had no choice but to carry on and see *which way* the river would turn. What awaited us on the great sea that was life. Ron was going too fast and Roland was beating on the dashboard like a drum, just excited as hell. Nirvana was blasting out of the tape deck and I could barely hear what Ron and Roland were saying as we zoomed past SeaTac and Southcenter. South, then North, to Mount Rainier. God, I loved that mountain. It always made me feel like I was home. I wanted to live

there someday, in her valleys, or in her peaks, maybe up on the ridge, in a cabin with leaded windows and dark, old, wooden beams running through the ceilings. There I'd write by lamp light, while the fire roared away in the fireplace, as I sat pondering in wonder the white howling landscape. And of course, I'd have a gorgeous, talented woman, who hung on my every word, had an exciting life of her own, and satisfied me sexually. And she would come to stay with me and my big dog when she wasn't busy travelling.

Roland and Ron were laughing about something and passing the pipe back and forth. It came back between the seats and I took a toke. Then I lay back, looking out the window, seeing the evergreen zoom by, and I was stoned and happy, and for the first time in my life I understood why all those kids had flipped out so when Cobain did himself. I finally got why Nirvana had driven everyone so mad. Why the media likened him to John Lennon and made such a god-awful damn fuss when he tragically chose to take his own life. I still didn't like it when they compared him with the likes of Lennon, but for the first time, in the back seat of that rented LeBaron, on my way to meet Redwing in the mountains, I realized that he had been Great. The poor, mad, brilliant, self-hating asshole had really made some *great* music. He'd created a little Universal Magic. And I was just now hearing it for the first time.

"What else can I write? I don't have the right." It was epic. Too bad he didn't stick around to write more.

Out the car window was a brilliant day. The sun-bright snow glistening. We pulled into the Paradise parking lot, got out and started throwing snowballs at one another. Ron beaned me a good one, right in the ear, and I had to stop. Ron and Roland kept it up, a great battle between two mighty warriors. We carried on like this for a while, getting in and out of the car to get warm, to get high, to play in the snow, and just to appreciate what a god-awful pretty day it was. There was no place as pretty as Washington when it wasn't pissing down rain.

In less than an hour, we saw Redwing pull up. He was piling out of a silver gray late model station wagon, waving like a madman. Mom and Dad who gave him a ride, beaming in the front, getting out to say goodbye, to help him with his bags. There was a boy and a girl in the backseat, and gear all over the place. Redwing got right out, and hugs went all around, then quick introductions to his ride.

"C'mere, I want you to meet these good people. I've been riding with them all the way from Idaho." We went over to the station wagon and said hello, the kids smiling and waving from the backseat, as Redwing gave Mom a hug and shook Dad's hand. He had their address and promised he'd send them his book, just as soon as it was finished. And he probably would. I hoped so. He was a crazy looking Indian, missing a front tooth. A juicy scar cut across his left cheek. I couldn't believe how well he got on with that nice white family. He had long, silver black Indian hair, a chiseled, thin face with full lips, strong chin, and a body that looked as though it could be dragged behind a horse without suffering too much damage. He could have been going on forty or fifty, it was impossible to tell. He looked half wolf, half raven. And he'd just hitchhiked all the way from Denver in little more than three days. I was duly impressed. He looked as tough as nails. He was a cowboy. When we got in the car, he told us all about his trip.

"Oh, it was great. Best time I ever made. I got stuck in Duluth Montana for about six hours. It was hotter than hell, and I was out of ciggies. Montana has got to be the worst place in America to try catch a ride." His skin was supple leather and he had a silver tongue, I could tell straight away. That's why that family had been so fond of him because he'd just talked like an eloquent Englishman with that rich, dangerous baritone voice of his. He'd charmed the pants of them. The rest of his journey had gone well, hitching rides with truckers and a traveling salesman, "selling these amazing space age portable telephones, you should've seen these things. All they needed was a dildo attachment, and there'd be one in every flipping' household in America." And he laughed like an old jackal. "I tell you though," he said getting serious again, "I can be feeling all hard and hopeless, like everyone on the planet is a stinking piece of shit, then I make a trip like this. And all across this country people are as sweet as cherry pie, lost maybe, misguided by the media and by their government, but the *people* are hardworking and honest, and for the most part, kind." Ron and Roland and I all nodded our heads.

"That's a refreshing story to be heard," said Ron.

"Yeah, it's too easy to take shit too seriously," Roland said. Roland was always saying things just slightly out of context. I thought his mind was just travelling faster than his mouth. I thought Roland was wise. He was probably just stoned. We were all feeling good. We told Redwing, whose first name was Robert, all about everything we had planned, how the show was coming together, and he'd better get ready, because we had some interviews with the papers and lots of work to do.

"Well, I'll be damned. Looks like I've arrived at the party just in time."

Roland beamed. "And how's fishing, Ron?" and "Seamus, I've heard all about you." He was a fast talker, with a voice like an old frog, and so very, very charming. "Where do you get a drink around here?"

"Now you're talking," I said. "I'll buy you one the minute we stop."

"I accept. Care for a ciggie? I bought a carton after that episode in Duluth." And he shook a cigarette out of the pack for me. Generic brand. I accepted it, though I had my own, just to be gracious.

"Dig these ashtrays," I said, pushing in the lighter.

"This is high style. This yours Ron?" Ron laughed and said no we'd rented it because his Maserati was in the shop.

"How about pulling it over and getting a drink."

"We'll wait till we get to town," Roland said. "Then there's a dozen places. We'll hit them all!"

"Well, pass that pipe back here in the meantime." I was smoking a peace pipe with an Apache.

Ron was making good time down the mountain, and we were all laughing and joking, and Robert Redwing was telling all kinds of crazy stories about his women back in Denver, and how he had another he was seeing on the side. And if one or other of them didn't shape up, he was gonna dump 'em both and get himself some new little thing.

"Hell, maybe I'll just move out here."

He'd been a sniper in Nam. "And if you think whitey is mean, you should know that the Apache used to bury people alive. Ant hills, we invented that," he added proudly. He'd been a race car driver, a railroad man, a hobo, and a businessman. And the way he told it you believed every word he said.

We got to town and decided to skip the bars and get to Roland's first, so Robert could drop off his gear and get spruced up.

"Hey, this is a great place you've got going here," Redwing says to Roland.

"Yeah, it's alright."

"No man, it's great! Just look at these windows." The windows looked out onto a back alley, a little patch of grass and two giant elms, which stood full and leafy and cool. It was an old building and the windows were made from thick, rippled old-fashioned glass. "Whatdya pay for this place?"

"Four fifty."

"That ain't bad," Redwing said. "That ain't bad."

And he scratched his chin, thinking, his head bent sidewise. Roland had beers in the fridge, which he passed around upon our arrival. He also had two bottles of red wine and half a pint of Canadian Club. So, we forgot about going out to the bars.

"Let's just stay here," Redwing said. "Bars are too expensive. Roland, why don't you call some folks and invite them over and we'll have a little party."

"That's cool. I'll call Polly and see what she's up to."

"Tell her to bring some more wine," Redwing said. He'd already finished a beer and was starting in on his second glass of red. I'd switched to wine too, after the first beer and the way we were going, we'd need plenty more if we were going to have company.

Polly came over with her new boyfriend, Dave. Dave was a tall lanky white guy with close set eyes, a serious face and a big head of long blond rock star hair. I couldn't see what Polly saw in him. Ron had fronted him some money for some gear and they were big buddies. Roland thought his band was the greatest. Somehow, I missed it. I didn't like his music, and I wasn't particularly fond of him. He was a nice enough bloke. He played guitar in one of the bands that would be playing in our upcoming show and before I knew it, Redwing and he were planning to do some work together.

"I've been wanting to work with a musician," Redwing told him. "Roland sent me your guyses tape and I think we could really *do* something."

"Cool," said Dave. And Redwing was positively enchanted with Polly, who was beaming in the light of such a great poet. When he spoke to Polly his eyes and speech became soft, seductive, and she was lapping up every moment. Dave was oblivious. Lecherous old bastard, I thought. We were laying around Roland's apartment, talking about writing, smoking grass, which Ron seemed to have an endless supply of. Ron didn't drink, but he could sure smoke a lot of pot. And I was glad he didn't drink. He was a pretty surly sort and built like a brick house. I sure wouldn't wanna tangle with him, under any circumstances. And it was refreshing to have one amongst us who was devoutly sober. Roland wasn't a big drinker either. He was a rotten drunk. He got too depressed. But he was having a good time tonight, drinking right along with the rest of us. And we were all bullshitting and thinking we were so grand, and poetry was king. And Redwing gave me something. He gave me a word. He knew it was the only thing he could give me, and with several drinks in us both he tossed it out there.

"Seamus," he said. "I wanna give you something.

It's my favorite word lately, and I think you'll like it. Maybe you can use it."

"Well, go on. What is it?"

"An-om-y," he said slowly, pronouncing each syllable. Anomie, spelled a n o m i e. It means something beyond apathy. When a society is so far gone, so apathetic, so lost, that it eats itself from the inside out."

"Wow, that's a heavy word."

"Do you like it?"

"Oh yeah, that's a great word. Thank you." And I meant it. I felt like I could use a word as dark and powerful as that one. Roland had told me that Redwing would help me with my writing. I was always looking for a teacher. And that was a word I didn't know. And what's more, he really *knew* what it meant, and that was the brilliance. That *was* the poetry. I only ever used it the once. I don't like to think of it, but now that I do, it still could be an appropriate term, where politics and people are concerned anyway. I'm an optimist but I think we're doomed as a species. My writing teachers all tell me, "You need conflict." Well, there it is.

Anomie

Don't talk to me about empty
Don't talk to me about
Bleeding heart
Pierced nipple misunderstanding
Let's talk tricky loser
Lice farming
Drunken love closeness
At four in the morning
Over God Book
Togetherness
Of a whole brilliant beginning

Don't talk to me about anomie
Talk to me
With eyes crisp

Focus,
If you talk at all

[Editor's Note: see Cirque, *Vol. 10, No. 2, for the first installment: "The God Thing, Chapter One."]*

Red Rock, Blue Rock   Jill Johnson

FICTION

Mark Crimmins

Spreader

Gechaka-Shedang! Gechaka-Shedang! The steel plates of the spreading machine clang into the reverse position when I reach the end of the cutting table. *Gechaka-Shedang! Gechaka-Shedang!* The table is thirty yards long. Ten feet wide. Four feet high. On each of its long edges there is a metal track. The wheels of the spreading machine run smoothly along these tracks as I push it up and down, up and down. The machine spreads a layer of nylon a few millimeters thick and eight feet wide on the surface of the huge elongated table. Thus my job title. Spreader. I spread material on the table. Or operate the spreading machine. Each time it gets to the end of the table, the machine has to flip the spreading plates so that it can lay the material in the opposite direction. *Gechaka-Shedang! Gechaka-Shedang!* The sound of the spreading plates registers at ninety-three decibels. That's what Tony, the Quality Control dude, tells me when he stops by every hour or so with his little gizmo for registering noise. The decibel meter. In accordance with Federal Regulations, he has to write down the sound readings, which in turn determine whether or not earplugs and headphones are mandated for the machine operator. For me, the earplugs are optional. Suggested but not needed. Because the noise is intermittent. Not constant. The loudest noise is that clanging of plates. Nearly a hundred decibels of it. *Gechaka-Shedang. Gechaka-Shedang!*

In all, I have to spread a hundred and forty-four layers of nylon on the table. That's a lot of nylon. The material comes on huge four-hundred-pound rolls that have to be lifted onto a special dolly with a crane down in the warehouse and then lifted by a smaller crane mounted on the factory ceiling from the dolly onto the spreading machine itself, where it rolls into place. Each roll has a thousand yards of fabric, so it takes about four rolls to spread the whole hundred and forty-four layers of material on the table. Each layer has to be lain flat on the one below it. If you have a kink in the material, then when the cutters come to cut out the patterns the kinks will make the garments have a flaw. An irregular line along the edge of the garment that will maybe make the sewers sew around the false perimeter and give the garment a little added slack. Maybe the customer will notice the

flaw and maybe he won't. But one thing's for sure. If the foreman notices the flaw, the kink, whatever, then that goes down as a mark against you. And if the foreman doesn't get it, the QC dudes will. That's assuming the sewer herself doesn't catch it. It's easy to track it to your batch. Each of the four spreaders has to sign off on the table when it's full, and then that table full of clothes is cut out by the cutters and the batch has your number coded on its labels. There's nowhere to hide.

But if you're a good spreader you don't need anywhere to hide. You lay a good smooth layer cake of nylon on that table so when the cutters put the pattern on top of the material and cut out twelve dozen pieces at a time with their hand-operated oscillating band knives, they have no problems and can see with a quick scan of the edges of the cut-out garment pieces that there are no loops or irregularities. Sometimes they'll give you a slap on the shoulder at break time. It's nice to get the acknowledgment.

"Nice spread, Mikey! No flaws! No irregularities! You make a cutter's life easy, man! One a these days, they gonna make you head spreader, yaknow?"

That's the way Andy talks. A buddy of mine on the cutting team. We became friends coz we both got these nosebleeds. At first, we thought it was the heat. Then we thought it was the altitude. Then we thought it was the dry desert air. But one way or another our noses bled like stuck pigs. Not every day, for sure, but most days. And sometimes they bled two three times in one day. Finally, one day in the break room, when we were both in there looking like walruses with tusks of tissue paper sticking out of our nostrils, Andy said he'd had enough.

"I aint bleedin no more, Mikey," he told me with his now nasal voice. It sounded like he had a bad cold. Coz of the tissues up his schnoz. "I've had enough a this shit. Bleedin on Monday. Bleedin on Tuesday. Bleedin on fuckin Wednesday. I'm gonna lose my job here if I'm not careful. Then what would I do? I gotta wife and kid to worry about. I'm a good cutter. I know that." He held out his hands. Only the top half of his left fourth finger was missing. "Lookathat! I practically got all my finguz on me still. Most the guys out there running outta finguz! Steve?

He's got what? Two fingers on his left hand, three on his right. I don't know how he operates that knife. He cuts off one more finger on his right hand he's finished as a cutter!"

Steve was ten years older than the rest of us. He'd been a cutter for a long time. That's why he lost so many fingers. It was just part of the job. Cutters end up cutting their fingers off one way or the other. Funny thing was, Steve wasn't worried about his mutilated hands. He was always talking about if he cut off that last important finger—the index finger on his right hand that you needed to operate the knife's key switch—he'd get a steel hand up at the hospital. A prosthetic limb. A metal claw. Then when someone made the mistake of giving him a hard time at the bars on the weekends, he'd pull out that hand and sock em with a full metal right hook and smash their face into pieces. He'd show 'em what a 'hard right' was, ha ha! The Frankenstein Punch! A full metal jacket! It was almost like he wanted to cut off that last finger just so he could get his claw.

But anyway, me and Andy bonded over our fucked up noses. But like I said, Andy had had enough. He wasn't gonna bleed no more. No more walrus jokes. No more of that horrible sweet taste of his own blood going down his throat and making him gag. What was he, he'd ask—a fuckin vampire of his own self?

"Nope," he told me on our break. "I've found out about this thing. This 'procedure' the doctors call it. They fix your nose real good so it don't never bleed no more. Not never! Some guy hits you in the middle a the face, ya nose don't even bleed! Imagine that! That'd freak the bastard out alright! He's just broke your beak in three places and it ain't even bleeding! Now motherfucker knows he's in trouble! He's picked a fight with a dude cain't bleed!" Andy reeled off with a "Wuhoo" when he said this, and punched the wall beside me with a carefully clenched fist. His hand went clear through the drywall. Dust and pieces of plaster fell to the floor. Fortunately, nobody was with us and nobody saw. In the big picture, it was just a small flaw in the plant's structure. What harm was that gonna do? That's the nice thing about working in factories. You fuck up and break something, it's no big deal. Just another hole in the wall. Andy was psyched about this medical procedure.

"It's called—get this—*cauterization*!" I remembered what the welders in the machine shop downstairs meant by that. To be honest it didn't sound too good to me. Andy got all excited about his new discovery though. "They take this, this like white hot piece of metal and

they shove it up your schnoz and they fucking *cauterize* the flesh, man! They seal it shut so you don't get no more fucking nosebleeds. It's like they weld your nose shut. And it's cheap. It takes no time and it costs like fifty bucks. It's not even a operation. So I'm seriously thinking of getting my nose cauterized, man. No more nosebleeds, Mikey!" Side by side, like nosebleed brothers, we looked at our faces in the reflection of a shiny steel panel. Andy gestured up at his tissue tusks. "Look at us, man! We're looking bad! *Real* bad! I get my nose cauterized. Fifty bucks and—pop! Gone! Say goodbye to tha Walrus! No more tusks! No more fuckin Beatles songs. No more jokes about not getting enough nookie. I know I'm getting enuff from Shirley!"

Andy's wife was the one who had found out about the cauterization procedure. She was so excited about it she was willing to pay for his treatment. He tried to get me to do the same thing. "We could go up there some Saturday and get our noses welded shut together, man! Like a coupla chicks gettin' their nose jobs, ha ha! We'd be brand new on Monday morning! Probly get a rise from Sparksy coz of how dedicated we was to our jobs! Think about how much more efficient we'd be! A factory's about efficiency. Nosebleeds don't enter the picture. It's all about the cauterization, Baby!" He whooped again and hit the metal sheet. *Thwang!* It sounded like the bell at the end of a boxing round. Andy, too, picked up on this. "The nosebleed is out for tha count, ha ha! Say goodbye to tha blood!"

But I wasn't quite as sure as Andy was about the virtues of cauterization. I told him I needed more time to think. I thought it over while I was spreading the nylon on the spreading table. That was one thing I liked about being a spreader. It gave you plenty of time to think. The machine pretty much did the job. You pushed it and walked alongside it and made sure there were no flaws in the spread. The truth was, even if there were flaws, you could just smooth them over with your expert spreader's hand. Spreaders aren't just labourers. They're *skilled* labourers. It took three or four hours, depending on how fast you pushed the machine, to finish a spreading job. So you had plenty of time to think. I'd use this time to think about my life. What I was planning to do next. All kinds of stuff.

In the future, I reckoned I wasn't gonna be a spreader forever. I dropped out of South High at sixteen and started work. Now I was already a Senior Spreader. Not bad for twenty-one. I figured by the time I was twenty-five I could be a foreman in the plant. Or maybe I would even quit the factory and try to go back to school. Finish off that high school diploma. Maybe even go to college as a mature student. If I did that, I could have a whole other life. I just kept laying the material down as I thought about my life. But right then I looked at the expanse of perfect white material I was spreading and had a strange thought—it was like I was laying down fold after fold of some huge scroll, a great blank scroll with nothing written on it. Maybe that's what my future was at that point—one great long continuous blank white page. I could write whatever I wanted on it. I'd sometimes have these thoughts while spreading. The supervisor of the sewers, Melody Stocks, said I was a thinker because of this. Nearing sixty, she thought I was intelligent, too intelligent to work in a factory forever. She told me to get out while I could. While I was still young. Before it was too late.

But before long I got back to thinking about the ins and outs of Andy's idea that I should get my nose cauterized. I hate to admit it, but a plan came to me as I walked up and down the cutting table beside my machine. I was soothed into a trance by all that repetition. The noise of the plant sometimes settled down into an even hum. Six hundred sewing machines. Four spreading machines. Ten cutters with their buzzing band knives. It all mixed together sometimes into a peaceful sort of harmony. White noise I guess you could call it. Some sort of fucked up symphony. A factory symphony! *A Symphony for the Working Class*, ha ha! During those long stretches, I found I could really think my way through things. I thought about Andy. It made no sense for us both to get our noses cauterized. And I felt a bit guilty thinking this, but it seemed to me that if Andy got his nose done, I could wait and see if it worked. I looked over at him briefly, bent over his band knife at Table Four. The truth was, cauterization sounded too painful to me. Andy'd mentioned that you got a big injection for the pain. I didn't like needles. I avoided injections whenever I could. You could call me an *injectaphobiac*. That's the word I made up for it. A lot of people had a fear of needles but nobody knew a word to describe that fear, so I made one up. I figured one day I could maybe get the word patented or put in *Webster's Dictionary*. Be like Benjamin Franklin. Get inventive. Sign a copyright or whatever.

So I decided to hold back and let Andy do the nose cauterization. I figured I'd wait and see and then I'd make my decision. I had a hard time looking Andy in the eye when we talked about it after that. He didn't realize that was why I was holding back. To let him be the guinea pig.

That's what I always liked about Andy—he was always straight up. He couldn't even see the ugly angle half the time. He just thought I was a scaredy-cat. Thought I just didn't wanna go 'under the needle,' as he called it with a laugh. We didn't really have that conversation with anyone else, but one day Neil, one of the older cutters, seemed to figure out what I was doing. "So, uh, how come you ain't getting this nose-weld thing, Mikey? Ain't you got as many nosebleeds as Andy?" I just told him I was too scared of needles, but he gave me a look that seemed to suggest he'd figured out my game. Neil was shrewd enough himself that he had radar for shrewdness. For calculation. For the hidden motivations behind the stuff we did. The real reasons behind the lies we told to cover our secret intentions. The lies we told ourselves.

Finally, the day came. The Friday before 'the procedure,' Andy was real excited and told us all about it all over again. He was so psyched about his new nose that he was like a giddy kid. He had a final nosebleed that Friday and called us all over. "I want you guys to see this," he said, as he shoved tissues up his nostrils. "My Last Nosebleed! Say Goodbye! Ha ha! *Say Goodbye to tha Blood!* It sounds like a boxer's book. One a them Norman Rockwell pictures. *His Last Nosebleed!* No more medical breaks for me! I'll be cutting out patterns so fast the rest of yuz won't be able to keep up! Not when I'm not held up by this goddam fuckin bloody nose!"

We were all glad for Andy and gave him a round of applause. He was gonna win the showdown fight with his own schnoz. While I was clapping, I caught Neil shooting me a sideways glance, but he didn't say anything. Andy left work in a fine mood. He ran out to his car, a beat-up old Vega. I never saw him so excited about anything. Right then, I regretted not joining him and getting my nose fixed up at the university clinic. Andy said they had the world's most advanced nose-cauterizing machine. I watched him speed out of the parking lot at the wheel of his Vega. Head forward, he gripped the wheel and leaned into his own bright future. Monday morning, we were all curious to see how he looked. To learn about the procedure. Andy was a bit late coming in, so we were all waiting for him when he arrived. When he walked in, he looked pretty much the same. But he wasn't smiling as much. He didn't have any bandages on. Just a Band-Aid across the top of his nose. He didn't have much to say before we turned on our machines at seven, but at nine in the break room, he gave us his account of what had happened.

"Okay," he said, energetic as usual while we

gathered around him. "First thing, this was fucking PAIAIAIAINFUUULLLLL! I'm talking bad fuckin news here! The doctor says, *Okay Andy I'm gonna give ya an injection. We're gonna burn the flesh inside ya nose and melt it, so ya gonna need some help with the pain.* Then he brings out this fucking huge needle!" He showed us how long it was with his hands. "He says, *Now Andy, you need this, okay? I'm going to have to stick this needle right up your nose and desensitize the flesh inside your nose. I need to prepare you for this. This injection is going right up near your optical nerves. The nerves up there are very sensitive. This injection is going to be incredibly painful!* I started sweating right there! Maybe I don't need this fucking cauterization procedure, I thought. I can just carry on shoving tissues up my schnoz. What's so fucking bad about that? Looking like a walrus suddenly sounded good. Plus, I don't think it's right that doctors tell you in advance if something's gonna be painful. They should just do it. You find out it's incredibly painful when it happens. But this guy made it twice as bad by telling me about it before it even happened. He seemed to enjoy scaring the shit out of me."

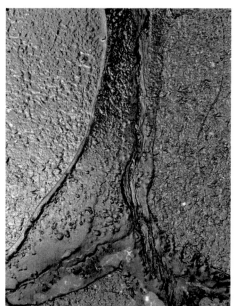

Andy continued with his story. Sitting and standing around

Tank Tar   *Jill Johnson*

him in the break room, we were all ears. You'd think so many guys who'd cut off multiple fingers in industrial accidents wouldn't wince during a story like his, but they did. All of us laughed nervously. Made faces. Covered our eyes with our hands like little kids. Some of us almost didn't want Andy to continue, but we couldn't stop listening once he'd started. It struck me while Andy was talking what a good storyteller he was. He'd often told me about his Grandpa from Jackson Hole, who told great stories about the outdoors. About rustling and ranching in extreme conditions. Sometimes I felt, when Andy was talking, that he must've got some of his Grandpa's genes. He could really tell a tale. And he had us with this cauterization story. He hadn't even got to the cauterization part yet. This was just the introduction. The Preface! He was playing up the pain injection for all it was worth. The way he described it, it felt like the doctor shoved that giant needle all the way up his nose and

deep into his brain.

I was sweating just hearing about it. Andy went on. He had us groaning, bending over, looking away, laughing. He told us next about the cauterizing wand. The doctor called it his 'magic wand.' Then the good doc, who sounded like a quack to me, explained to Andy how the procedure was not always successful. Sometimes it didn't stop the nose bleeding—the bleeding just continued after the wound had healed anyway. If you were really unlucky, the doctor explained—covering his ass from lawsuits we figured—your nose actually bled worse than before.

Andy was ready to leap out of the doctor's chair at that point and sprint back to his light blue Vega. But he had a dilemma. He'd already endured the excruciating pain of the injection, so now he figured it would be a waste not to continue. Otherwise, he'd have just gone to the clinic and got this excruciating injection for nothing. That made no sense. The pain he'd endured so far was like an investment, he said. The doctor told him that *in the majority of the cases* the procedure worked. But Andy realized that could mean it only had a 51% success rate. He didn't like the numbers. By this time, he didn't trust the doctor, who gave Andy a last chance to change his mind. Neil said the doctor was using reverse psychology, but us younger guys didn't know what that meant. Anyway, Andy was freaked out by all the doctor's moves. Maybe the injection itself, he said, was starting to fuck with his head. Maybe it was affecting his judgment. How could he know?

Myself—for reasons I'm not going to go into here—I'd always had a mistrust of the medical community. Suffice it to say that I'd seen the slimy side of the profession. As far as I was concerned, cutters and spreaders were straight up types of people. The kind of down-to-earth folks you get in the garment industry. Maybe they had a few missing fingers, but they were honest and you knew where you stood with them. They had no pretense. No vanity. They didn't get passive aggressive on your ass. Doctors were different altogether. In fact—as far as I was concerned—doctors were like a different race of beings altogether. But that was just me.

Or maybe it wasn't. Andy was beginning to think the doctor was some twisted bastard who got a kick out of scaring his patients. Maybe he got a kick out of inflicting pain. Look at the way he made them anticipate. It was like he was making them go through it twice. Then he would say all this shit about how the pain might accomplish nothing. What the hell was he thinking when he said all that shit? It wasn't like the bastard would return his fee if the procedure failed, was it? Andy said it again— the doctor was like some fucked up Wizard of Oz. He took up his cauterizing wand, which looked like a long, slender, soldering gun.

While he was telling us all this, I noticed something had changed in Andy. As he related the incidents with relish, his left eye was twitching a bit. The part of his nose he'd had cauterized was near the top of the left nostril. The twitch near his eye was not too far from where the procedure had been done. Danny noticed it too and mentioned it to Andy, but Andy just brushed it off. That was just a temporary side effect, he said. It would go away in a coupla days. The doctor told him it was nothing to worry about. We all looked at each other when he said that, but nobody said anything, and he went on.

So—squinting with that newly twitching left eye—Andy told us about the cauterization. The doctor had told him with relish that the point of his wand, his *Wizard of Oz Magic Wand,* as Andy was calling it now, would heat up to seven hundred degrees. It was imperative for Andy to stay perfectly still as the doctor put the white-hot metal welding wand into his nostril and then slowly inserted it farther and farther up his nasal passage until he got to the point where he was going to apply it to the supersensitive flesh and melt it into a new configuration. Even then, at the most painful point of the procedure, it was vital, the doctor told him, not to move. Otherwise irreparable damage could be done to surrounding tissue and nerves. In spite of how excruciating the injection had been, Andy told us that the pain of the cauterization was unbelievable. His twitch going faster now, Andy told us how he heard the skin singeing and could smell the awful stink of his own burning flesh. Danny nearly barfed up his Quaker Oats when he heard that. He caught them in his mouth but he had to swallow them a second time. The rest of us weren't doing much better.

Now Andy told us about the other pains he had endured in this life. The spiral fracture in his femur he got playing football for West High was nothing compared to

this. He'd shattered his tailbone on a rock that protruded through the ice while he was sledding down a glacier at full tilt up in Montana. The pain of that was nothing too. The only pain he'd had even remotely like this was when a dentist had fucked up a root canal and left some dead nerves at the bottom of the sealed-up cavity in his tooth, down beneath the cement. When this developed into an abscess, Andy has actually passed out from the pain. A doctor had told him he could have died if the abscess had burst into his brain. Not even the strongest opiates could quell the pain of that abscess. But the cauterization pain was worse. And it was sustained. The Fucked-Up Wizard of Oz seemed to take forever to perform his cauterizing magic. Perhaps it was only a few minutes. Andy had thought it was going to be just a second or two of pain, but it was more complicated than that. The doctor said, over Andy's screams, that he needed to make sure. Or was he just deliberately inflicting more pain on Andy for some dark reason of his own? Who could know? It certainly crossed my mind. A couple of the guys shot me looks sideways during Andy's story that suggested they might be thinking the same thing. Neil glanced at me, too, nodding slightly.

We were relieved when the second buzzer sounded, announcing the end of the break. I noticed that my shirt was saturated with sweat when I went back out to my spreading machine. After the Edgar Allan Poe horrors of Andy's harrowing story, I was glad to be back to the simplicity and order of my machine and my table. The clanging plates at the end of each layer of nylon I spread seemed to hammer the story I'd just heard of existence. *Gechaka-Shedang! Gechaka-Shedang!*

Then, when I looked over at Andy's table, I could see him cupping his hands and catching the drops of a new nosebleed. He glanced over at me with a look of dread. But when I caught him later near the water fountain, he assured me that the Wizard of Oz had told him there'd be some bleeding after the procedure. Was I watching Andy lie to himself? Well, under the circumstances, what was he supposed to do? The bleeding would last for a week or two and then it would stop. But here's the thing. It never did stop. Andy's nose kept bleeding just like before. If anything, it was worse. For a while he kept believing it was just fallout from the procedure.

But finally, Andy accepted that he'd gone through all that pain for nothing. He took it quite well. To me he always seemed slightly changed after he endured the horrors of that procedure. It was subtle, to be sure. But he'd lost his enthusiasm. His spark. He never did, though, lose that twitch in his left eye. Danny told me once that it was permanent neurological damage and never to say anything to Andy about it. We all agreed we'd try to ignore the twitch and never mention it to Andy.

As for me, needless to say, I wasn't getting my nose cauterized anytime soon. I never did get it done. My decision to let Andy be the fall guy saved me a lot of pain and suffering. Plus, my nosebleeds just stopped of their own accord after about a year and never returned. I felt bad for Andy, but I hadn't hurt him myself. I put most of the blame on the doctor. Perhaps also on Andy's tendency to believe in things. His excessive trust. In uncomfortable moments, however—though Andy himself was too nice a guy to say so—I realized I had stood by and let him do irreparable damage to himself. Was this the only time I let someone else suffer to gain an advantage for myself? Or was this the only time I caught myself doing it? How could I know? I felt guilty, though, especially given the fact that Andy had come out of this with nerve damage. A twitch. A slight but permanent disfigurement. In a strange way, when I spoke with Andy after this, that twitch in his eye always seemed like a sort of accusation against me. But I managed over time to ease my conscience. Back and forth I walked along the tracks of the cutting table with my spreading machine on its creaking wheels. In the end zones of my runs, the clanging reversal of the spreading plates would drown out my worries. My fears. My guilt. Sometimes the banging plates sounded like the strokes of a hammer on an anvil, a hammer pounding my inner unease down to some unfathomable and uncharted place where I never wandered, never wanted to explore: *Gechaka-Shedang! Gechaka-Shedang! Gechaka-Shedang!*

Paul Haeder

Johnny Boy (JT) and Black Kettle

JT loves drawing sandhill cranes. Extruded from memory, JT sits on the sagging bumper of the Ford RV as he pushes capillaries of charcoal into the sky he delivers on the sketch pad paper.

Unending fire sky, he tells himself. He wants to imagine the sky this way, Turneresque, electric, something like all those village buildings he left behind in Huehuetenango what seems like a life time ago.

He steadies his hand and fingers, pushing and pulling, like an archaeologist digging through strata for evidence of life. He has no need to jump up and start over with colored pencils, Prismacolor pens, or sloppy acrylics.

The celestial rainbow of cirrus is a constant wash in his blinking moments, in between drawing birds of El Bosque and remembering war. The elegance of this bird—Antigone canadensis—JT knows is lost in his sketching, but each time a Rocky Mountain sandhill crane lifts, bouncing on air, dipping back into the water, JT understands the limits of art. It's easy to fold back fifty years.

A half century passes, from a youthful JT, soon a Government Issue grunt, then lifted out of Indochina with near-spiritual mortal wounds, into London to visit an aunt in Surrey. Then off to France. It's a dream and nightmare, December 1968. A 23-year-old's dream to see Paris.

Walking for hours in Saigon, JT finds himself in the cubby of a wood carver, Viet Nguon. In an instant of hormonic synchronicity, the Las Cruces boy is being told about Southwestern Native American masks by a bamboo-thin man in black silk ensemble. This master of wood has long graying hair cuffed into a foot-long viper down his back. He doesn't display a traditional Fu Manchu beard of aging guys. Rather, this man's sideburns are something out of Dickens–Vietnamese lambchops. Curly hair like the dogs sold in markets for stir-fry.

Viet's store is on a side street near An Dong market, and the alley-sized foot-and-bike path is devoted to shops where wood carvings and wood artisan wares are manufactured and sold.

The artist Viet has three hundred masks in his cramped shop. JT is all eyes, and for the New Mexico kid, each crazed mask seems like magic.

The Vietnamese artist speaks English. "You like? Many hundreds more I sell to many kinds of people. Where you from soldier?"

JT wants the real blood of these people—words, emotions, gestures, laughing and chatter from these Homo Sapiens he was told was "always the enemy…left or right, north or south, boy or girl, they are your enemy, Thomlinson. "

The lucidity of his nights sweating is always about the sound of war. The screams and moans of machine-gunned farmers, VC, somewhere in the elephant and canary grass. The rice paddies at night. Groans. The odor of flesh, burning shit, tires, and napalm and diesel. It was his companion now, extracted from the field, ready to ship out and be done with the war with Vietnam. I'll never be done with Vietnam, he told himself. Even now all the way to the middle of New Mexico Chihuahua desert.

"You come from where?"

JT stumbles in his response: "First Division, but ready for home. Attached at Tan Son Nhut," JT says as he straightens his back, in deference to the elder. The man is in his sixties, JT estimates, but that's not always easy to gauge for so many Vietnamese–older guys sometimes look younger. Maybe he is eighty. Hard to tell.

"I see, I see. Bro', Big Red One. It says Thomlison. Family name? My name Viet Nguon. Call me Viet. I ask where you family come from, no care about patch on arm?"

JT's surprised–then, looks down at his fatigues, the name patch. JT touches the BRO shield and number 1 on his arm. He still never got used to the fact he had been drafted 18 months earlier, and his whole life was green, black boots, humping a rucksack, laying mines, carrying an M-16.

"Uh, New Mexico. Las Cruces. United States." JT still can't recall the last time he spoke to a civilian Vietnamese. Sure, the yelling and cursing his unit dramatized out of fear, that wasn't the same. JT, remembers words, grunted words, gaseous words, lifting from the dark green of Vietnam, scattered dying enemies. Children screaming. Babies heaving. Groans. Water buffalo slogging. Civets. Roosters. Chinese music on transistor radios. Cicadas.

"You have people with beautiful masks. Fantastic features. What you call serpents. Those people in your homeland, named Hopi, Navajo. Great masks. Here, look, one I do like they say, kachina—like a bird. What, you call raven?"

Viet gives JT the water melon sized mask. Amazing details of the bird's beak and nostrum, the eyes, blue-black, the wood almost alive with feature cuts.

"I go to your country with books, no? Inside words on page. Masks, a magic of people. You put on. Put on. Here, mirror."

JT reluctantly takes the mask, which is light, and he touches the fine carved spaces. Black feathers are slicked back, like a mane flowing to a person's neck. The corvid's eyes have two perfectly drilled openings so the mask wearer can see.

"It's okay, sir." JT says trying to hand back the mask.

"No, good stuff, Thomlinson. Magic. You put on. You can be new Thomlinson. No more corporal, no more jungle, no more boom and fire…but bird man. Try on. Magic!"

Viet puts a calming but firm hand on JT's shoulder. Surprisingly to JT, Viet is tall for a Vietnamese, almost 5' 11", two inches shorter than JT.

JT knows the signs of panic, claustrophobia, are telltale – sweaty upper lip, flushed neck, slurred words. He's feeling the acrid instant coffee hit his windpipe.

"It okay, Thomlinson. Bird goes on this way," Viet says, helping lift the mask into place. "You know, black plague? Your ancestors had bird masks. Put sage and perfumes in long beaks. Chase away bubonic plague. You know this history?"

JT imagines all these bird men, fat, big Frenchmen and others walking around with prods to keep away the plague victims. "Un, no, not that. But I remember my mother taking me and my sister to Santa Fe. I remember the dances. Lots of costumes. Masks. Just like this one. And others, sir." JT presses the concave of the mask into his head as Viet secures the headgear with a beautiful silk purple ribbon.

"Raven. Powerful. Not what plague doctors have in seventeen century. This powerful…they call crow talisman."

JT is guided by the artist Viet to the mirror near Viet's assembling table where he carves and designs masks.

"Maybe Thomlinson clan knows raven good animal, help people. Make world for them. Raven trick too. Steal shiny objects. Raven is child, cause loud trouble for others. But wise. See, Thomlinson, see magic of mask?"

JT looks at the image in the mirror — tall, thin GI, wrinkled uniform, with this magnificent piece of art, carved and adorned with black and purple feathers. He sees that boy, in El Bosque del Apache. Mother taking the children to the wildlife refuge to watch sandhill cranes and snow geese winter over in the desiccated land around Socorro.

JT knows the transformation from soldier into this Vietnamese man's magic bird will be his talisman. Memory molded into whatever is left of his feelings about killing Vietnamese. The goo of death and stench of heaving Americans in a foreign land disappear for a moment, maybe forever in this crystalized moment.

"You see, you feel. New you. Raven, crow. We have in Vietnam, same clown birds. They come with death. Silly creatures. Smart. Last ones standing after Big Red One bro's come in with mortars and fire tongue."

JT stares for what seems like ten minutes. Viet vanishes. The mind, JT thinks, plays tricks. He squeezes his eyes shut behind the mask, and he sees himself flying. Black bird at El Bosque. Jumping around all the other birds. Trickster. Pest.

+-+

You know son, either way you look at it, we are fucked, says JT's mother, looking like cracked pasta months from her death from breast cancer.

Vagabond lives I gave you and your sister. I am okay with you leaving, hiding in Canada. Mexico. Or you go over there in the bloody morass and come back hardened, but with a chance at something new.

Their mother was an ornithologist for the US Fish and Wildlife Service. JT and his sis' Roberta always got the Rachel Carson and Jane Goodall of things.

Look for the birds when you can, Johnny Boy. If you go overseas, look for birds and listen to the people who know their birds. If you go, dear, you will have bird stories only I can dream of…El Bosque is fantastic but not like all those old-world jungle species. It's going to be heaven.

+-+

When JT takes off the large, bigger than human life-sized mask, he feels tears running down to his open collar and pure white cotton undershirt. Viet is there instantly, with a wooden carving of the same sort of bird. It fits in the palm of his hand. He hands it to JT.

"You take. You hold this when you got back. New Mexico. Big land of colors I see in movies, no? You go see birds for new light. Vietnam. One day, Thomlinson clan and Viet clan come together. You go to Paris, like I study art. Ho Chi study art in Paris. Go to big museum of African work. Trocadero. Ethnology. Go see masks."

JT never paid Viet because Viet never took the corporal's money.

Six months later, JT is in Paris, bumming around, absorbed in the street art. Bumming hashish. And he finds the Trocadero had been demolished in 1935.

But he does find those masks and other ethnographic materials Viet Nhung talked about. At the Musée de l'Homme, housed in the Palais de Chaillot.

JT carries the rucksack and the journals his mother would have wanted to see if she had survived another wintering of the sandhill cranes. The entire list of sightings of birds throughout his humping through lowlands and jungle and alpine forests would have put her on Ornithological Cloud Nine.

Not just an artist's obsession, but an offering for a mother's memory. More than 880 birds in Vietnam, and Corporal Thomlinson comes back to El Bosque with more than 340 captured in notes and sketchings.

A bird professor at University of New Mexico was blown away by the lonely corporal's bird list and his descriptions and drawings. "You've got to get a doctorate in birds, man. This is crazy impressive."

He follows in his mother's footsteps–this time state game and fish. Entire weeks in wilderness. Entire lifetimes to find the birdman's magic.

It is birds that saved me, man. So many of my buddies from Vietnam, gone. Three sheets to the wind. Hunkered down in some flop. Lots of heroin. I did nothing more than listen to Viet and push something like magic into my being. I never got to be the fucking artist of my dreams, of that magic, but, still, the art of this, out here, now, in

Zoom Gathering   Monica O'Keefe

"A smell of mold and neglect caught me by the throat. I was so depressed that I would have chosen to leave immediately,' Picasso said. 'But I forced myself to stay, to examine these masks, all these objects that people had created with a sacred, magical purpose, to serve as intermediaries between them and the unknown, hostile forces surrounding them, attempting in that way to overcome their fears by giving them color and form. And then I understood what painting really meant. It's not an esthetic process. It's a form of magic that interposes itself between us and the hostile universe, a means of seizing power by imposing a form on our terror as well as on our desires. The day I understood that, I had found my path."

the boonies, with birds. The other wildlife. Some marbles still in my head pushing 74 years old. You can't call this a blessing, but man, I have had my mother next to me every single day. She was right...I would come back, transformed. I know this is a so-called sacred moment, and I am grateful, but what saved me was not a higher authority or power, but the true magic of masks and birds —He wrote this during one of his AA meetings, that famous 20-year coin award.

JT still has the Picasso quote taped up to the tiny wall of the RV where the small bed is slung over the cab of the vehicle. Something profound enough for a drifting American ex-Vietnam soldier to have written down in his journal next to the birds of Paris he spent time cataloguing and drawing.

He found the quote somewhere on the Paris streets. Someone he shared wine with. A Frenchman who recognized in the young JT a transcendence from tool of war to a drifter in time and space...to magic seeker.

"You want to be an artist?" this fellow asks. "You enjoy Picasso? *Oui*, when Pablo was young, no pennies in his pocket, in Paris, he kept his eyes open for African masks at the Trocadero Museum. It was not an impressive musee. But the young Picasso, he fell for the magic—the charm— of Africa. Here, his actual words from a book. I give you them now, Johnny Boy:

Sandhill crane. Omnivore. Average life span in the wild: 20 years. Body: 31.5 to 47.2 inches. Wingspan: 5 to 6 ft. Weight: 6.5 to 14 pounds. More than 500,000 sandhill cranes amass at Nebraska's Platte River in spring.

Sand Hill Crane and Sand Creek Massacre. JT can't shake the mnemonic. In November 1864, Colonel John Chivington and his Colorado volunteers massacre a peaceful village of Cheyenne camped near Sand Creek in Colorado Territory. Chivington the Methodist preacher placed himself in the center of the Indian wars as his opportunity to gain recognition to win a government office. Chivington burned villages and killed Cheyenne whenever and wherever he could.

JT was there, days after Calley and his men from Charlie Company 1st Battalion, 20th Infantry Regiment unleashed the My Lai Massacre. Three hundred or 507 dead?

This day, this war crime, a war crime that was exposed by soldiers and condemned by the U.S. government in 1864. Sand Creek Massacre unleashed decades of war on the Great Plains. Even locals are unaware of what had happened in their own backyard.

The hundreds of troops charged the Cheyenne village of around a thousand. A chief raised the Stars and Stripes above his lodge. And others in the village waved white flags.

In response, the troops opened fire with carbines and

cannon, killing more than 150 Indians, most of them women, children and the elderly.

Before departing, the troops burned the village and mutilated the dead, carrying off body parts as trophies.

A 104 years later, these 1st Platoon members testified in court that the deaths of individual Vietnamese men, women and children took place inside Mỹ Lai during the security sweep. Livestock was shot as well.

JT can't forget the testimony of PFC Michael Bernhardt describing what he saw upon entering the sub-hamlet of Xom Lang:

I walked up and saw these guys doing strange things… Setting fire to the hootches and huts and waiting for people to come out and then shooting them…going into the hootches and shooting them up…gathering people in groups and shooting them…As I walked in you could see piles of people all through the village…all over. They were gathered up into large groups. I saw them shoot an M79 grenade launcher into a group of people who were still alive. But it was mostly done with a machine gun. They were shooting women and children just like anybody else. We met no resistance and I only saw three captured weapons. We had no casualties. It was just like any other Vietnamese village–old papa-sans, women and kids. As a matter of fact, I don't remember seeing one military-age male in the entire place, dead or alive.

Band Number: 599-05468

JT goes to the small RV and pulls down one of his first big color sketches. He brought to life one of the old timers. One of those Rocky Mountain sandhill cranes with the band on his leg for more than 36 years.

It was JT's last foray in the Wildlife Service. December 2006. In El Bosque.

The Sandhill crane started life on the Wyoming border, on the Thomas Fork of the Bear River.

Band Number: 599-05468. One of the oldest Rocky Mountain Sandhill Cranes. The bird was banded with its brood mate on June 29, 1973. The year his sister died in a car wreck. The year he began banding birds.

A two-chick brood is normal for Rocky Mountain Sandhills.

The magic of birds and what JT's mom inculcated in him pushed him through Vietnam, through the dark nights of booze and massacres.

JT was there to sketch the animal when it was banded with its sister.

Then he was with it for last rites—Band 599-05468. For its 36 and a half years on the planet, the creature flew from Border, Wyoming—where he and his sister were banded at age 44 days—to the staging area for sandhill cranes the San Luis Valley of Colorado and then down the Rio Grande to Bosque del Apache. That's a one-way trip of 700 miles.

If one were to assume this crane returned close to its nesting grounds each spring and back to Bosque del Apache each winter, the bird made the round trip 36 times, as well a final one-way trip where it was found. That is a total of 51,100 miles in a lifetime, or the equivalent of circling the earth more than twice.

JT thinks about the bird often, what the Fish and Wildlife guys call Band Number 599-05468.

The day he sketched the chick, JT knew a different name would stick for him. Not Band 599-05468. But an anthropomorphic one—Black Kettle.

Named after the Cheyenne Chief, Black Kettle, who survived the Sand Creek massacre. Black Kettle, the chief who had raised a U.S. flag in a futile gesture of fellowship, survived the massacre, carrying his badly wounded wife from the field and limping east across the wintry plains. He was a peacemaker, and in 1865 he signed a treaty, resettling his band on reservation land in Oklahoma.

Three years later, Black Kettle was killed, in yet another massacre, this one led by Colonel George Armstrong Custer.

Corporal Johnny Boy Thomlinson remembers. Each memory captured somewhere in his 74 years of sketches. ◙

Doug Margeson

The People With Sincere Lips

They called it the Dog and Pony Show. Not much of a title, that. Banal. Unimaginative. Prosaic at best. It did, however, do a reasonably good job of exemplifying the people who coined it, for whatever imagination and originality they once possessed had been leeched out of them long ago. And they didn't even know it because the awareness to know it had been leeched out of them long ago, too.

Anyway, each year, the people with the sincere lips came to Associated Amalgamated to put on the Dog and Pony Show and each year all employees were required to stop whatever they were doing and listen to them.

The old hands knew the routine and always made sure to find comfortable chairs in the back. That way, they could doze unnoticed.

The young man was new to it all. He had never seen the Dog and Pony Show and reasoned that good manners dictated he politely listen to the people with sincere lips.

The people with sincere lips asked for money; not for themselves, but for The Charity which, as near at the young man could discern, paid for every program for solving every form of physical, mental, social and spiritual woe known to humankind.

But the people with sincere lips made the young man uncomfortable. Inexperienced though he was, their dewy eyes, their concerned tones and, yes, their pursed, slightly smiling and, above all, *sincere* lips made him uncomfortable. But the young man—the polite, inexperienced young man—ignored his instincts and listened to them with an open mind.

After a brief introduction, the people with the sincere lips set up a screen, turned off the lights, and switched on a rickety movie projector. The old hands tried not to snore.

The young man dutifully watched the movie. It was about all the wonderful things The Charity did for the Less Fortunate. Specifically, it was about a wealthy person who spent his spare time taking handicapped people for rides on his yacht.

This interested the young man. As a boy, he had spent his summers at the exclusive country club in his town, caddying for wealthy persons. They were not the sort to take handicapped people for rides on their yachts.

As a matter of fact, most of them were rude and insulting; browbeating caddies about whatever was bothering them at the moment, or about nothing at all, whenever they felt like it, which was often enough that the young man—the boy, then—was confident in the measure he took of them. They were assholes. He seriously doubted they would allow less fortunate people past the gate to the yacht club. The less fortunate might exude their unique miasma, a pall of poverty and misery that would taint the patrician environs. Wealthy persons had to be careful about such things.

But the film saw it otherwise. Such nautical noblesse oblige was typical of the world The Charity wrought, the narrator said. Then he went on to recite how The Charity was making all better the afflictions of the diseased, the destitute, the decrepit, the deranged and the dumped on.

The film ended with a montage of less fortunate and wealthy persons smiling at each other on the beach at sunset, all to the strains of a stirring aria by Barry Manilow. The music rose to a properly stirring crescendo and the narrator assured everyone that he knew just how much the assembled viewers wanted to contribute part of their paychecks to The Charity.

The lights came on and the old hands woke up. One fell out of his chair. No one noticed except, perhaps, the people with sincere lips. But they didn't let it show as they busily passed out envelopes and brochures, all the while cooing about how certain they were that the employees at Associated Amalgamated just couldn't wait to contribute part of their paychecks to The Charity.

At this point in the proceedings, the young man experienced a revelation. It was as though a divine power suddenly tapped his consciousness. The movie was merely a commercial, the revelation said; no different than commercials extolling the wonders of products for grooming one's arm pits. They had little connection to reality. They simply tweaked one's emotions—the emotion of pity, in this case—and then played upon one's need to be an accepted member of the group. Everyone in this group was happy to contribute part of their paychecks to The Charity. The people with sincere lips said so, so it must have been true. Surely, no one wanted to be an outcast from such a noble assemblage.

But the young man was not happy to contribute part of his paycheck, particularly when he saw what The Charity considered a fair share of his earnings. He once had read that in certain neighborhoods in New York, large men in dark overcoats asked businesses for roughly the same percentage of their earnings so that unpleasant things would not befall them.

But surely, this was something different. Besides, the young man felt he should do something to help the less fortunate. It was only right.

Uncertain about how to proceed, the young man went to an old hand for advice. The old hand chortled phlegmily at the young man's naiveté.

"Hell, just ignore all that shit," The old hand said. "Just pledge ten bucks a year, like we all do." That way, the old hand gurgled, their boss, the senior assistant regional manager, would get a 100 percent participation plaque to hang on his wall, the company's name would be read aloud at the next Chamber of Commerce meeting and appropriate stability would be assured in the universe for the next twelve months.

The old hand forgot to tell the young man the most important part: that, as with large men in dark overcoats, the ten bucks was not requested. It was expected. This omission would prove significant.

The young man was disturbed. The people with sincere lips were unctuous and shifty and the old hand's approach seemed like so much well-camouflaged cowardice. The whole affair was off kilter.

So, he decided he would not contribute to The Charity. Perhaps he would have things better figured out by next year. Then he would see. Meanwhile, he forgot about it.

The next day, he was summoned to the office of Mr. Drone.

Mr. Drone was the sort of person, quite common in American business, who somewhere early in life had his personality surgically removed. Without any personality to hinder him, Mr. Drone made a perfect corporate man. He obeyed all directives. He accepted all policies. He questioned nothing. If he had any awareness that he possessed a soul, he sublimated it to insensate obsequiousness to the sociology of the corporate world. That there might be other values or ways of life never penetrated his psyche.

Mr. Drone told the young man to close the door, never a good omen, and then asked why the young man

Marking Time   *Sheary Clough Suiter*

had forgotten to contribute to The Charity. Politely, the young man said he had not forgotten. He had decided not to contribute.

It was as if Mr. Drone had been strapped into Old Sparky and Tom Hanks flipped the switch. He jerked upright, his eyes wide, his mouth slightly agape. He stayed that way, seemingly paralyzed, for a good fifteen seconds.

Then, choking as if he had received a karate chop to the throat, he said, "You w-w-w-what?"

And the young man explained again. The whole business raised issues of personal ethics, and he wanted to think it over a bit. Maybe he would contribute next year.

Mr. Drone was not familiar with the concept of personal ethics. The mention of something so foreign caused his head to snap oddly to the left so that his ear nearly touched his collarbone. He stared at the young man with the expression of one observing a person conducting an unpleasant bodily function in public. He stayed that way for an even longer time than before, so long that the young man eventually got up and left.

Within a day or two, the young man started hearing dark rumblings about the catastrophe he had caused. The senior assistant regional managers did not get his 100 percent participation plaque. The company's name was not read aloud at the Chamber of Commerce. The leaders of other companies sniggered at the absence. Never in the course of Associated Amalgamated's history had such a thing happened. The very future of western civilization teetered on the brink.

Large piles of tedious busy work began appearing on the young man's desk. The young man's fellow junior executives pointedly avoided him in the elevator. The old hands whispered and chuckled whenever he passed by.

The young man endured. We learn from our mistakes, he concluded. He would just have to work some extra hours for a while. It would all blow over.

And eventually it seemed to—more or less.

A year later, the young man saw that the people with sincere lips were scheduled to manifest themselves at the offices of Associated Amalgamated. By this time, the young man had become sophisticated enough in his concepts of personal ethics that he saw nothing particularly distasteful about contributing ten dollars. He was becoming an old hand.

Then, one day, he found an unfamiliar folder on his desk, a very thick folder. It was a manual for operation of the campaign for The Charity at Associated Amalgamated. The young man had been assigned to conduct it—in addition to all his regular tasks. In previous years, a committee of six or seven people was assigned the campaign full-time, and even then it was considered the most back-breaking shit job in the company. Associated Amalgamated had more than 4,000 employees working in gawd knows how many locations around the state. All must be given the Dog and Pony and Show and all must contribute to The Charity—and it was the young man's responsibility to see that they did.

The young man didn't ask why he had been drafted. He knew. Everybody knew.

So he ran the campaign. By dint of herculean effort, he managed to get everything done—through lack of sleep that turned into bronchitis and the loss of a wife, the prettiest, sweetest human being he had never known, a wife who could not understand why he was never home and, when he was, so sullen and withdrawn that if he spoke at all it was to lash out at her. She became afraid of him, moved in with her sister and refused to answer his calls. Ever.

As it turned out, the young man actually did a reasonably good job of running the campaign. He learned how to display sincere lips. But once the campaign was over—as in the next day—he left Associated Amalgamated. Eventually, he got another job; a number of other jobs, actually. He had no particular interest in a long-term career. He did not want to become an old hand.

Wherever he ended up, the young man always looked forward to the day the Dog and Pony Show arrived. When it did, he made it a point to step forward, take an envelope and then, after making sure the people with the sincere lips were watching, drop it into a metal wastebasket with a loud clonk. Sometimes, he took a wastebasket to the room ahead of time just to make sure.

When he performed this little ritual, his face took on a distinctive expression; dark and evil, the glowering, maniacal leer of the seriously crazed. Stay away from him. He'll rip your lungs out, Jim. It was not entirely an act. The young man meant it, at least enough that, indeed, no one fucked with him.

Perhaps he was crazy, perhaps not. In any case, the young man enjoyed his act. In addition to the pleasant conceit of self-righteousness, he enjoyed watching the people with sincere lips. Sometimes, they would snap upright, as if Tom Hanks had just flipped the switch. Or they would stare at him as if he had conducted an unpleasant bodily function in public. Or, once, the women with sincere lips skittered behind the men with sincere lips for protection. Then the men with sincere lips tried to skitter behind them. The young man really liked that.

One day, while on his lunch break, the young man was browsing a nearby bookstore. A title caught his eye: *Let the Bastards Freeze in The Dark*. He bought it right away. His didn't care about the book—although he later heard it actually was pretty good—just the title. He cut off the cover, framed it and when it came time for the people with sincere lips to stage the Dog and Pony Show, he put it on his desk facing the open door. If anyone asked about it, the young man would hunch over in a twisted, depraved posture and flash his maniacal leer. The leer was enough to make the other person eager to talk about something else.

In the course of his affairs, the young man ended up meeting an official from The Charity. He was an august personage, weighty with the self-importance of corporate dignitas. The young man told him about his experience at Associated Amalgamated.

The august personage harrumphed and said, "Well, we certainly don't condone that sort of thing. But, as I'm sure you understand, we can't control what businesses do within their own walls. We regret you had such a negative experience."

The young man, who wasn't young anymore, cackled a long, demented cackle, the sort of thing you would expect to hear from the terminally mad. All other conversation in the room abruptly stopped. Then he leered at the august personage, his eyes vulpine and glowing, something straight from the bowels of hell. He started stalking toward the august personage, his body hunched and coiled.

The august personage's lips, although not sincere, trembled a little. Then he backed away slowly, measuring each step as if he was in a minefield and, above all, never turning his back on the young man. His lips continued to tremble all the way to the door, which he closed behind himself slowly and gently as if trying to not set off an explosion.

The young man continued to leer—madly, viciously, demonically, his face cramped into in a mask of contorted depravity. He even panted a little. Stay away from him. He'll rip your lungs out, Jim. ◪

Russell Thayer

The Pie Safe

Magpie Bates stood over a spattering iron skillet, a spoonful of lard losing its form and opacity as it spread, getting ready to brown a mess of ham steak and fried eggs. Biscuits rose in the oven, and she exhaled a cloud of smoke around the cigarette in her mouth, her cropped red hair pulled behind her ears, a full apron covered with roses tied around a trim waist, protecting denim trousers and a crisp white blouse. Her bare feet felt the chill December morning on the speckled black linoleum of the large corner apartment's homey kitchen, and she liked the raw touch of the floor on her bare skin.

Sugarpie DeMarco sat in one of the two chairs arranged around the chrome-edged table by the window, lolling in a silk robe, legs thrust out like tongs, her black hair a wispy tangle, her skin a muddy brown, eyes closed, head flopped back. A cup of coffee steamed in front of her. She wore slippers, but nothing under the robe, which had fallen open.

"Lord," she said. "When do I get some eggs?"

"Hold your horses, Sugarpie. Why don't you put some clothes on for breakfast? It'll be a minute still."

"I'm gonna take a bath after I eat. No sense doin' all the work of gettin' dressed."

"I guess not," said Magpie, still a little damp from her own luxuriating soak.

The joints had jumped the night before. Saturday night. Magpie's ears still rang a bit. She thumped piano in a tight jazz combo currently headlining at the New Orleans Swing Club. Sugarpie sang in front of a popular big band, the house crew at the Can-Do Club. It was late morning, and the girls planned to relax a bit, maybe unbox a new jigsaw puzzle, maybe an afternoon movie followed by an Italian dinner with checkered tablecloths and red wine.

The comfortable apartment they shared was known around San Francisco's Fillmore scene as "The Pie Safe" because no man had ever stood barefoot in the kitchen, with its grand view of the bay, and felt the sunrise on his face. The Safe was meant to keep two fresh, warm pies protected from vermin and insects: drunks and hopheads from the clubs, musicians looking for a bit of carnal release after a long evening of stimulating jazz.

"Are you sure you want to do this?" asked Magpie, now seated at the table, talking around a mouthful of warm ham. "A Christmas party? Frankly, I'm trepidatious."

"You is, huh?" said Sugarpie, buttering a biscuit. "Look, hon. We'll just invite the boys in our bands. And their girls. A happy thanks for all the work they put in behind us."

"All of them?" Magpie sighed. "You've got at least fifteen men in the Topliners." Magpie was friendly with only a couple of them.

"They're good boys," said Sugarpie.

"They seem like a rowdy bunch," said Magpie.

"They like to have fun. Did anybody dance at your show last night? Anybody have fun trying to understand all that technique you throw around like hot darts?" Sugarpie liked to needle Magpie about the innovative bebop she adored, how it demanded people sit still and listen rather than enjoy the music on their feet, in their hips, spinning in each other's arms.

"The stuff we play," explained Magpie to deaf ears, "doesn't inspire dancing. You know that. The syncopation, the chord progressions, improvisation. It—"

"I like to swing," said Sugarpie, yawning as she got to her feet, holding her robe closed. "You the cook, baby. You plan the menu. I'll try to make my bed and help you clean a little. Should we get the mule tuned up?"

An upright piano stood against the interior wall of the living room. It would be the highlight of the party when Magpie accompanied the guests for some rousing Christmas songs.

"I'll have the man swing by," said Magpie with a smirk.

Cow Hollow was a middle-class neighborhood, a good distance removed from the Fillmore clubs, but within walking distance if one were drunk and needing fresh air. When exploring the local rental options, Magpie had gone to see the landlord by herself, telling the man that she would be sharing the two-bedroom apartment with her sister. When she told him what she did for a living, he claimed to have a taste for jazz music and smiled back at Magpie when she smiled. She hoped he would still be smiling when he found out that her beloved sister had a less rosy complexion. The three-story building was situated on the west side of Divisadero, surrounded by shops and good restaurants. It was a new building, with an elevator, but they could afford it now that they made regular money. The few neighbors Magpie had talked to in the hallway claimed to like hearing the two women sing and play in the afternoons. Half the apartments were still empty. So far, no trouble. A strong deadbolt kept the door secure.

"How much alcohol can we afford?" asked Magpie as Sugarpie ran water for her bath.

"Tell yo' buddy Otis to swipe a few crates of Lucky Lager from the club. I'll pick up a dozen bottles of brown liquor. You gonna whip up some of yo' precious cakes and whatnots?"

Sutton I   *Annekathrin Hansen*

Magpie nodded. She enjoyed cooking in the apartment's modern kitchen, and she missed the sturdy English sweets she was raised on as a child in Hong Kong. Coming to San Francisco after liberation from a Japanese prison camp in Manila, she'd worked for two years as a short-order cook and waitress, her quick mind taking in the fast, delicious cuisine of her new home. Fabricated into a classical prodigy by an overbearing mother, Magpie had never lost her feel for the frenetic pace of the ragtime and boogie she secretly shared with her father, and she listened wisely to the way jazz was changing. She and Sugarpie had found each other while hanging around the clubs looking for gigs. Both women would turn twenty-three during the coming year, their careers off and running like the Southern Pacific's Daylight Limited.

"Which evening works best for you?" asked Magpie, flipping through her datebook.

"I can't think right now," said Sugarpie, a washcloth covering her eyes.

"We rarely have gigs on a Thursday," said Magpie, "so let's make it the twenty-third. We'll open the door to the Safe at seven. How does that sound?"

"You crack the whip; I'll make the trip," said Sugarpie.

* * *

On the morning of the party, Magpie's friend Leonard knocked at the door of the Safe. Once it was opened, he dragged in a small tree, nudging a box of decorations across the floor with his foot. The guest was soon upright in a stand, watered, and the apartment began to fill with the smell of a mountain forest. After helping Leonard decorate the tree with colored glass balls, Sugarpie hung silver strands of tinsel from wall sconces and doorknobs.

Magpie kissed Leonard on the cheek as he left, then began to arrange her confections on a folding table next to the piano.

"That man loves you," said Sugarpie, nodding with significance as she collected the empty decoration boxes.

"And I love him," said Magpie, pulling aside a curtain with her finger to watch Leonard get into his car.

"He's old enough to be yo' father."

"And that's just how I love him, Sugar. So, mind your own business."

Throughout the afternoon, Sugarpie tidied the living room, arranged a dozen borrowed folding chairs, and ran to the grocery for odds and ends while Magpie worked hard in the kitchen rolling out Chelsea buns and glazing the lemon drizzle cake she loved so much. The day before, Magpie had constructed a pineapple upside-down cake and two large Bakewell tarts.

"Looking forward to some spotted dick?" asked Magpie.

"I ain't," said Sugarpie, "but I am lookin' forward to yo' lip-smackin' whiskey sours. We got enough ice? I bought lemons and a jar of cherries. I know we got bourbon."

"I'll prepare a gallon jug in your honor," said Magpie, wiping her brow with the back of her hand.

"I feel loved, too, Magpie. Merry Christmas."

"Merry Christmas to you, Sugarpie. The Safe looks beautiful. It sparkles just like you."

At five o'clock, Magpie's friend Otis showed up with two crates of beer. He stepped into the apartment with reverence, the stacked crates jiggling musically as he carried them into the kitchen, where he began to load the icebox.

Magpie watched him work. He was a large, handsome man, dark skin smooth on his face and neck, a thin mustache cut just over his lip. Head bartender at the New Orleans Swing Club, Otis had always been good to her, as good a friend as Leonard, and just as inappropriate as boyfriend material. It was, she thought, just the way she liked things right now. Having friends was the best thing in the world.

"This a nice place you got here, Magpie. You be careful tonight."

She took his arm as he left the kitchen. She could tell her touch electrified him.

"I want you here."

"I'll be here, then," he said.

* * *

After midnight, the acrid smell of reefer hung like swamp mist in the air. The living room windows had been thrown wide to cool the writhing mass. The caroling had ended with cheers, the last bottle of bourbon drained and pitched onto the floor. Magpie, a walking ornament in the green satin dress she liked to wear onstage because someone once told her how good it looked against her shiny red hair, kicked the empty bottle against a wall or someone's shin, then stumbled to sit on the piano bench, lifting her legs to spin toward the piano. Settling into a sultry blues, Magpie turned her head from side to side, watching the bright teeth and wide smiles weave through the low, buttery light. A few voices mumbled a simple "yeah" back at her as she rolled along, feeling as happy as anyone had a right to be as the night broke toward morning.

After half an hour, Magpie stopped playing and stood up to light applause. As she wove toward the bathroom, a horn player in Sugarpie's band, a guy named Peterman, reached out and roughly squeezed one of her buttocks through the silky fabric of her dress. Magpie turned to scowl at him.

"There ain't much to hold on to, girl," said Peterman, "but maybe if I grab 'em both." Laughing drunkenly, he pulled her close and reached around behind with both hands to squeeze her again, pulling her against his groin. Hubert, the guitarist in Magpie's band, jerked Peterman hard away from her. Peterman squared to face Hubert. Magpie rushed to hold down the fists of her guitarist.

"Don't break your hand, Hubie," she whispered. "It's not worth it."

"I don't like seein' that boy touch you like that."

"I appreciate it, but an unpleasant touch doesn't hurt like a broken hand. And you have mouths to feed. Why don't you come with me to the kitchen?" She walked between the contentious men as she guided Hubert out of the room. After taking the last beer out of the icebox, she made Hubert sit at the table and promise that he

would remain there. As she came out of the room, she was surprised again by Peterman, who put his hand at the back of her neck and pulled her mouth to his. She pushed him away after tasting the bourbon on his tongue, and the room grew very quiet as Otis rose. Ronnie, the leader and saxophonist in Magpie's band, also moved toward Peterman, but Magpie pulled him back.

Otis confronted Peterman.

"You got no call to do that."

"Aw, hell, Otis, she don't mind a little kiss. This ofay princess, she just like all the pale girls who come down here to swing and sway. She cat around onstage, playin' her little heart out 'cause she like our music so much." Peterman grabbed his crotch. "When all she really want is that mean black snake."

Otis grasped the front of Peterman's shirt and squeezed the collar so hard against his throat that his eyes bugged out. Magpie felt a rush of spirit leave her body as she thought about what the man had said, wondering if other people thought as much about her motives for living her life the way she chose.

"Please leave my home," she said. "Otis. Let him go."

Otis released his grip, and Peterman smiled as he collected himself to move to the door. His voice echoed as he moved down the hallway.

"And her boy Otis do whatever she say 'cause he feel her down there, too. I know you, man. I know what you after."

Sugarpie angrily stomped her foot.

"All right now! Party's over!" Her voice began to quiver by the end of her short speech, and she rushed to her bedroom to slam the door.

Magpie began to usher the guests out, hugging the men she performed with, avoiding eye contact with the other men, and especially their now stern-faced wives and girlfriends.

"You should go, too, Otis," she said after the room cleared.

Otis grabbed his hat and moved slowly through the door. Magpie watched him call the elevator.

"Lock up," he said as he stepped inside.

Before Magpie could close the door, Sugarpie came out of her bedroom and looked around at the mess.

"Every good party gotta have some crazy," she said with a sigh.

"I guess," said Magpie, hearing the stairwell door close.

"Behind you!" screamed Sugarpie, her eyes gone

wide.

Magpie didn't have a chance to turn before she was thrust onto the floor. Falling upon her, Peterman pinned her hard with his knee. Soon, he was fighting off Sugarpie, who seemed to be all over him before he managed to sling her away. Magpie could see out of one eye that Sugarpie went down hard, smacking her head on the polished oak floor.

As Peterman began to tear the back of her dress apart, Magpie unexpectedly felt his crushing weight come off her spine. Rolling over, she looked up just in time to see Otis clout Peterman on the jaw, sending the brute backward into the keyboard of the piano, where he bounced away after an explosion of dissonance to stumble over the stiff legs of the overturned piano bench, then fall toward an open window. Flailing for the sill, Peterman's hand slipped off the wood as the weight of his meanness carried him out into the night air.

"Spill your brains, you son of a bitch!" screamed Sugarpie as she ran to the window. After a moment, she stepped back, her hands covering her open mouth.

"Oh, no," said Magpie.

"You pushed him out, girl," said Sugarpie. "You got to take the fall for this."

"No," said Otis. "This is my doing."

"No, it ain't," said Sugarpie. "It's her doing, and she got to say she pushed him."

"I grew up in a prison, Sugar. I can't go back. I've finally got my life in order."

"You ain't never goin' to prison, you blue-eyed fool. The man came back here drunk and crazy. He came for you and maybe me, and Otis stopped him. He put his hand on yo' ass. Folks can vouch for that. That shouldn't be enough to kill a man, but that's how it works in this world."

"I don't like it."

"Nobody like it, Magpie, but right now I ain't complainin'."

Magpie sensed the presence of Otis beside her. She held the torn dress against her chest. The Safe felt as though it had been blown open. Forever.

"What would happen to Otis?" Magpie asked.

"The cops might do any goddamned thing," said Sugarpie. "If they let him off, Peterman's friends are gonna get Otis for sure. And he got his little girl at home."

Magpie turned to look at Otis, her brow wrinkled.

"Jocelyn," Otis whispered. "She's five."

"You've never told me about this. Do you have a wife?"

"She died before she even held our baby. My sister, she live with me. She look after the girl."

"Shit, Otis," said Magpie.

"I didn't mean for him to go out the window," he said.

Magpie glanced around at the disordered contents of the Safe. On chairs and tables, even the floor, plates held half-eaten pieces of her English heritage.

Sirens wailed above the unmistakable sound of excited people on the sidewalk.

Magpie turned to Otis.

"The hallway stairs exit into the alley," she whispered. "Hurry."

After Otis squeezed out, Magpie closed the heavy door. As she lifted her hand to turn the deadbolt, she heard the sound of car doors being slammed. Realizing she couldn't lock the door right then, with officers soon in the hall, she looked at the chipped polish on her fingernails and noticed her hand was shaking, her perfect life split open like Peterman's head on the sidewalk. ◪

Against the Sky   *Jack Broom*

Web 2   Daniela Naomi Molnar

POETRY

John S. Argetsinger

Looking Back

Looking back I am lucky I am not dead
She kept her cigarettes hidden in the family van
Her husband was the head of the SWAT team
This was small town Alaska
Nobody locked their doors
My only contender was the light with the sensor
I would wander up to his house and without him knowing
Sneak several cigarettes out of the van and slink back
Out into the darkness
It was exhilarating to know I was sneaking into a cop's garage
To steal his wife's Marlboros
The captain of the SWAT team at that
I never told anyone what I was up to,
Sometimes making a trip back twice in one night
I am lucky I didn't get shot or killed
Those were more innocent times, not much happened in that town.

Rust   Jan Jung

Gabrielle Baalke

Tithe

I pull a twenty from my wallet
and decide that it is
too much for a tip;
I leave it anyway.

The waitress who has left
our glasses empty and her own
apartment, roommate, husband, home
in order to serve us

receives the tenth I meant to leave
last Sunday, but thoughtlessly forgot
in my blue jacket pocket. The
bill that I've been holding in reserve

now sits within the plastic folder
on the table at the restaurant,
where the waitress will retrieve it,
fold it, spend it, possibly even

tithe it, as I had meant to, placing it
alongside envelopes, and dollars
dropped by fumbling, generous, knobby,
newborn hands into the winnowing basket

where it will be used, collected by the priest,
pressed into needful palms, presented
as an offering, a firstfruit—too little,
perhaps, but given, nonetheless.

The View From   J. Leslie
Within No. 2, 2019

Landscape 1   Cynthia Yatchman

John Baalke

Wrangell Mountains Triptych

Sketch 1 - Edges

7:30 a.m. pickup at Copper Center Lodge. Just two today
for the trip to McCarthy, women, in their 60s, both
from Berkeley. Karen and Miranda for now, as I don't
remember names. Stopping in Chitina, I had to pick up
Howard's rafts and rowing frames, left the day before,
return them to his place at the end of the road. Deflated,
folded (so to speak), and stowed alongside Spirit Mountain
Artworks, the silvery-gray jumble of rafts and gear was
loaded in the van, and we were on our way, across the
braided Copper. I explained how the CR&NW railroad
once hauled high-grade chalcocite from the copper mines
at Kennecott, made a turn here and followed the River
south to Cordova.

Sixty miles of gravel ahead, surface like a washboard,
the occasional railroad spike dredged from the past by
a DOT grader. We wound through the curves clinging to
the Kotsina bluffs. One morning - weeks earlier - there was
a young woman wandering along the road here, shards of glass
in her hair. Said her car went off the road, but it was nowhere
to be seen. Gave her a lift back to Chitina, within moments
she began to come out of shock. Broken back, yet she climbed
the ninety-foot cliffs, having survived the end-over-end flight
of her Subaru wagon over the edge, miraculously landing
upright. Months later, I received a letter, and a photo. She was
shirtless, canoeing some remote river in Arizona, back fully
healed. Said she had no memory of the crash beyond
fumbling with a cassette tape while driving, people gathered
around her, a gentle hand on her brow.

Miranda, Karen, and I pressed on, making the best of a sunny day, not aware that another passenger had joined our journey in Chitina. We passed the somewhat unremarkable Silver Lake, and the trailhead for Nugget Creek and Dixie Pass, until we came to the Kuskulana overlook. At seventeen miles in, it was a perfect stop for photos of the historic bridge: a steel, cantilever-style span, built in 1910, and 238 feet above the river. Karen (as we have named her) had a Nikon SLR with telephoto lens at the ready. However, as we prepared to disembark the van, I noticed a Red-backed Vole make its way from the seat onto Miranda's shoulder. Unsure how to break the news of this wildlife sighting in a tactful manner, I waited until we were out, and doors were closed. The ladies took it all in stride: stowaway vole, trailing it through the Dwarf Dogwood and wild roses, camera clicking, roar of the glacial Kuskulana flowing through the canyon below.

Sketch 2 – Bearings

It may have been 1989, likely late August, mid-morning. William was driven; a sort of renaissance man if you will. He fully embraced whatever he tried: big game hunting, taxidermy, aviation, cross-country trekking, etcetera. So it came to be that Will wanted to see McCarthy, and everything else that would fit into two days and a night. We drove his Ford pickup nonstop to the Dixie Pass trailhead to make a start. Will figured the 17-mile round-trip with 5,000-foot elevation gain could be managed in six hours if we scrambled. He wanted to get into the mountains, and get up high to scope out Dall Sheep on the ridges. Going minimal – and to Will this meant what can be fit in pockets – we briskly set off across the tundra bench, and two miles along dropped down a bluff to Strelna Creek. The way was nothing more than a well-used game trail meandering up a valley, and after the first fork, boulder-hop, and stream-crossing, it became less than that. After a few miles of this creek hopscotch, Will was ready to break the drudge and ascend the nearest peak. Soon we were thousands of feet higher, edging our way around a rocky precipice, the only sound, blood pounding in our ears. Scent of dry shale on our hands. Sweat cooling quickly as we stood gathering our bearings. Horizons, here and there, etched in our minds.

Carb-jitters on the ramble down. But blueberries, wild and
everywhere, staved-off the pangs. We plunged in voraciously,
and meeting the creek again below, indulged our thirst
in the icy current. Late afternoon arrived as we regained
the pickup, and our journey on toward McCarthy. Another
forty-five miles of gravel, then camp for the night along
the moraine of the Kennicott Glacier. In the twilight, we
rounded Fireweed Mountain. At road's-edge stood an older
man watching a small pond where a bull moose fed on water-
weeds, now dunking, now lifting its head. Said he was waiting
for it to step out of the water, then he'd take it; thirty-aught-six
with scope rested on the gate of his truck. We wished him luck,
and went on to make camp. Marinated mountain goat back-
strap is what Will brought, and we roasted it over an open fire,
stars burning, cool early autumn night. Next morning, we
crossed the Kennicott River using the trams, rolling on a cable,
pulled with a rope. Historic McCarthy was granted a glance
before we fast-walked four-and-a-half miles to the old Kennecott
ghost-town. One thousand people called this place home in
the 1930s, lived their everyday lives alongside immense glaciers,
circled by high mountain peaks. We wandered through the
hospital, down the maze of levels in the mill, beneath the steel
cables and buckets which brought the chalcocite from the miles
of tunnels above. Will wanted to venture up the trail beyond,
to see the Root Glacier, and the Stairway Icefall. We did, then
traipsed the distance back to the trams, packed up, and left.
Rounding Fireweed Mountain again, we soon saw the hunter's
truck, still there, and the hunter himself stepping out of some
willows. He was bent and wheezing. His heart he said. Had to
get his nitro pills, said he shot the moose; said we could have it
if we packed it out. Through an alder thicket, across wet
hummocky tundra, slippery algal mud, to the far side of the pond
where the animal, barely gutted, lay in a small grove of poplar.
Will removed the entrails, accidentally cut my hand when his
knife slid too quickly between skin and rib. I bled a little and
he proceeded to quarter the bull. Then I packed as much as I
could carry, making eight, maybe ten, loads of flesh and bone,
on a warm, buggy August afternoon.

Sketch 3 - Words

"Ten peaks over fourteen-thousand feet, and over forty peaks
over ten-thousand feet, making Wrangell-St. Elias a world-
class mountain wilderness." I knew this well. It was part of
my repertoire as an interpretive ranger. Interpretive meant
I spoke in terms of the park to visitors, answered their every
question. It also meant I had arrived at the apex of my junior
high *career* essay: park ranger. Check.

Boondoggle. That's what we called it when we got out of the
visitor center and into the park. "Six-times the size of Yellow-
stone." It was a big place, and we had to know what we were
talking about, right? Sean was law enforcement, stationed in
Chitina, and we were headed to the upper Kotsina to check on
a reported illegal hunt. I was the spare man, the expendable
movie character who carries a radio, but no gun. We unload
the two ATVs from the trailer - three-wheelers, it's the mid-80s,
so, they're safe enough, not even a thought otherwise. Twenty
miles on an old mining access route will put us in the shadow of
"Mount Wrangell, a massive andesitic shield volcano, still
active, and some three-times the volume of Mt. Rainier in
Washington." Gear, gas, Sean's shotgun, and we bumped along
down the trail. In May, I had been dropped on the north side
of the park at "Chisana (pronounced Shushanna)." It had once
been the largest log-cabin town in Alaska, and site of the last big
goldrush. Now, it had two-dozen residents at best. I was there
to help Jim and Bob move timbers from the airstrip to their work-
site. An historic architectural survey had been done, and several
old cabins were to be restored. Logs and beams had been milled
to specifications and ferried by DeHavilland Otter from Northway.
Every few hours, the plane landed with another load. It was slow,
methodical work, and then waiting. Day after day, getting to know
the landscape, the bold cross-fox that visited, the ghosts
of miners and cabins gone bust.

Sean led the way as the trail made a steep, boulder-strewn descent
toward Elliott Creek. I remember unintentionally nosing the
front tire into a rock, how it flattened under the momentum and
the rear-end lifted uncomfortably in a way an ATV should not.
Easing all three wheels steadily beneath me, I was newly attuned
to the feel of earth and machine when we arrived, raging Creek
before us in the valley bottom. Three-wheelers were light, and fat
tires would float. We roped off and walked each ATV through.
Getting wet was inevitable. Climbing out and around the ridge,
then descending again to the glacial gray brown Kotsina, we
edged along cut bank until the forest overgrowth thinned to willow
and scrub spruce. Two rough cabins fifty yards apart, tucked in
the alders; one occupied, the other not. We settled in, and Sean
put his uniform on. Badge, holster, gun. He made contact, asked
questions, took down names, scribbled some notes; I held the radio,
I was the spare man, the interpretive ranger, ready as ever
to express the superlatives.

Fall Flames   *Jim Thiele*

Thomas R. Bacon

Posted From The Northern Province

As I write, shorter days drift to winter,
life's seasons insistent, hints of silence
woven into the icy air, a song
of inevitable circumstance.

Japanese Maple leaves blush brighter red
as green undertones of sun shiver back
into the ground for sleep and I watch clouds,
and shadows of clouds, reshape mountain sides,

flocks gathering, swirls of wind flying south.
So much to see, I live distracted. New
frost glitters from roof tops and blue sky
reflects the colors of sea in currents

of time passing. That's what I have to tell
for now. Daylight fading, hope you are well.

Christianne Balk
Two Poems

Smoke

Drifts between us and the mountains, turning
the sun into a smudged globe almost small
enough to hold. Around us, a thousand
thousand acres burn, swaths of croplands, barns,
prairies, towns, hillsides, valleys, and forests
reduced to fuel by fires so hot they raise
their own weather, thunderstorms and lightning
fanned by the winds. We cry for help and stand
our ground, men, women, and children wielding
rakes, buckets, shovels, and garden hoses
until the troops tell us it's time to leave.
We know we can't call this an act of God
as we drive, bumper to bumper, past walls
of flame three stories high, praying for rain.

Red Sun In The Smoke   *Deborah Chava Singer*

Spring Basin   *Cheryl Stadig*

Snow Lake

Take me in your glacial heart

And hold me

stunned above silty beds

of soft, crushed stone—

shake my limbs numb

rock me

in your breathless clarity—

nudge me through your ice and show me

how to crawl

wide-eyed towards your gravel shore.

Gabrielle Barnett

Milepost 107, shortly after fall equinox

Hands at the wheel, skirting the inlet,
a hint of amber, then fire-burst
slides out from behind the fore-land, just south of west.

Luminescent orange swept up in cloud
suspends time, elongates a moment
called to attention by a fleeting angle of light.

Coincident positioning of horizon, sun
and self, arrests preoccupation with arrival, diffuses
chronic brooding over turns taken wrong, or terrain left unexplored.

Space expands, opening distant vistas
to a jagged cordilleran silhouette sharpened
by back-light, while the home sky rests, coastal pastel and gray.

Shades of Coleridge intrude, unveiling lands
fantastic, destinations unreachable save through imagination,
incantation, or devil's bargain; so sublime merges with ancient lore.

Beckoning across the endless sea of always beyond
a glimpse of illumination awes again another who failed
to cherish the thing at hand, until it slipped from sight.

Cook Inlet Landscape   *Janet Clemens*

Falls   *Deborah Chava Singer*

Rachel Barton

The Sky is Falling

Once, when I am just a girl, and we are living in Skookumchuck, BC, where the Kootenai runs into rapids, my father catches a tiktáalik long as he is tall, the freshwater ling's fish bones almost thick enough to use as picks in the cascade of my mother's blue-black hair. She is sunning it dry one morning when two boys ride by on a sorrel bay, bareback, laughing as they struggle to keep a purchase on the horse's dark mane and one another. Three times they ride past our house, searching for another glimpse of Mama who is too busy to bother with them.

So I'm thinking about the woman in my dreams, her back to me through the window, her long wavy hair, and the sound of the piano beyond the edge of the curtain enticing me to follow. Who is playing? I don't know but it feels like our home in Indiana so maybe one of my sisters; we all took turns on that bench. I move from window to window, the music like falling rain, but she doesn't turn to me so that I can be sure. The woman with the wavy hair doesn't turn, so I start to feel left out like this is a scene I cannot enter, a sister I cannot reclaim. I want to cry.

My husband tosses his cap with the mildew stains back into the wash pile. He had left it in the car where the windows fog with damp every time he slides behind the wheel and out of the rain. Still, he is surprised the damp has penetrated the thicker seams and cultivated the growth of mold. He doesn't want that on his head, mold spores so close to his brain and all. He doesn't want that. He reaches for his wool fedora, a tacky brown and white plaid whose worn fibers were "pilling" even before he found it at the thrift store. It keeps his head warm in the rain.

I want to say *Skookum* to startle someone like maybe I mean *spook 'em* but stronger and stranger. I know they'll give me a look like my brains are leaking out of my ears but at least I'll get to say it out loud: *skookum!* Just say it. It's a lot of fun. Or we can talk about the weather: *It's raining! Oh my gawd!* Like that's so unusual. Don't you know? This is Oregon, and even if we *have* had two dry springs in a row, this place is all about water which Kesey already covered in exhausting detail in his big fat novel that only pretended to be fiction—the timber may be gone now but the rain is real enough. Get over it.

Jennifer Bisbing

The Missions

Why didn't you pay the fee
The box just wanted five and the land could use more

You stealing again?

Did the ranch hand leave the barn light on
Or are you in there now

building your escape plan?

What do you hope to find
out past the highway signs?

A glimpse of the whistling woman
A golden eagle's yellow shoes

Barn Storm   *Gary Thomas*

Kristina Boratino

Vintage Bait

I fell in love in my small town antique store—
finally discovering beauty in the fossil.
Leisurely feeling my way around the
crooked nooks and crannies of his past.
Detailed, delicate flaws silently yearn to be noticed.
I've always preferred colorful and complex to simple; stale.
Slowly savoring, and tracing the firm spines of vintage hardbacks simultaneously stirs and settles
my soul. Yet, as the amber
sunset glow sneaks in, hidden lies find their voice.
Dusted courage floats heavily, as my fingertips
fall into every hill and valley of a cold,
chipped fishing lure.
Catch.

     Release.

Coming Home   *Sheary Clough Suiter*

Mark Burke

Stories She Told

Last-born girl's duty, mother gone,
she stayed at the stone farm
after her brothers went east for work.
Barn roof caved by the snow,
mortar falling from the log-house seams,
she tended to her father,
boiled his oats and salt cod,
talked to him about the snow, the leaks
though he couldn't answer.
She made up stories, what we all do,
invent, sometimes without knowing,
how a stranger would walk the dirt-road,
come to call, singers clapping
when she sprang the sword-dance
across the scraped linoleum, spinning alone
through the kitchen's coal-oil shadows.
She held her father's wake in the house,
neighbors drank up her father's screech,
the priest brought his useless prayers,
they all told stories of the deaths,
the mad, the lost, promises on a mass-card
left with the body on the front-room table.
So much turns on the choices,
hard to see past the first steps on the road.
She had to choose before winter came,
cut her own firewood,
stuff cloth in the window gaps,
wait to hear the scrape of any footstep
along the dark hall to her room
or go to work in town,
lie, say she was younger,
the air sharp with rumors of war,
make the most of the months
before all the men were gone.

Window Blocked   *Jill Johnson*

Dale Champlin
Two Poems

Down on Her Knees

Callie's on her hands and knees looking
for her thong, her mascara and the key
to her Harley—the bull rider passed out
on top of the bedspread—jeans shoved
down around his boot tops.

What was his name? Marvin or River?
something with a V in the middle—
those names didn't sound quite right though—
it wasn't much fun the way he blacked out
as soon as they finished—flopped onto his side.

Mostly men treated her like a stray cat
or the punch line of some dirty joke—
snapping her bra strap and trying to grope
her whenever she got too close, the same
way boys have since she got tits.

After a six-pack of Coors she couldn't
remember if they even kissed. Last night
her blood rushed so hard she could hear
it drumming in her ears. Thoughts came
to her slow as a porcupine.

Not Obscene   *Jim Thiele*

She couldn't care less about civilization
the way she loved scrub oaks—
kingfishers bright as the brightest blue—
hibonite blue—fishing the river bottom,
and ducks butt-up in the shallows.

She hadn't asked if he was a native—
reminded her of a coyote in a trap
vulture-bit and bedraggled—kind of lost
the way boys in her high school
looked in the middle of a pop quiz.

A Dove! Callie Said

—after Li-Young Lee, "A Dove I Said"

Mother, she said.
What she meant to say was *waterfall.*
What she meant was *a pool dimpled by rain.*

Bread, she said.
What she meant to say was *arroyo steeped in moonlight.*
What she meant was *waves of meadow grass pulsing against the foothills.*

Prairie, she said.
What she meant to say was *heartbreak and despair.*
What she meant was *sleepwalking.*

Bed, she said
What she meant to say was *wild horses.*
What she meant was *nightmare.*

Damselfly, she said.
What she meant to say was *tumbleweed.*
What she meant was *night wind.*

Book, she said.
What she meant to say was *river.*
What she meant was *a breeze arriving from nowhere.*

Callie took a bead on her circumstances.

Family, she said.
What she meant to say was *unnamed future.*
What she meant was *a promise that her life would come true.*

End of the Run   Cheryl Stadig

The ranch house was the repetition
of the mourning dove coo-cooing on Callie's roof—
rafters open to spilled night sky.

Scoured by fire, Callie's heart is spread to embers.

The end, she says.
What she means to say is *the beginning.*
What she means is *it's time to leave.*

Dale Champlin's poetry collection Callie Comes of Age *was recently published by Cirque Press.*

A Million Mountains No.9, 2021   *J. Leslie*

Nancy Christopherson
Two Poems

Sculptor

The wind brought the Arctic air
the clear sky—blue today—and stars
brilliant at night and blew the snow
into drifts across roads blew the deep snow.

Once, on the north rim I skied in
then lay down on the snow and made
angels. I wrote PEACE I wrote LOVE
inside their bodies. I wrote LOVE beside
them drew arrows through the
centers of their hearts. Do you know
what I mean. On the way back
out a coyote I could see followed me
paralleled my tracks about
a hundred yards off. I suspect
the rest of the pack trotted along hidden
undetected behind big pines
and barren brush. Mostly the snow
field was open. Light snowflakes
in number and beauty flashed.
I looked into the Creator's face for
the second time—overwhelming
simplicity—there is no plan. I took my
skis off. The animal removed its fur coat.
Each of us exposed to the elements.
Cold beings hungry for anything
that sparkled or moved. We just stood
there.

Philips Resevoir, Watching the Cranes Come In

I can hear them before I spot them, slow flapping in—
wings
flashing in the distance almost white—the ruckus they make

rubbing ribbed glottides together, not snapping just
rattling,
calling out *trill coo, purr-cooing.* I know they have arrived

and will settle to rest a while before lifting off again, to
circle, higher, higher,
climbing higher to get up over the mountains bearing north.

They will cross the Northern Cascades then the tall
coastal
ranges of British Columbia, or the wild northern Rockies

of Alberta, the green-white coastal ranges of southeast Alaska
to push on
past Denali. Such a long route—but these are elemental beings,

which makes me smile as I remember that they
mate for life,
are symbols of fidelity and longevity, even immortality—

in some cultures. These tall beige-gray wading birds
with
bright red caps and round amber eyes which nest in the marshy

Arctic tundra—and I, who have lost nearly everything
having been
pushed away from the table as it were—the idea of

them migrating gives comfort and a reason to beam—
there are yet constants
in life. Cars and trucks roar past in the background along

the two-lane asphalt to John Day. I realize the natural
world
survives just fine without me—in fact thrives—without

Mountain Cranes   *Jim Thiele*

any human involvement at all, if we'd just
leave it alone.
I should leave immediately and never come back.

First published in the online journal Kosmos Quarterly, *Spring Gallery of Poets, Spring 2021*

Place 18   *Daniela Naomi Molnar*

Jennifer Dorner

The House on Reedway Street

had everything I could ask for:
a tree swing, our dog, cats
that came and went. Stormy's
hot pink Power Wheels convertible
gouging new potholes in the road,
and the Endicott's paneled walls
and foundation raised
above the floods. It was Oreos
and orange slices in the kitchen
with its red Formica counters.
Shake 'N Bake chicken on Fridays
and school clothes from Emporium
at Mall 205. Maybe I am thinking
of one of those years before I learned
what we didn't have. When rich
meant simply the delight of mud
puddles splashing or reflecting
shadows on my face. And work
meant piano lessons after
swimming, stretching my fingers
into chords over the chipped keys
in time with the metronome
for my teacher, Gordon, who drew
clef notes on sheets of music,
left-handed, with his triangular,
lumber-store pens.

Gene Ervine

The Juncos Left: Jim Sisk 1943-2021

"The juncos left last week."
You mention walking to dinner;
attending to comings and
goings has helped us see.

Now you are "going South"
so we need to observe more.
Since you have been here,
there is much to track.

As I reflect, the geese flock
ready for winter pastures,
farther north bunchberry,
and birch leaves are turning.

Those birds may beat you to
the land of the meadowlarks,
whose songs you first learned
on evening walks with your dad.

You will come home
to a place of the familiar,
seeing children of old friends
you learned before Alaska.

Those geese will pivot north again,
and there are new buds forming
behind fading leaves on birch.
We yearn for your return, too.

One Leaf   *Cynthia Steele*

Amelia Díaz Ettinger
Two Poems

The Seven Poles at Minam, Circled Chief Joseph Dreams

We did not know the history of this place
at the top of the curve, Minam Pass.

We used to stop or slow the car
a ritual to watch honeybees

swarming on red basalt.
An unnerving need to pause.

Not knowing we were showing our respects
pausing at the ghost of seven poles.

At first it was just him and me,
the children joined the ceremony years later,

making the climb in the safety
of our car, claiming this territory,

their glee at those small bodies seen then unseen
in bright sunlight. My son called it the Yellow Dance.

Mesmerized by the living spectrum
movement and the distant buzz of time,

back then I wondered if the rocks tasted of honey;
now I wonder if the honey was heavy with rocks.

Clarno Ridge   *Matt Witt*

Larix laricina not a slag

My Tamarack does not curve, it bruises the sky
her straight and unwavering touch, sharp

as a splinter in the eye of a cloud, she cuts.
At his height he whispers, she listens,

the braggart recounting his past fury
from inglorious gray to white ruin.

The tamarack relinquishes no secrets,
exposes her delicate branches, a disarray

of eyelashes. A common harlot, below lays
her robes. A surprise cover for rocks and lichen

under the appreciative eye of the sun,
a yellow that is his own reflation.

My Tamarack talks with a Black-backed,
a growing family inside her watchful eye.

Tough skin alive with extravagant percussion,
a generosity, nobility to a tyrant.

A hot rendition of her own to cloud, sky, and sun.
Under her flaking leather bark there is blood.

New Earth 14   *Daniela Naomi Molnar*

On Top of the World   *Janet Clemens*

Chase Ferree
Two Poems

The Double

There'd be ample light if only
I could adjust the aperture to fit
the man singing alone in the outfield,

the moon and its double, the crow—
broken leg lifted, foot dangling beneath
its breast. Undertail, fluffed as if for warmth

like terry cloth or polymer vest,
each fiber distinct, blown out.
Facing down the gull, this over-eager

welterweight reminds me of a dog
until I wonder if the gestures find
their energy in pain.

What could have harmed this fidgeting creature,
far from the others that gather so thick
that their calling soars across the lake?

What is a call but a conversation?
What is a leg to this being with wings?

Hand-wringing

In his throat, my ever human father holds
a complicated truth no more. It sounds

harsh to hear him say it, tears clotting his voice.
In the woods once, my breath and steps hushed

at his side. A sudden bird against the sky. Conscious
of my sight I swung my barrel, took the shot. The bird

pitched. Gloves off I came close to the bleeding dove
a caught cry on the wind. Sunlight between the trees. Afraid

of its slow death, my head to my chest, my cold hands
cramped, I couldn't. This dying dove, a crooked coo

in its throat. My ever humane father held
its head and breast and cranked each hand counter

to the other—all sound halts.

Robin Leaving   *Jack Broom*

Castles of Ice and Mud   *Design by Leslie Fried & Carly Egli*

Leslie Fried

Palace at Fish Creek

*In your longing for your giant self lies your goodness,
and that longing is in all of you.*
            —Kahlil Gibran

Walking in winter
over Fish Creek
I saw something strange
under the ice
markings pale, scratchy
black-and-white a sort of man
and woman, huge
sprawled silent
jaws, fists and hips twisted
in sleep deep breathing
among the roots, tubers
and rotting algae.

I felt them stir as March blew in
pushing and pulling
rolling over making heat
under fading white
elbows and knees
barely concealed
by slush and rubble
cracks to rivulets
making space dragging winter
to its end making food
from lichens and pine cones
last summer's litter
earth soup
iridescent yellow.

In April
the bedclothes rose
over Fish Creek
the sort of man and woman
stood up above the trees
crowned and gowned
in seaweed and shell
and roared a windy farewell
lumbering north to a colder place

Warmth rippled from up to down
cattails sprouted fuzzy tufts
like baby birds
lifting their crowns to the light
from nests of moss, lichen
and rockweed
ducks and geese flapped about
this way and that
barking, hissing "ha-ha!
the snow is going, the ice is going
we will soon take back the lagoon."

Spring to summer to fall
sumptuous meals were had by all
krill, herring eggs
clams, worms
and snails highly prized
a mad marketplace of acrobats
and dive bombers
I saw it: death, birth and so on
until the fall rains'
last big letting go.

The saga of succession
a sunken palace
rock walls incised
with reds, greens and browns
forms living and dead
from land and sea
a marriage bed adorned
with yellow grass
swan's down and bone
bent, curling in obeisance
to love making of the first order
earth's lust for new.

Winter is coming
I'm walking to the bridge
to check for signs
shift in shadow
pulse beneath the cackle
of departing geese
and distant apparition
of two beings
crowns of shell over slick eelgrass
gliding south to sleep
in a palace of ice
a long silence
before jubilation.

Which Way   *Jim Thiele*

Brigitte Goetze

How to Get Filthily Rich

An apron helps but is no guarantee
that the applesauce in its hot, manic way
will not escape the lid's determination
to dampen. Even with the most careful attention,
watching the angle of exposure, you will get splattered.
So, prepare yourself, wear that old blouse,
its color bleached over the shoulders, already mottled.
Besides that, the right equipment is a necessity.
You can can on your stove (as long as you don't have
one of those new-fangled glass-tops), but, take my word for it,
springing for an electric canner, holding a whopping 10 pints,
will just gladden your heart—it boils in a jiffy,
giving you ample time to sit on the patio with your honey,
allowing a glass of red wine to round out the evening.

In addition to the canner, seriously consider a second food dryer.
After all, you want to get rich, and that means, you know,
efficiency counts. Once you are set up,
filling another nine trays with the fruit of the season
is just a little bit of extra effort,
for which you will have plenty of energy with just two
squares of extremely dark chocolate. Boy, do they kick
the sweetness of little bits of perfectly ripe pears
into high gear. You can anticipate that cold and rainy
day when those dried slices are better
than any store-bought candy—in any way
you can imagine. I am not yet done

regarding that canner. I can assure you
its voluptuous belly gives you ample space
to speed-blanch 20 lbs of green beans for freezing.
Not to speak of the 70 ears of corn, that sucker takes
ten ears in just one layer. Oh, I almost forgot
to mention the shelling peas—we sweet-talked
our local farmer into raising them with the promise to buy
every single pod she can grow. Takes a few evenings
of shelling on the patio, but we both would be—almost—willing
to promise our firstborn to get that boon. If you never did
eat garden-grown shelling peas--you are truly deprived.

Corn Stalk Post   *Deborah Chava Singer*

Now, as the folk song celebrates, there is nothing comparable
to home-grown tomatoes. Truly vine-ripened, they burst
in your mouth with a complexity of flavors and just the right
balance between sweetness and acid. Last year I canned
about 120 lbs. No—full disclosure here—not all from my garden,
to get my fingers on that mother lode, I had to join,
become a member of the club. For crying out loud,
a CSA doesn't aspire to exclusivity. Besides, like any millionaire,
you just have to write a check. No big deal. Anyway,
who wouldn't want to fully explore that vast versatility?
Those love apples offer a plethora of preserving choices:
juice, sauce, paste, canned whole in their own juices,
(pieces of which will add color and tang to your hearty winter soups),
salsa, sun-dried (well, that's just a marketing term—they use electricity
and you can, too), and for the thrifty, the more extravagant
concoctions, like green tomato relish. Yup, we like to be tomato rich.

Speaking of condiments. Fermenting is the easiest,
least-labor intensive way of getting wealthy. For sure,
making sauerkraut is a messy affair—I own up to that—
(though it really saves you $$$), fermenting pickles
requires almost no clean-up and is basically effortless.
They'll stay crisp for a year, kept cool, if you acquire
—again you can't get rich without investment—
a second fridge—just see it as a mortgage:
initial expense, long-lasting benefit. In truth,
growing cucumbers is easy: two hill-beds
and a generous hand with a watering wand
will give you all the pickles you can eat.
Besides, that fridge has those boxes on the bottom
where you can store your apples, you won't have to buy
fresh fruit until March. I am not kidding!

Okay, I could go on, speak about black-, blue-, rasp-, and strawberries
(the latter you got to grow yourself, those "new" varieties even
from the farmers market don't cut it. Believe me, there is a reason
why gardeners propagate heirlooms), Italian prunes (nothing you can buy
will be as tasty as those you lovingly blanched before drying), sweet and hot peppers,
and—well, I think, you got my drift. When you survey
your filled fridges, freezers (by now you have more than one,
akin to real estate moguls who buy when they see a good deal),
shelves and cabinets, your heart will swell with gratitude
for the bounty which has come your way.
Now, this is critically important:
if you want to be rich for more than one year (you do, don't you?)
putting in your share of sweat is not sufficient. Remember,
honest entrepreneurs admit, success is at least 80% luck, so…
stay in Gaia's good graces, honor her law:
gladly share her cornucopia.

Paul Haeder

Seeking Solace behind Writer's Mask

sayonara The Year of Beginning a Century of Buffoons and Devils

gum tree outside
spasmatic limbs
roots reaching sky
great blue heron squadrons
above filagree tips
agate sheen murder
crows by a dozen
espying me watch

powder blue, fog, rain,
monsoon, electric
sunrise, I hear tidal churn down
road, closed-tight window
hermetic darting beta
at fingertips, clacking away
words flow staccato breathing

"have typewriter, will travel"
2020 world stagnated
viral fear like storm
troopers, 24-7 virus
TV, social media
rotting from top
down, mercenaries
one and all
shekels by nanosecond
magic of the markets
evil more than Dante's
evil dredging fear
Goebbels and Mengele
half-woman/half-elephant
carnival actors, bloated
faces of racists
geriatric Brooks Brothers
criminals, laughing KIA

a distant foghorn
helicopter scanning
Pacific king tides
sneaker waves
conjunctions of sun
moon Jupiter
Saturn solstice
guiding double star
galvanizing superstitious
boys and girls
lining up for a billion
jabs, Gates & Company
devils limp-wristed
richest criminals worldwide

Anna hummer
dissipates forbidden
thoughts momentarily
drawing air on silhouetted
gum tree barren
more depth of being
against the millions
of Eichmann's setting
death schedules
school children hijacked
stuck to Lazy Boy middle
managers, while Black
Lives Matter, fieldhands
speaking mother tongues
choppers, butchering
their own lives
as Rachel Maddow
Lot's are stench detritus
gesticulating multi-millionaire
commentary, press-titutes
by another name

shine on, Pacific yews
dawn dews, word
is lynx is wandering
Bay Side streets
black bears dance too
Anna hummingbirds dive
bombing for fun, elk the
only reindeer in sight

the locust gum tree
traps winter lamentations
buds ready for springing
into hollowed light
I write seeking
dissipated destiny
barely hinted at
peregrine greeted me
at bridge arch
I'll take any sign
the Gregorian calendar
forever wrong
thirteen moons
blue moon

Wolf Moon
Snow Moon
Worm Moon
Pink Moon
Flower Moon
Strawberry Moon
Buck Moon
Sturgeon Moon
Corn Moon
Hunters Moon
Beaver Moon
Cold Moon

I'll watch gum tree
moons passing
give me Indian
names, so I forever
erase the deadly
viruses of Capitalism
our reckoning
with bat viruses
cooked up
in the devils' labs.

Great Blue Heron at Juanita Bay   *Jack Broom*

Jim Hanlen

Wheat Field with Crows

The crows are painting too.
Their strokes leave black
spots for wings. Look,
the wheat field is twisting
itself, trying to take flight.
The sun smears its yellow
finger. The wind has bent
the day into afternoon.
What holds this canvas
in place? Some black spots
are cawing off canvas.
Stand and look. The fury
will make you stagger.

Bird at Dawn   *Matt Witt*

Sarah Isto

Post from Peru, March 2021

No word from you since August.
And from your country
only dismal news reports:
pandemic blooming,
beds overflowing,
scant equipment, doctor strikes.

Now in my email, your name.
I brighten at the festivity
of the first paragraph—
triple exclamation points, a hug emoji,
your "hahaha" at receiving
our Christmas card yesterday.

I see you as twenty years ago
living with us for a high school year,
always delighting in absurdities
delivering them up like jokes,
eyes widening at the punch line,
the first to laugh.

In later years we mailed and skyped
but met only once at a conference
after you decided to follow my path
to medical school—colleagues
who never quite slid off our
temporary mother-daughter tie.

My eyes move down a line
to your unadorned second paragraph:
"Our health system has collapsed.
We are supposed to get a vaccine
(Chinese, 74% effective) later this month.
People are dying every day.
The worst is most are
younger than 50 years.
Not enough doctors or ventilators.

It seems like the end of the world here.
Thank you for remembering me.
Love always, C.Y."

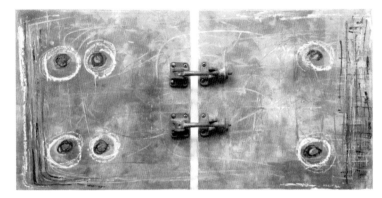

Barely Holding On   *Tami Phelps*

Brenda Jaeger

Sustain

I
Guitar and my heart beat,
flamenco dancers circling edge of sound
"Listen to me!" say my castanets

The front of the guitar strums
fingers let you know
there are two

Sound and heartbeat
throb to the drum of heels
a flash—it is over

II
When I sing the Fado
I know nothing
but Death will sharpen
the rusty sword I call
my life

III

If the grain is open
sound will linger
sustain will hover
wood and skin-covered bone
can bring out what is buried deep inside

IV

If wood is dense
the beat of fingers, of skin-covered bone
will bright the notes
send them out, a fast trampoline—
will go before the dancer,
will lead the way,
say the final word,
absolve the singer
confirm the composer

Once set in motion
there can be no end--
shape of earth
depth of the sky

V

Ebony, mahogany, sapele,
rosewood, spruce, walnut,
birds-eye maple, koa, and cedar make
each syllable a note, a clack of heel on the floor

Strings of steel, strings of nylon wound in silver,
all work to keep the world a-spin

Homage   *Brenda Jaeger*

Marc Janssen

On A Jetty Unnamed

With swift moving fingers, salt coated and cracked, he maneuvered the translucent strand through the hole at the end of the hook. Then the almost invisible line was slid back around itself like a snake writhing around its own body four, five, or even six times. The end was found again and forced back through one of its own loops and pulled tight.

It's late and the ceiling has not fallen in,
The clock has not stopped,
The morning has not come
And he wishes he were a fish,
Sighting invisible stings in the sky.
Somehow, with knowledge of the world, he would survive.
He sees his thoughts coiling up upon themselves
Slipping through,
Pulling tight.

Realizing he forgot to put a sinker on, he bent over once more and retrieved a teardrop of lead with a circle of steel on one end. Bending the line into a loop he squeezed it through the hole in the sinker, wetted the thumb and forefinger with his tongue and again tasted the salt left there from the waters of Pickering Passage. Pinched the leading edge of the line three times before finally pulling it through. Then threaded the line with the hook, pulled, and repeated.

It's late.
He can feel the sun rising in the earth like a bubble about to burst from the surface.
And he can feel himself drifting.
A lightness settles on him.
There is a feeling of weightlessness as if he were suspended on unconsciousness.
A fast shiver jolts his body as if to remind him he could not fly from the comforting confines of the bed.
Eyes closed, he sees the earth far below him. The clouds part to display the pattern of the landscape to the Pacific, the Main Street lights glowing iridescent and ghostly in the rising fog; the fan tops of palm trees like ragged umbrellas; the red tile and brown shingle roofs with flickering lights peeping between mini-blinds as red eyed watchers laugh to early morning talk shows, and swallows perched on telephone wires for the night and killdeer set in the middle of soccer fields like land mines waiting for the passing of beer carrying wayward teenagers, and there is a terrible pain in his chest, his heart hurts and burns, and calls out, and he wants to lift even higher to smell the breeze from the late blooming honey suckle on fog obscured Santa Barbara Island; to see the glow of oil rigs set like Christmas trees on the black and green water near Carpenteria, or the freighters sunk low in the water from Seattle to LA, and their low growling engines, and their wake.
He had never seen a wake trailing away from a really big boat before.

He grasped the cork handle of the pole and let the hook and line swing before him in lazy arcs. Put his thumb on the bail and drew the tip of the pole slowly behind him, the line rotated drawing invisible cones in the air. His arm, cocked like a catapult, sprang forward causing the line to go straight and high. Just before the apogee, his thumb slipped down and he watches as the sinker carries the hook into the sky and down into the oncoming waves.

Marc Janssen's poetry collection November Reconsidered *was recently published by Cirque Press.*

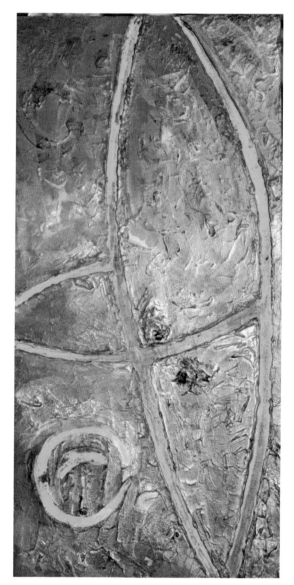

Eric Gordon Johnson

Dog Dish Rock

There's a trail on the mountain
I hiked as a boy. Now
the house sits next to it.
On the way up our dogs leaped up
and lapped rainwater from a bowl
atop a boulder midst berries blue and crow.
We picked there often
and she asked that her ashes
be spread below the rock.
I put down dog Lupine
two weeks after she passed.
Both their ashes lie there now. So
I stop on the way up
with new dog Daisy who drinks
rainwater from Dog Dish Rock.

Copper   *Nard Claar*

Penny Johnson

Short Lives of Animals

Because my quilt squares are Tibetan prayer flags with more in common with a kite's tail and the past is so far behind   I search for consistency in the shadows of trees   a tiny black and white photo with lacey edges of my mother   dark-haired bent-back   like a spring twig   bathes me   hairless my mouth oval in shock this Adirondack stream a lung-sucked baptism predestines a future of freezing water among hemlock and maple.

Because other women baste their quilt squares with a running stitch in effortless speed while they make up an endurance   painstakingly anchor fabric in microscopic nubs   I return to Routt County lodgepoles and roads the snow sits solid only before noon and glares white as lightning until spring melt comes so furious both geese leave home spinning in circles as they float downhill before aspen shiver pale spring leaves.

Because I can't cover with my own quilt but mother's brown with yellowed ivory saved solely for bone wrenching nights my cat on the pillow beside me I remember the time my niece's face soaked with tears asking   why can't they live long enough   live as long as we do   realize I am the serviceberry tree felled limbs damming this creek   it is not that they live so short but that we live so long and our fruit is simply to

bear witness.

Tree Shadow   *Jill Johnson*

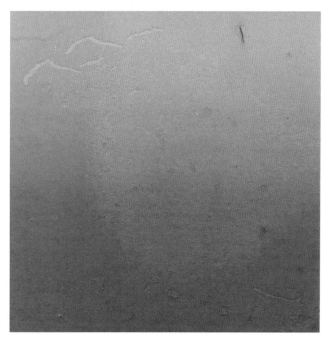

Midnight Sun   *Annekathrin Hansen*

Marilyn Johnston

The Year That Was (and Still Is)

While the cutting winds blew from the east
as we foraged for the last vestiges of garden
bounty, we measured what to pick and what
to leave in scissored order, while the moon
waxed and settled us in our yards. Even
the apples, at least what hadn't already
succumbed to the spotted wing Drosophila Fly,
fell from the tree, half-eaten by the herd of deer
that bedded down at dusk under its limbs.
Car keys neglected for days, we threaded our
way around the field, walked the perimeter
of the neighborhood; as we carried our wrenches
and screwdrivers around the house like unlicensed
workers, trying to tidy up things that were broken
down, afraid to let someone outside our pod in.
And in the end, too uncorked and wary of wine,
we'd spend our restless nights forgetting the order
of how days of the week fell, each one blending
into the other. Finally now, with news unevenly
clipped together and tweeted about
"The Year That Was," we can pretend sun
is finally coming through clouds; and, as if
momentarily blinded, even if no warmth falls
on our face, we can be grateful—hold our
head up, searching for the light.

Carol Levin

Only Got Bones & Joints

Sam Shazam's a whisper
　　　of information to carry
　　　　　you into activity,

even though extremely informative, he is
　　　breakable. Only bones & joints, & can't
　　　　　compare to being alive & kicking.

He can't make head or tail of our crippling
　　　muscle spasms, our heartaches tender
as melon's flesh, our heebie-jeebies,

　　　　　or the invigorating verve of our
　　　　　rib-tickling doubled over belly-laughs.

Behind my chair Sam Shazam hangs
　　　from a rod
　　　　　naked arms akimbo, organs missing

as if shadows blot licks of light.
　　　I nod at his broken
　　　　　occipital joint's

connecting couplet where, still,
　　　the skeleton, Sam Shazam,
　　　　　demonstrates

axial bones & joints
　　　of vertebrae that bear our weight.
　　　　　There's wily arm attachments at

the sterno-clavicular joints, graceful curves
　　　toward the clavicle's finale, an ingenious
　　　　　link of our whoopee *synovial ball-*

&-socket joints also known as, glenohumorel joints.
　　　There's chewy jaw joints & rotations
　　　　　in dancing hip joints—& fingers, & knees—

Ah, Sam you've got them all.

Doddery man-made Sam introduces us to our design
　　　though he's a little broken now
　　　　　like some people I know and some I love.

Gravitational Pull　　　　　　　*Sheary Clough Suiter*

Joe McAvoy

World's shortest poem with the longest title

August 19, 2015, Oregon, Under a Star-Lit Sky
With a Good Book, Sitting in the Adirondack Chair My Son Built For Me, Allison Krause and Union Station
Playing,
Cold Amber Ale, Air Crisp and Fall-Like After a Scorching Day (August Being a Confused Month Weather-
wise), Crickets Serenading, The Basketball Hoop Staring at Me Across the Driveway Saying "I Raised
Your Children" and I, the Atheist, Confused on Whom to Thank,
Nevertheless….

…..thank you

Rainbow Clouds   *Matt Witt*

Karla Linn Merrifield

Long Strange Climate Trip

Yesterday afternoon at Site #2, I dropped
pink windowpane acid, tripped out
at Monument Lake in the national preserve.
Blake le Tent blew over and away,
my camp chair came to an abrupt end leaving
me with wind, clouds, a rainbow sun
and the water's blue circumcised eye.
I climbed the fully erectile cell tower.
I moved into a pendulous breast gourd martin house.
I discussed the fortunes of the planet
with a recombinant saurian.
Time flew northward on blue heron wings.

Suddenly I was airborne,
a cypress seed planted far into the future
as far north as I could imagine going
from the Everglades and remain
on the North American continent.
Far, far out. Over far eons.

Treeless
tundra
begat
the boreal
begat
the temperate deciduous
begat
the subtropical wetland
forest
where I took root,
I grew on Ellesmere Island—
above the Arctic Circle

What was once
the world of ice
is the world ending in fire.
I stand alone in my dome,
last tree on Earth,
burned alive, burned alive.

After The Fire No. 1, 2020   *J. Leslie*

James Merrill

I Went to School Today

Salvador Dali was instructing, painfully, the concept
of relativity. "Everything is relative to something else;
this chair is relative to that corner. And the corner is relative
to the hall, as well as the clock on the wall down that hall."
Einstein was sweeping up after the children's lunch in the cafeteria.
The chemistry lab had been converted to a plant for recycling bubble
gum, so the kids could learn the importance of making tires.
I asked Dali something about black holes, and he told me,
"You must paint something like that with white; break it
into parts first." So I drove home, prepared to apply
my new-found knowledge to the canvass of my life
in the suburbs. I parked the sedan in the driveway
and looked toward heaven.
I see the color of the sky in your eyes just before it rains, but
after you've been crying. You meet me at the door, your heart
dripping on your sleeve. Furtively you look out the door, then
beckon me in. Your cheeks match the color of the rose I'm holding
out for you. I step over the threshold of a dream into my life. Inside,
the walls are the color of a hardboiled egg, where the yolk appears
just under the surface. I reach into my pocket and find
the ticket from the movie we saw last night—now
just a stub of the time.

Pushing Winter   *Julie Lloyd*

Thomas Mitchell

The Old Red Wool Coat

It was never anything special, simply
an old wool coat that my father wore,
one that seemed to adapt to his every
moment. Sometimes he reached
for a Chesterfield from the folded pocket,
or a shiny lure when he was fishing,
a swallowtail or a niggle to drop
in the deep mystery of the American
River. Maybe it gave him a sense
of who he was, ambling through life
as he lumbered down a street
at the far end of town, under
the telephone wires, over the girder
bridge where the space between
the foot planks revealed the rushing water
below, walking from one malaise
to another, the moods that were there
no matter what he tried to do about it.
I remember once at the dinner table
I noticed a brass button missing from
the broad hem of his coat. It caught
my attention but I was afraid to ask.
Years later, after he died from a failed heart,
my mother told me he had tied the button
to his line as a makeshift spinner
on a fly-by-night fishing trip.

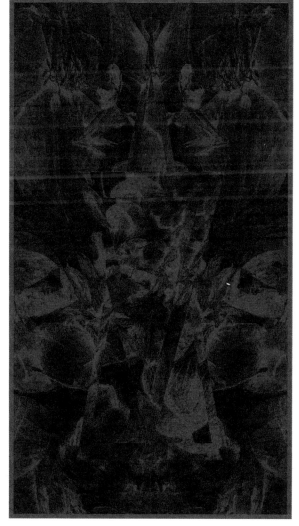

Beauty 6   *Julie Lloyd*

Susan Morse

The Quilter

for my sister, who gathered the family quilts

She began on a Singer treadle machine,
cutting simple pieces at first, rocking
her foot backward and forward like those
Gees Bend women from Alabama*
with their call-and-response stitches singing,
"housetop" and "bricklayer," singing their
visual histories into being, hand-to-hand
laid down from one generation to the next.

My Sister's Quilt   Susan Morse

>   In her early years, she did not
>   know of her own heritage, the great
>   aunt on her grandmother's farm,
>   an Oklahoma quilter, piecing
>   the traditional patterns: *Hunter's
>   Stars, Kaleidoscope, Wedding Ring*,
>   the pictures becoming more intricate,
>   more intimate as the occasions fit,
>   choosing the essential working
>   colors and textures, coarse
>   or smooth like life, learning
>   the slip knot for anchoring.

Later she learned to paper piece
each triangle first, add fans of light,
or design the concentric squares
which could close in
upon a body if she let them.
Two husbands came and went,
years passed humming
along with her machines.

>   But her knowledge continued
>   as she studied those years,
>   arranged the width
>   of her own borders, wove
>   colorful tales like the women
>   before her, each covering
>   caught up by needle and thread
>   and the rocking feet of all
>   the journeys she envisioned.

**Gees Bend, Alabama is famous for the women who have hand quilted
stories of their lives for over a hundred years. They exhibit their quilts
through the Souls Grown Deep Foundation.*

Anne Carse Nolting

Glimpse Into Eternity

After my son died
the wrong knee started hurting,
south wind blew, my car sailed
over the top of an ancient rhododendron
and got hooked on a branch.

In the store people parted before me
as a red sea might
when someone like me starts walking
where she shouldn't,
and others stared at me searching
for something they couldn't understand,
expecting something else.

After my son died
I lay in the hammock rocking his ashes
and slumbered.
Mom, you always have missed my childhood,
I became a man and went on to the next stage,
and here is yet another.
Who is to say what you and I know?

He talks to me now
the way I talked to him, waddling home
after work through Sitka rain, belly big,
substance of his ash somehow, miraculously
organized in my womb.
Mystery embraced, coming and going.

As an 11 year old, he told me:
"In the future I will be a wave"
and he squirmed out of my arms
into the world.
And lest this world forget, he said:

"Remember, your value as a person
derives from your inner soul and spirit.
Nothing from the outside has the capacity to lessen
or hurt you.
You are a sacred and special person,
and it all comes from the inside."

After my son died
the coroner's report noted
he looked much older than 38 years,
which should not be a shock;
he was always an old soul, one who snuck in
over the threshold of another star.
It is his eyes, people say. So passionate,
a glimpse into eternity.

"Feel the sea, Mom," he said, "let it rise up,
cover you with all the love in the universe,
and know my love for you will always, always be forever
much much more."

quotes by Ben Carse Nolting

Silty Waves   *Susan Biggs*

Al Nyhart

To One Experiencing Sentience

For Brian Greene

Perhaps you weren't expecting it.

  Maybe you thought it came with the goods,

that all those protons & particles

  would do the math for you,

that all you had to do

  was capitulate to the elegance of increasing entropy

& observe how the babushkas of Chernobyl

  walk heavily between rows of new potatoes.

Bead   *Nard Claar*

Mary Odden

Do you recognize anyone, asks the Capitol Police

#1   Yeah, I think so.

First, just as he wants it, the guy in the fox and coyote furs. The horns, behind the Speaker's podium. I recognize the fur, remember the animal in the trap with its foreign eyes. Not then the protagonist. I remember, in shame? That I believed in its death, a trade, its little life for one of my urgent ones. After 100 hats, there's a box of furs I never sewed and I am sorry. While they waited in darkness, dead in vain, this guy was born, his beautiful body smooth as a bullet, his sculpted torso available for autograph. His eyes, under a fortuitous gift of brow, I have been taught by Goldwyn-Mayer to recognize. Those eyes are heroic and clear as Dolby super vision, blue as newly broken glacier. Every cleared field of his muscle is tattooed with the memes of freedom. Freedom, that box o'socks. I am a western, too. Ranch kids good as New York's best, now in their dotage, came to teach my classes in suits, came to the podium in suits, now recognized by no chair have proceeded to caskets in their best shoes, too mute. What is it we expected of shoes? I wore a flower; it's what I learned to mean. Meme is still a new word for me. It's good they don't recognize him, a great-grandson empty as a word of praise, cute in horns on Christmas morning, still in his pajama bottoms, still digging in the pile for another present.

Comes the Fall   *Tami Phelps*

Barbara Parchim

A Small Passing

We found the snipe lying under the artichoke
already rampant with new growth.
Cradling her body in my hand
I marveled at the most substantial part of her
the long beak — a formidable tool,
used for probing the boggy meadow.
The rest — long legs and brown mottled feathering —
so light and showing no sign of injury.
Age or sickness may have brought her upslope
to shelter under spiky umbrella leaves.

I buried her in the comfrey patch.
I was thinking comfrey for comfort,
a balm to soothe the bruise of regret —
such a brief life, no less remarkable than mine.
Come June —
the alchemy of a small bird
and a blue-flowered healer.

Little Dipper   *Jim Thiele*

Diane Ray

More Begats

1.
Rogue rockets into Israel
   that begat an errant bomb
      that begat struck back

2.
that landed tiny Yasmeen
   pocked with shrapnel
      on the world's page

3.
the dazed toddler mumbling
   Nothing happened
      unaware

4.
Mama
   is no
      more

5.
that sounds
   another
      clarion

6.
and a truck
   incinerates
      an ancient street

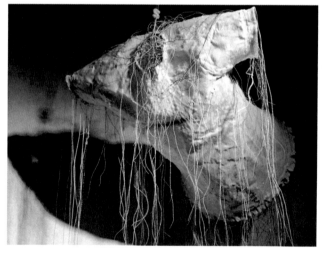

Flight of the Innocents   *Sheary Clough Suiter*

7.
as an old man
   strolls
      Yerushalayim

Michael Eden Reynolds

decadesdecided™

How to Deice your Glacier

1. Unplug the glacier.
2. Remove everything from the glacier and store someplace cold.
3. If you have towels, put them down.
4. If you have children, show them where you've put the contents of the glacier in case you are gone when it has thawed.
5. If you're pressed for time or experience compulsions, chip away at the glacier with a metal spatula.*
6. Waiting is hard. It won't be long.
7. If there was cake in the glacier, please eat it now.**
8. If you are still here when the glacier is completely defrosted, replace your cold goods.***
9. Plug in your glacier and resume normal operation. It won't be long now.

Ice 2   *Nard Claar*

* We do not recommend you do this, but we know that you will.
** Icing may contain nuts.
*** Rubber boots not included.

Richard Roberts

Hills Above Plains

Wailing winds born mourning in caves of these drab hills
forlorn hills humbled by horizon mountain ranges
manless hills where light-eyed coyotes den and lie watching
far down upon nervous highway threads between towns
these sere hills of the plain, borders of manland,
shunned by flatland man
to admire town church spires, shrink from seeing
above his fields grave hills – home of his direbeast and viper.

No gold here, no lumber tree, no elk or trout, no picnic papers
in these limbo lands of final wildernesses
unsettled and unsought where lone strangeseekers
find boulders of glacial surge, strata lines
of eonic lakes, earth-hue finger painting by mythmen
upon sandstone windcave walls, carvings on rock ramparts,
find flint weaponheads of stone age thrust,
wind-bared skulls of genesis, find final undoing abidance
confirmed by hillwinds telling.

Crack in the Earth   *Matt Witt*

Zack Rogow

Lord Byron to His Daughter Ada

Missolonghi, Greece: 12 April 1824

My dearest daughter, no doubt you ponder
How you came to have a father reviled
By the press, gossips, your mother; who'd squander
His choicest of years, from England exiled
To Venice and Ravenna, to wander
And never glimpse how time has changed his child.
So I'm sending you, my señorita,
This *apologia pro sua vita*.

Accusers say I chase every passion,
Boy or girl; that gaming I just accrue
Mont Blancs of debt; my gilded coach I fashion
After Bonaparte's; sired a child or two
On the side; no pleasure do I ration.
It well could be that every word is true!
I hope those who claim I'm the fount of all evil
Concede at least I'm a handsome devil.

Blue Gardenia   *Julie Lloyd*

"Most selfish writer who e're walked the earth."
Aye, that's I, they jabber of no other.
And yet I sailed to Greece, to midwife the birth
Of a country free and united, mother
Of gods and soft marble—for all that's worth.
Each faction would rather knife the other.
With fever freezing, at thirty-six my life
May end before I put an end to their strife.

I've heard that you have quite a head for maths—
From *moi* you could have never gained that skill.
All children should stumble toward their own paths
Leave parents' dreams for parents to fulfill.
My absence I won't excuse, nor calm your wraths.
You felt them when I left, you feel them still.
But a poet for a parent—you could do worse.
You never knew your father—you'll know him from his verse.

Joel Savishinsky

Dogs Outnumbered the People: Colville Lake, Northwest Territories

Dogs outnumbered the people
better than three to one. If
demography is destiny, the fates
would have laughed and barked
their regrets. But even without fatalism
on their side, the animals' chorus
rose through the early evening,
calling the stars to order, taking
attendance of the planets before
the moon grew small in its ascent.

Under the cover of skim milk light,
I would visit the cabin next door,
the family whose daughters had sewn
my old-style parka, whose elders
made me welcome and gave me
my first lessons in *deneké*, the people's
Athabascan dialect. The grandmother
would butcher caribou as I butchered
their language, my atonal efforts always
good for a laugh, her patience seemingly
as tireless as the months-long Arctic night.

Queen Anne's Blue   *Julie Lloyd*

The comfort was mostly wordless,
the fire's hiss in the stove telling
its tales, the rasp of a file as I
sharpened first my ax and then,
unbidden, picked up four from
the household and did them next.
Someone would lay more wood
on the embers, adjust the flue, or
lift the kettle of tea from the grate
and top off their metal mug.

A sneeze.
        A sigh.
                A smile or a nod
                could silence the solitudes.

Alone,
 together,
        again,
  while outside,
far above paths lined with old snow,
the aurora crackled, breaking the sky
into bright candy and brittle music.

Spoon Petals   *Tami Phelps*

Tamara Kaye Sellman

In the Safeway Parking Lot

(for J.)

two young men brush their teeth
from inside the protective wings
of opened car doors, check side
mirrors while grooming with paper
napkins, the wagon's windows
fogged, condensation of breathing,
the back seat still pressed flat

April's cold but golden sunrise
after two days without rain reminds
me of her sudden exit, the sometimes
daughter who's made the same deal
who wants the comfort of a roof
but is not permitted because heroin
severs a family clean like a cleaver

I am not a morning person otherwise
but were I to take a trip to the ocean,
I might want to go before the robin sings,
cruise by the vacant side lots of stores,
a casual spy for the lost girl, imagining
the toys left in her pockets: tampon,
toothbrush, matchbook, compact

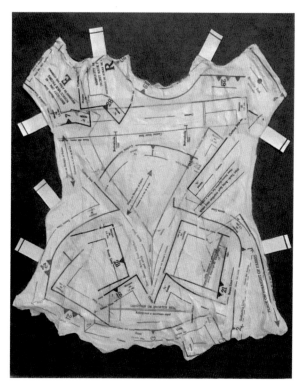

One Size Does Not Fit All   *Tami Phelps*

Tom Sexton
Three Poems

After Reading Hinton's Anthology of Classical Chinese Poetry

At the end of another cold May,
blossoms on the apple show

a bit of pink. They open white.
We were once the youngest couple

on our street now we're the oldest.
A friend about to fly to Paris says:

"Money is a kind of song, an aria."
No one has ever returned to Peach-

Blossom Spring, I'm tempted to say.
Instead, I turn my tongue to stone.

Forgotten Collars   *Gary Thomas*

Transfiguration of Our Lord, Ninilchik

for Suzie Fair

I held a crown of gold over the head
of a bride to be many years ago
in this small gold- domed church on a high bluff.
When I caught sight of it today, my thoughts
turned to her driving here from Anchorage,
on what was then a narrow winding road
when her every thought had become an anchor
and every other road led straight to Hell
or Hades, she was proud to be a scholar.
She'd climb the long muddy path to this place
where the priest would be waiting to unlock
the door before *leaving her in God's hands
for as long as she needed.* Somehow, he
knew when it was time for him to return.

When she stepped out of the church, the mountains
and the wide inlet seemed about to merge.
She mentioned this to me once, only once.
I imagine them making their way down
to the village, smiling, making small talk
laughing when one of them slipped, almost fell.
Years away from this place, surrounded by
brooding mountains, she ended her own life.
Between white crosses, fireweed in bloom.

April in Ketchikan

Wind-driven rain was falling so hard
that walking was like wading upstream.
"It's a shower," the hotel clerk said when
he handed me their only umbrella.
"Rain's expected later this afternoon."
Perched on the hills above the main street,
the old houses have bragging rights.
One with glowing shingles leaned toward
its darker neighbor as if to discuss the azaleas
tumbling down from every nook and cranny.

When a gust of wind turned the umbrella
inside out, water ran down my arms and neck
filled my pockets and then my shoes.
The next gust bent it like a straw.
When I turned back toward the New York Hotel,
a mill worker leaning out of his pickup truck
yelled, "only fairies carry umbrellas in Ketchikan,"
then gunning his engine he left me in his wake.
A raven watching my progress seemed to find me
amusing before it opened its umbrella, flew away.

Ghost Ferns   *Jim Thiele*

Merna Dyer Skinner
Two Poems

Secret-Keepers of Easter Island

I must tell you of the wild horses of Rapa Nui—
thousands of feral creatures, who, in daylight,
meander coastal ridges of volcanic rock—
indifferent to drop-offs, to surging seas below.

I must tell you of the Rapa Nui man who arrives
each morning at Anakena Beach, dressed in fedora,
fleece, and fatigues, homemade rake in hand.
In silence, he combs the white coral sands
in straight lines and swirls, erasing traces
of warring ancestors who long ago swam
and slaughtered here.

And, what of the rows of moai heads,
balancing red discs like uniformed soldiers?
(Two of the five eaten away by erosion). Stoic male faces—
stone lips and round eye-holes staring inland,
their white coral eyeballs and red scoria pupils—
broken fragments later found buried deep in the sand.
What had those eyes witnessed? Why were they removed?

Mostly, I must tell you how black the land,
once the sun slips into the sea. When, driving at midnight,
a canopy of slate clouds blots out the moon,
and I can see no farther into the misty night than my headlights
allow—a herd of wild horses steps out from the darkness.

Ambling across the rutted dirt road, they never look my way,
as if my patch of light is not there. Phantoms dissolving
back into the night—mysterious, silent—
neither a neigh nor a whinny, only the soft shuffling—
hundreds of hooves upon the ground—and tokerau,
the wind, in from the ocean, whispering "shshshsh"
over the tree-barren land.

She Could Have Lost a Hand

Sea-legs wide, on the aft deck, my mother readies her lure—
threads fishing line though eyelets, loops filament

into one tidy knot, pulled tight with her right index finger,
its tip cut deep, scarred, decades ago, into an upturned smile.

–Like tying your shoes, she tells me. I know
the story: she's running—late for her first day of school…

her sister ahead…the shove…outstretched fingers
reaching for the heavy door—its iron latch catching

skin and bone, bites hard. With a flick of that finger
she releases the reel's lock. *Best to use a light line,*

she says, *if you want to fool the biggest fish.*
Her cast, graceful as a ballerina's ballon,

sends filament arcing into the blue—taut, slight, never slack—
a distant splash, then a click—the bite alarm set.

Her small frame, like a soft wave, settles into the deck chair.
Light chop laps the hull—occasionally, lazy clicks sound,

as drifting currents coax the chaser further out to sea.
Sitting beside her, I dangle my feet, close my eyes

lulled by serenity— across my thin lids, sunlight flickers
through the weave of my straw sunhat.

Aftermath　　　　　　　　　*Sheary Clough Suiter*

Then—zzzzzzzzzzzz—something big—running out the line.
The pole's tip, like a mad divining rod, dives toward the sea.

Bracing her stance, Mother cranks the reel,
bowing forward, giving slack, rocking back—

as if in frenzied prayer, holding, reeling—losing line to the fight—
straining tension rips the reel away—unspooling into the wind her line.

She grabs gloves—frantically— wraps the windborne cord
around her left hand, pulling with her right, wrapping, pulling,

calling for the gaff, bringing the beast in sight—
in reach of the hook—over the gunwale, onto the deck.

Her bloodied hand useless—she grabs pliers with her right,
reaches into the battle-lost gaping mouth, wrenching free the lure.

With a gutting knife, she releases her nylon-bound hand—
slices open the Bonito's belly along its silver seam,

reaches in—culls entrails—flings them to the gulls
fishing in the blue above.

Kathleen Stancik
Two Poems

Hope

> *Hope is the struggle of the soul.*
> —*Herman Melville*

Hope enters the meadow on delicate legs
lowers her head to nibble a patch
of wild iris piercing the hardpan,
violets sheltered by thistle.

Night seeps into turbulent air, the yellows & blues
hand-painted on lupine vanish in darkness,
return polished at dawn, color packed tight as pollen
dressing the legs of honeybees.

Some days, Hope feels unripe, a hard green fruit
on a plum tree. Some days she's lush:
a flint of sunlight slips into the meadow
ignites tassels of seed into bonfires. She bolts

then settles, dips her delicate head to the pond,
lips like lilies, floating, sublime,
ripples radiating like birdsong.
An eagle skims by, trout in its talons.

Hope crushes green shoots under her hooves;
cattails bend with the weight of a hawk. In the damp
of the night she pillows her treacherous head
on the razor-sharp edge of desire.

In Loukes Garden I   *Annekathrin Hansen*

Yesterday

the smoke arrived
carrying a forest
in its suitcase.

Place 19   *Daniela Naomi Molnar*

Richard Stokes

December Storm

Forecasters call the assault atmospheric
rivers of rain. Torrents pour from gray skies,
from melting alpine snow-packs.
The slope behind my house wakes in anger,
shutters and shakes like a wet dog.

Water and mud roar down every wrinkle.
Root wads of wind-toppled hemlocks
tear stream-sides. Sediments clog channels.
Boulders laid by glaciers roll and slide.

In early morning darkness I listen to the roar
of water rushing through the house-side culvert,
remember when another angry stream
jumped the banks, slammed the house,
filled our basement with soupy mud.

A massive mudslide down the block shaves
off a deck and sluices logs, debris
and a trailered boat downhill.
A stream gobbles hunks of my neighbor's lawn.
Ninety miles to the north a slide takes
six houses and two lives.

The frontal assault ends, but the sun
still hides in gray gauze. The surface
of the lake in front of our house is placid,
but the mocha-color tells a tale of mud.

Water still hurries over freshly exposed rocks
as I walk upslope to check on lurking dangers.
I have the uneasy feeling I'm tiptoeing
across a sodden beast that may any minute
try to shake itself dry.

Doug Stone

Fog at Yachats

Fog strolls off the ocean
like an old uncle coming to visit,
dapper in his silky gray overcoat.
Hands clasped behind his back,
he walks up the beach, across the highway,
carefully edges around houses on the hillside,
then opens his arms to the firs.
They crowd around him, welcoming him back.
The whole forest weeps with joy,
tears glistening on every branch.

Foggy Marina at Ilwaco   *Jack Broom*

Mark Thalman

The Locomotive in Odell Lake

I untie my 14 footer called the Kokanee,
set the choke, and jerk the starter rope
until the Evinrude sputters, catches—
Pulling away from the dock, I watch stones
drop off into darkness.

Trolling past Trapper Creek, I recall
a faded photo of the small sawmill
that opened in 1924
to supply thick timbers of Douglas Fir
for framing Southern Pacific tunnels

between Oakridge and Cascade Summit.
Workers transporting the mill's locomotive
weren't ready for high waves
when they ventured from Shelter Cove.

Clearing Breezy Point,
the barge, an angry bull, began bucking
and before eight seconds were up,
the engine was thrown overboard—
sinking out of sight.

Without a steam engine, Pott's Sawmill
forgot about trying to build tracks
to harvest trees. Instead, they cut old growth
along the lake and rafted logs to West Bay
to be sawed into beams.

The engine is probably on its side,
silt caked thick, while salmon
swim past the smoke stack and pistons
like steam trailing down the tracks.

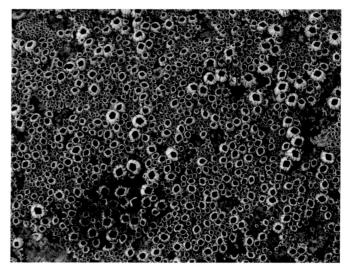

Abandoned   *Jim Thiele*

Lucy Tyrrell

I Dwell in Possibility

after Emily Dickinson

I dwell in possibility—
bare limbs counting leafless
hours, thin foliage tracking scent
of spring, photosynthetic cells
summing summer
until sand disappears

through scarlet hourglass.
I garner those requisite ten
thousand practice hours—
breathe lilac air, suck water
through filigreed rootlets,
master deciduous pattern.

After scores of years—
I stand rough-barked, firmly rooted,
cradle woven nests of song,
slip out bands of wood, spread wide
my hands for tender shade.
I gather paradise in leafy poems,
interstices of empty sky.

Lunch   *Jim Thiele*

John Van Dreal

Crimson to Pink to Gone

The slippers were once deep, alizarin crimson,
now so worn the hue is faded—
patches of light pink and rust-red almost translucent
as they cling to her feet.

She won't let them go.

She once proclaimed, "My ruby shoes will turn to wings,
giant calligraphic extensions that carry me to
checkered marble floors and crushed
velvet furniture."

That was a dozen years ago. Just before
the last of a string of emotional crises
ending with her wandering off at dawn, found
later with unsettled eyes and facial expressions
twisted by disoriented confusion, covered in
duck feces and river slime, hunkered behind a
downtown alley garbage dumpster.

That was the impetus for intervention, hospitalizations,
medications, even the consideration of electroconvulsive
therapy.

She's stabilized now—held just short of catatonia by
the right pairing of medication and supervision.
She rarely speaks.
She almost never listens to others.
She spends her waking hours drawing with colored
pencils—flowers and birds, mostly, on watercolor paper.

His love for her has paled but his devotion has not.
He still sits with her, often eyeing the slippers.
He won't let them go either.
The nurses know this and add stitches
when threadbare material splits or tears.

Two Thoughts   *Nard Claar*

Nativity Scene   *Jack Broom*

Jeanine Walker
Two Poems

To Hold a Cross

He reaches for her hand. The pregnant woman.
One dog, one cat, a man named Juan and a woman
named Rosie, who stands with her stomach
pointing toward the apartment in which they might live.

It's a small place. I no longer
pay for gas. Inside, they remark
how it's been painted
recently, though the former
tenants' scuff marks
are still on the walls.

She tells him the baby is kicking. He suggests
it's the chili from lunch. I point out
the late-night restaurant just opened across the street.
I thought it would be noisy, but it's not.

Rosie says it's not. Juan
moves his hand from hers onto
her belly. I feel it, he says.
I tell them the tenants
on the other side of the house
keep their music down.

Juan glances at me. His eyes move
to the wall's drilled hole that once held
a cross. Two crosses, three,
the former occupants left such reminders.

Then his eyes close. He kneels
on one of the carpet's remaining stains,
ear to his wife's belly. The dog
and cat wait in the car.
I know there are far more
than three of us here.

Walking Home in a Drizzle During a Drought

Watch what water you drink
during a drought.
Memorize his winking eye
from a window.
Beware rides offered from trucks.

The steps you step grow wider.
Everyone must pass the bridge before returning.
Look at the riverbed so dry.
Two bikes parked at the no parking sign,
two children off in the dirt.

Pay attention to your shoes. The rain
won't distinguish you from the next who wanders.
One man hums on his stoop beside a sign
saying, "Quiet People." Consider then
the woman walking with three bags full.

The road in front of you, it widens.
A dog rolls a suitcase from house to car.
Your passenger is your imagination:
you take no others.
The legs you started out with are not these legs.
Your feet ache like fallen trees.

On your porch the black kitty meows.
Her paws are the wet stones of gardens.
You pull her onto your lap
to welcome yourself back
and she lets you.

What affection. Even if later
you'll find it false, take it.

Welcome   *Jill Johnson*

Anne Ward-Masterson
Two Poems

New Hampshire 1957-1975

All the stories 16 years of formal
schooling taught me:
written by Homer, Shakespeare, Yeats,
Whitman, Hemingway, Steinbeck, Salinger…
Those stories everyone should hear at least once?
They are not mine. They are a glittering borrowed gift
meant to be memorized, and left unclaimed by me.
The sorrow in my soul
passed down for generations
by ancestors stolen from Africa
their names tossed into the depths of oblivion?
THAT sorrow
needs stories to wipe away its tears;
But, dad and I knew no "our" stories.
Did not know the language our ancestors
cried out in; As they were stolen
away from their lives,
to enrich someone else's.
The language cut out of them
placed in gilded wooden boxes at
the feet of Jesus

as tribute. My ears never heard, my mouth never knew
the shape or taste of their names on my tongue.
My soul only ever lifted up faceless
first ancestors to G-d.
On another branch
my grandmother's five times
great grandfather
free and fishing on the Maryland
shore gave rise
to a dynasty of sorts:
a succession of three wives
bearing thirty children all told.
And the Jones family (a slavery fairytale)
brought to D.C. after the war, given a mule
and $50, left to live whatever lives they
could make for themselves.
They worked in the
Treasury Department…
their exact jobs lost
a dropped stitch
in the family record.
Knowing these scraps
of family stories thin on details,
faded with retelling
is almost more painful than
knowing nothing. Holding the tattered
remnants I know
about my black ancestors
scarcely connected by the tenuous
strands of national narratives
on slavery, Jim Crow, redlining
leaves me longing
for what my Irish cousins have:
a village where I can visit the bones of my ancestors,
a pub to visit distant cousins, a church where I can sit
where my ancestors sat.
In moving to NH,
the color of their skin,
was the first thing people
knew about my grandparents.
It was too easy to compare them,
we later generations, to night,
all the dangers unseen.
The evil that would snuff out
the Paschal Candle. Our private selves,
retelling whispers of remembered scraps
of our family history, when overheard,
had our stories distorted and betrayed,
we endured trial in the man-made crucible

of the gossips in a small town.
Torments invented by people who claimed to
"Have no problem with black people," as long as we
stayed an abstraction.
So, we made our own fairy tales.
Of Old Crow
wily and mischievous, both.
With the gloss of magic
across his wings looking like rainbows
in the sunlight. He would search out
little black girls, their young fathers with old souls,
especially on rainy days.
To fly above the heavy cotton-wool.
Flap languidly in the kisses of the sun.
Or hold conversations with Chickadees and Pickerel:
about the thrift of bees, the craziness of Chipmunks,
the feast that comes immediately after the
haying machines cut swaths of grass,
leaving them lie in August sunlight.
It is only as an adult I let myself know,
these stories my dad and I
traded back and forth,
buckled side by side
onto the taped-up bench seat
of his rusty pick-up, brought us sanity.
Were talismans we held tucked under our tongues
against slights, racial epithets
of classmates, co-workers,
teachers, congressmen.
Until the next rain storm let us build a new world
in the rusty mobile living room of my dad's truck.

Web 1   *Daniela Naomi Molnar*

Onion   *Susan Biggs*

Heliotropism

Midsummer
11pm
The sun still gives color
To the sky
The leaves on the trees
Its golden fingers
Reach past the hem
Of the blackout curtains
Tendrils of laughter
From children playing football
Follow easily in their wake
You stand precariously
One foot on the lid of your toy chest
The tangled curls of your head
Tucked between the curtain and window
You strike me as a flower
Bending its petals to the last
Rays of sun

Patty Ware

Jesus died ~~for our sins~~

the now I am living through
is proclaimed by Christians
to be Lent: *Repent and believe in the gospel*
smudged ashes on my mute forehead; I open
my mouth to seek, what—solace? understanding?
the celibate collars preach of prayer,
giving alms, fasting; yet I cannot
quell this dull ache of doubt
turned to throb, like a crack
in an aging tooth whose fissure has creviced
into its root

I was never good at Lent,
though the nuns created contests
to see which student could pin the most purple
crosses on the class bulletin board,
each a symbol of sacrifice; back when giving
up candy, or soda, or not fighting
with a sibling earned accolades
from wimpled women, my fragile conscience
guilty too soon, crowding out
an insistent impulse to raise my hand, to inquire why
would Jesus want us to suffer?
Jesus died for you, the nuns would say
solemnly, and we'd reflexively bow
our heads, as if ashamed of simply being
the children that we were.

Do not put on sackcloth and ashes
Jesus said, lest others know you are fasting, rather
make yourself pleasant to behold, not
like the hypocrites—and so I try
not to wail too loudly, to bear up
though the woman who bore me
is battered up both sides of her body,
from her fall during the dark shield of night
from four days of ripping
out her IV's in the hospital.
She cries out to her own mother
dead more than a decade—
tells me, *I am tired;* I say I am praying
for you, mom. *Tell Him*, she whispers,
I am ready.

If I were to abstain
from every sweet morsel, or stop sipping
crisp Chardonnay, would that bring God
closer, would it make these flood waters
recede, this baptism now become
my drowning? Do not speak to me
of sin or suffering; I am tired
of hearing it isn't too late
to make for myself
a meaningful Lent; I want
no more promises of joy
of the miracle of Easter resurrection

somehow, I never understood
that in the garden of Gethsemane,
even Jesus—our Savior—
prayed for a different ending.

Forgotten Collars   *Gary Thomas*

Margo Waring

Poplars and Alders

Where I lived when I was five,
poplars were the street trees,
tall, thick trunked, furrowed brown bark.
In spring little girls in pastel sundresses,
embraced by the resinous smell of balm of Gilead,
gathered their sticky sweet catkins, red, fuzzy, soft
from sidewalks to pound into imaginary pies and cakes,
food for future husbands and children.

Now, closer to my end than to my start,
red alders edge the lane at my house.
Smooth mottled bark, ashy gray.
Toothed leaves come late in spring.
Each fall, I rake the curled brown leaves
crackling in the wind, releasing
a sharp smell of decay, sign of coming frost.

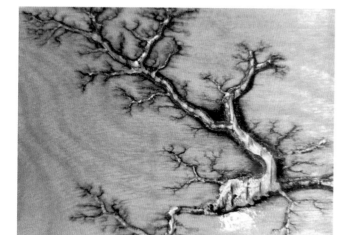

Grain   *Nard Claar*

Margo Waring's poetry collection Growing Older in this
Place: A Life in Alaska's Rainforest *is forthcoming from
Cirque Press.*

Tidal Reflections   *Monica O'Keefe*

O. Alan Weltzien

Man with Mop

Grad school on pause, broke back home
I wring the mop in the bucket then swab
the hall in tight figure 8s. Third shift at a local
community college where, Masters in hand,

I should teach. I empty waste baskets, push
the vacuum in a classroom and at the front
desk I box anger, release the white-collar
daytime bubble, head down until the 2:30 a.m.

lunch break. One guy holds a Masters in art
history but we never talk. Around 4:00 a.m.
skunk hour, I remove used tampons
in the women's bathroom, wipe down surfaces,

eyes scan for anything out of place, and I
dream those long reading lists trailing
each grad class like kite tails, my return
months and miles ahead, wait shift's end.

I drive home as dawn edges the Cascades'
silhouette, toss and turn until Noon
and my fingers still grip the mop's handle,
out of joint with daylight's world and myself.

Tonja Woelber

Light

Dark is foe in backcountry,
Black cloth wrapped tight
around the mouth and eyes.
Tree roots, rocks, uneven ground
are danger. A limb hits the chest
like a rifle butt.
Deep night fools the senses:
direction lost,
friends and enemies
cannot be told apart,
the sound of breath a threat.

Night can suffocate in a tent,
make visions of blood-scored fangs,
piercing claws.
A plane engine miles up
could be an avalanche
frothing down a mountain,
tossing boulders,
ending in eerie silence
on the valley floor.

A headlamp, a match, anything
to fight against the dark,
exhausted fear,
the half-sleep of the terror-crazed.

There are times
anyone would give
his last rations, his boots,
his only weapon,
for light.

Mountain Monster   *Jim Thiele*

Christian Woodard

Go that way

Until there's no more
water. Until you're on your own
recognizance. Search out the skins
that your grandparents molted:
a doehide skirt in Idaho Falls,
a plaid business suit.

Thus, doubly divested, piss
your complicity into any old stock
tank, the thin trickle sipping
at its own reflection. By then
they'll arrive,
a herd of moonlight disguised
as pronghorn. Join them. And drink
and drink.

Look up, over your shoulder. But no—
it's not Monsanto. It's not
the Nazis.
                    Normal people
with small concerns have already
refined shame
to its thinnest distillates.

They barter what remains
for diapers, for salt.
Cold black ooze for a sack
of dried beans.

Not far from here, the last bear rots

its long smear of oil
down a creased coulee.

Beyond the Trees   *Tami Phelps*

John McKay

The Skies Wept: Reflections on an "Academic" Discussion (*4/8/04, University of Alaska Anchorage*) of the Stillborn (*d. 4/27/04*) Cantata for Rachel Corrie (*d. 3/16/03, Palestine*) by composer Philip Munger (*b.1946*)

I.

After the combatants and curious have gone
I find myself strangely drawn
back to the music
practice room.
Room 124
dim
silent
except for
angry echoes
still reverberating, hateful
missives caroming off walls spattered with
invectives, venom dripping down beige semi-gloss.

Unspoken support sticks to the grungy tan rug.
Dollops of frenzy froth
still cling to blue
cloth chairbacks.
Reason
peeks out
from its hiding places
in the corners, and retreats,
seeing neither escort nor safe harbor.

At my approach,
snakes and roaches,
newly hatched but millennia in the
making, meander from pools of bile vomited
there scarcely an hour ago. They do not scurry before my
shadow or discouraged steps, but slither languorously and amble
presumptuously, as if knowing they have been given permission and protection.
The tightly composed uncomposed composer of seven movements, prickly, defensive, anxious,
is still there, incorporeally, having spent his explanation, still
searching for acceptance and redemption.
No redeemer was recognized.
The skies did not open.
His dry eyes
wept.

Fear, zealotry, and ignorance still hang
heavy in the air, in particles too
thick for the ventilation
system to have
stirred
and completed the process of exchanging it,
spreading it to every corner of the Arts
Building, from where it would seep
out into the rest of the campus,
to join what now
clings,
in barely detectable moles, to the cheeks and hair
and clothes of those who left that
room, fanning out through
the community, once
our community,
spreading the
stench.
The chalkboard in the music room hangs mute,
its cleft staff bearing no witness that might
be judged, no scales,
tonic or catatonic;
no chords to
give voice to
the discord;
no rests
for the
weary.

II.

Reading between the lines of
          an
academic discussion may not be a beau-
          ti-
ful thing to behold, and for the
          Semi-
litera
          te
Can be perilous, at best.

III.

Images still flash about the room,
strobe memories
peeking and
flitting
from silent baby
grand to hushed kettle and
bass, to mute chimes and speakers:

Leaf and Lichen   *Matt Witt*

The imperious solon, in his flag toga,
from his little grandstand, smilingly
slips his shiv between the ribs, makes
clear that in this land of the free he
will never associate with this unworthy.

The unctuous demagogue
        from the synagogue,
      worrying words
    like prayer
  beads,
Twisting words
      into double
      helixes to
      pass on
Code for generations, as long
        as it will play and then
        return to the coda
        for as long
      as it
will play
        and then
        return
      to the
Coda.

The patient handsome brown beaked man, the *Let me speak* eloquent
Semite of the wrong tribe, *May I speak? No. Let me speak, I am
in my own land a second-class citizen.*
As it should be. Shut up
Towel-head.
Now impatient,
out of control, in the fertile desert
of this academic haven he finds the oasis a mirage.

The lieutenants of the absent general
hoping to avoid riot, nervously twisting their watchstems.
The poets, the artists
wonder what's
next, the books?
Next, the meeting halls?
Next, anything that gives *offense?*—which,
as the elegant maven of civility notes, is quite unnecessary.

They have constructed verbal cages within and around
cages and banging words against the bars
argue about who is in captivity.

O, Absolom!
O, Rachel! O, Linda,
Thushara, and Phil! No
one's crying uncle, there are only anti-'s.

IV.

This may be a free country, but
remember it has
a Mainstream.
You may
choose
to travel it
in either direction,
but it only flows one way.

Stay vigilant, you
who pee into our mainstream
who wash your impure thoughts in our mainstream
who set up your false gods of tolerance and compromise on the banks of our mainstream.

We will hold you under, until
your lungs are filled from our mainstream, until
they runneth over, and every note seeking refuge in the least of your airsacs
has been replaced with the purifying waters of our mainstream,
and you will float peacefully, silently

with
the
current.

V.

Swords
beaten into
ploughshares retain
at some sub-atomic level
the memory of their ancestry.
These massive steel blades not only rip
through desert crust making way for olive groves and lemon trees but rip
through homes planted in heat, springing up,
bitter harvest, to nourish our enemies,
weeds to be mown before they
mow us, and blow us
to praying
pieces.

Praying for
peace is illusory,
the forwarding address is uncertain,
and cramming pages ripped from our sacred
texts down our throats will
not satisfy our
hunger.
Demography, that bastard prince of the democratic
kingdom must be exiled, or better yet, crushed
beneath the blade of
preservation.
Human shields
or
human bombs,
you must choose sides;
are you of the tribe of Withus, or of the tribe
of Againstus? How long before we will not be taken
to task for grieving the wrong death, for grieving all death?

                    VI.

I say you can't-hate-a Arab or Jew
You say cantata, can too, can do.
Can't hate a
cantata
cantata, fermata …
hold that thought …
let's call the whole thing off.

                    VII.

(No movement detected)

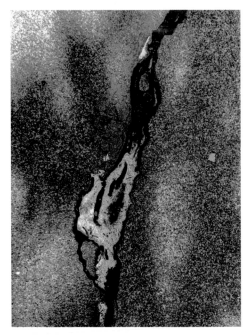

Street Patch   *Jill Johnson*

Oregon Grape in Snow   *Matt Witt*

Sandra Yannone

Let No One Stand Alone

for Rachel Corrie (1979-2003)

The day I reconnected with evil
again, driving south on I-5 to escape my own
mini-series of headlines in Bellingham, the news
from Rafah broke, horrific, like all history
emerging, that she had died, clutching
fistfuls of dirt, that day when she stood

her ground alone, bulldozer and American college girl, a stand
off, March 16th, 2003, and NPR reporting that evil
had prevailed in not so many spoken words. Outside of Everett, I clutched
the story's every word and the steering wheel harder than a car owner
should, my knuckles turning whiter than history
recorded, each mile driven bringing news of worse news

as western Washington blurred by. A Caterpillar D9R now news,
conflicting reports, as the operator keeps standing
by his story that he never saw her, like all of history
buried, a corpse shouldering its dirty shot glasses of evil,
like everything that history swallows and disowns
to keep its truth underground, soiled—
 all those clutch

plays for convenient blindness, the way a small girl might clutch
a stolen chocolate bar in her not-so-naïve fist. The news
that Sunday afternoon so disorienting that I couldn't own
it over all these years. And for days after, everyone I knew stood
shell-shocked on the campus bricks, mourning that something so evil
could befall upon an Olympia family, community, in spring. We became history

unforgettable, togethered, in those distorted budding days, and history
would repeat weeks later when a friend, originally from Ireland, clutched
his armchair's armrests like the side of a lifeboat to survive evil's
swells just hours after speaking at her memorial. He tried to keep the '80s news
from Belfast at bay so as not to confuse everything he stood
for from everything crumbling beneath Rachel's own

sure feet, but he couldn't distinguish his own
grief over losing Bobby's sister, whom he loved, from this new history
still fresh in his mind like butchered meat. He couldn't stand
anything now resembling the girlish present, and clutching
his mug handle, I witnessed a man unraveled by more than news
while we drank strong Irish tea, his heart having been evil's

good next-door neighbor for far too long. He stood up, alone, clutching
his own singular history, weeping, wishing Rachel had made her story
farther away from the news, and from that man-made blade of evil.

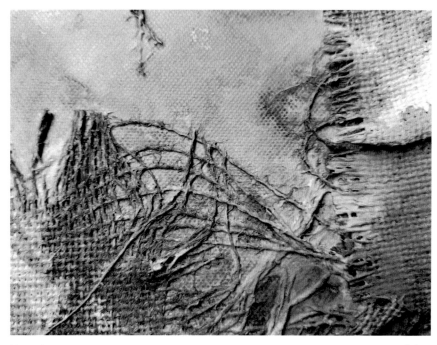

Unravel   *Nard Claar*

In Loukes Garden III   Annekathrin Hansen

FEATURES
REVIEW

Paul Haeder

A Review of Sean Ulman's *Seward Soundboard*, Cirque Press, Anchorage, AK, 2020

Musical Riffs and Paint Splashes of Sean Ulman's *Seward Soundboard*

The Music

> *Life is for the living.*
> *Death is for the dead.*
> *Let life be like music.*
> *And death a note unsaid.*
> —Langston Hughes, *The Collected Poems*

Here's a situational recipe for pure enjoyment while imbibing on beer, food and storytelling through a not-so imaginary alpine glen feast of Sean Ullman's 2020 *Seward Soundboard*:

- one part Bebop Dizzy Gillespie on I-pod
- field full of arrowleaf balsamroot in bloom
- eagles above with multiple attempts at talon locks
- cedar plank near alderwood fire with sockeye fillets baking
- basket of huckleberries
- cold-water stream at your feet
- 7.7 ABV IPA just uncapped
- four people sitting around dusky fire passing around rhubarb and apple cobbler
- a giant round of Gouda sliced with Bear & Son six-inch blade and antler handle
- no sounds from interloping roads
- clear sky, no high-tension power lines
- undivided attention of four friends while you start sounding out and riffing with Sean Ulman's words
- final course of a little "We'll Make It Through" by Ray LaMontagne

Oh yeah, all of that with a dogeared volume of this Cirque Press gem.

There are variations on this around the campfire story telling feast scenario, of course, depending on if you are, say, there in Alaska where I spent time (Hyder), or Southeast, in a place like Nelson, BC, or further down the road, Bonner's Ferry, or in Nez Perce land, on the South Fork of the Clearwater in Idaho.

This gem of a book — cloned fiction, sort of Pictures at an Exhibition of Seward — drips sea-full air and glacial tremors for all to ruminate inside, thanks to the creative juices of Ulman, who acts as bellwether for understanding the ebb-flow and syncopation of this Alaska town. Qutalleq in native Alutiiq, the population of Seward hovers around 3K. Seward was once Mile 0 for the starting point of the original Iditarod Trail (now it begins in Anchorage and ends in Nome).

His book is a canvas of many changing hues a la J.M.W. Turner or Austrian artist Tina Blau. The silver tone photo paper of a W. Eugene Smith. A narrative poem of beat Lawrence Ferlinghetti. Juxtaposing of Phillip Glass and Neil Young singeing the air.

Ulman's carried both tone and tenor in his remarkably simple ode to a quirky town by chiseling a narrator on a quest to dazzle us with poetic whale songs as part of a living mural. He is in touch with alleyways, bars, hikers and marathoners. The book is a lyric poem, and a day-in-the-life of a town's eccentricities, proclivities.

Even though we surge along in his synchronous cavalcade of filmic shorts, Ulman's writing harkens back to Hemingway in that this creative writing aficionado from Massachusetts (b. 1981) follows some simple rules of describing the essence of Seward — short declarative sentences. Subject-verb-complement!

He's a fan of alliteration. That style forces the reader to lift into the Alaskan clouds or envisage the great Resurrection Bay to Seward's west. The weather is felt, heard, tasted, smelled. The pleasure of Seward is Ulman as wanderer. Voyeur of a town. He ended up in Alaska in 2007.

Like the circadian rhythms of bears or bald eagles, Ulman draws a town through the very corpuscles of its spirit: people, land, and a lot of birds. Music flows as the narrator is troubadour of reflection and admiration of the characters that make up part of the synoptical elegance of a place.

This slim book is, again, a read one undertakes with the glow of a wood-burning stove while hunkered down near Mount Hood, or, in a palapa at midnight along the Caribbean in the Yucatan as the ocean sprays a hundred acres of light from bioluminescence. I'd say, during my far-flung adventures in Vietnam as a journalist and wildlife support team member, if this book would have been published 25 years ago, I would have hauled it into the bio-reserve where I was studying. Read in bursts and spurts, sort of a grace note to my day, as I sipped tea and chugged rice wine before hitting the sack for another day deep into primary forest.

In a very literal sense, Ulman sculpts locals and the traveler/tourist into his field of vision. At times, his writing is a macro lens into humor and down-home observations. Other times, Ulman/narrator is there with a telephoto shot, capturing rare moments of feather quivering near an avalanche's heaving dervish of snow clouds.

The people of Seward must be high-fiving Sean daily, because in one sense, this is a Seward Home Companion, "where all the women are strong, all the men are good-looking, and all the children are above average" (no aspersions to Sean by alluding to Garrison Keillor's long-running show).

The Map

We have a 150-page book in three-part harmony, and each section is anchored to light, shadow, soil, rain, snow, endless darkness, infinite days that capture this part of the globe. Seasons brought to the reader through upwelling of wind, ocean, reflections ricocheting off Resurrection Bay. He comes in with a Terrance Mallick scene setter many times, for example:

Fireweed dyed valley floors with burgundy stars.
Tips curled into delicate sickles, bent to breezes and belched cottony-winged seedpods.
Languid breeze ribbons shipped strollers nose-baths of brine.
Coils of woodstove smoke smote ramblers' brains, wracking rambling musings.
Ravens clucked.

This is on page one, and he gifts us two main characters — The Lightseeker and The Returner. Both of them weave their own stories/POV into the fabric of Seward. The Lightseeker is a man hunting spectral truths, collecting beams of light, contemplating stars and glassy bodies of water. The Returner is a youngish woman, back in Seward after years in California. Her aging parents are etched into the granite and conglomerate bedrock of Seward.

Lots of chummy dialogue. The narrator is a wispy wren, rolling through windows and doors, carving space into glades and soaring over the heights of mountains. Seeker of the people, and always returning to the fabric of a community stuck up north, this avian god I envision is the muse and talisman of Sean Ulman. A community of locals doing life's work as fishers, outfitters, service employees, retirees and even prison guards, Seward is an ecosystem which Ulman keeps simple. The place is a veritable ramshackle of tourists around Fourth of July (30,000 swelling the streets and eateries and bars).

The Chamber of Commerce puts 300,000 as the number of annual visitors.

Humanity is labeled by the narrator for what they do in civilization's vast employment realm — painter, homesteader, baker, prison guard, clerk, barista, volunteer trail groomer, and on and on.

Here, one fellow, during two days of snow in September: "A bleary-eyed, coffee-drugged plowman laughed like a madman as he sang, 'Let it snow, let it snow, let cash flow...'"

Ulman's narrator is sure to catch the artist's angle of repose, as well as the writer's emancipation of thought and feelings while looking through the wispy clouds into the blinking sky and into the snowcapped peaks:

> Beyond eastern mountains, at the end of a pink and orange cloud-speckled sunrise, a ribbed cloud shelf (a sunny-blue flue), funneled to a cubed sky compartment.
> This cloud catacomb was an ephemeral factory for poems.

Whimsy and jazzy. As I stated, there is that free-jazz/ outside jazz element to this wordsmith's phraseology. There is Ulman's compact writing style. There are the archetypical humans peopling the scenes as the flighty narrator hits this or that scene in snap-shot style, catching people in action. The feast of visuals is what drives each page to be turned and turned.

The reader, is there, witnessing the goings on, and many of the pages fill up with this or that town person, this or that townie" goings on, this or that petite town drama unfolding.

The words exchanged are sometimes arranged for people jaunting about running into friends, and sometimes the townies unleash soliloquies. Other times crisp, short dialogue chatters on the page, for example, between two "sunglassed Nordic skiers" or, for example, with The Returner as she flirts with "the therapist."

Again, the protagonists are Everyman and Everywoman,

who are the stalactites and stalagmites of the journey through the Seward soundboard (lowercase 's') — a slice of rough-hewed heaven with a whole lot of people jonesing for endorphins vis-à-vis mountain biking, trail hiking, running marathons, swimming, and kayaking.

Threaded into the basket that is the soundboard are spirit people, those specters who take on the same avocations, defined occupations and place markers for Seward. The ghosts are watchers.

He takes minimal peeks into the real stewards of this place, the Native people. Here, a whimsical passage: "A Native woman, without intending to, did not say a single word all day, including a dream (during a long nap) in which her dream double was being abnormally chatty."

Authorial Intent/Tensions

That little flowing sentence above draws me into Gabriel García Márquez, the magical realism of dream time, *curanderas*, shamans and, of course, in the case of North America, the spirit worlds of Native people.

Sean Ulman

The persistence stage left and stage right of entrances/ exits of birds populating his book gives more credence for someone like me entering literary dreamtime as I seek colliding tribal forces and my own "talk walkabout" through animism many of the original people of this Turtle Island have taught me.

> Plants panted.
> Birds bit bugs and berries, chirped contact chitter, shat turds.

This bit of humor folds into another interesting scene — the guard at the Seward Prison (Spring Creek Correctional Center). This fellow ditches his shift to instead hike to Godwin Glacier. Hours later, he returns with a bit of ice from the ancient flow. He hands it to the warden. Deposits his keys and ID into his superior's hands, along with the melting ice chunk.

Ulman's book ends on Labor Day, and then September 15, when "at 6:04 a.m., an 8.1 earthquake bolted the ocean floor 250 miles southwest of Seward."

The various characters in the town consider the possible tsunami after-effect. In those last eight pages, we get people of Seward and tourists living out fears, hopes, dreams, ruminations as, of course, no tidal wave appears.

Again, Ulman bookends the novel this way:

> Jovially clucking back (the first vocal sound she had made in two days), the Returner knew with thawing certainty that there would be no wave.
> Flapping shiny, black-tongue wings with astounding synchronicity, the ravens rolled on toward Seward.
> The Returner watched them until they shrank out of sight, then started running down the trail, back to the cabins, to pack up and head home.

A Common Language

The people out west, well, sure, are a different breed apart. True of my time in Arizona, New Mexico, West Texas. And, Alaska, the western most illusion of dreams and hopes, boom and bust.

> *One cannot be pessimistic about the West. This is the native home of hope. When it fully learns that cooperation, not rugged individualism, is the quality that most characterizes and preserves it, then it will have achieved itself and outlived its origins. Then it has a chance to create a society to match its scenery.*
>
> *—Wallace Stegner*

Ulman sows life into Seward. He goes with the flow, hooking into the mundane and pedestrian, blowing colorful swirls of glass with his gift of word play and observation. I imagine Sean out there with camera in hand and notepad at the ready, not capturing life but rather galvanizing himself into life. Grafting what he sees while teaching writing for Kenai Peninsula College and running a writer's group at the senior center. ◪

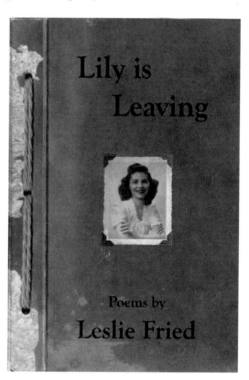

REVIEW

Frances McCue

A Review of Leslie Fried's *Lily is Leaving*, Cirque Press, Anchorage, AK, 2021

No Sorting Grief

Grief is sloppy. Art tries to make it tidy. For sorrowful poems, songs and paintings to relate, they need to be laid out within a structure and left to expand in the minds of viewers and listeners. In lies the irony: craft has its confines so that it can liberate its subjects. Grief has its quiet lulls and its rage-filled tirades; it has its disjointed moves, its recurrences, and its counting of the hours. As the only culturally-sanctioned form of madness, it's never a straight line of events but rather a quarantine inside devastation and magical thinking. I wonder if those who feel that grief proceeds in a step-by-step process are longing for the structure of art and haven't found it yet.

Of course, an artist or poet can overdo formal matters and deaden the emotional experience that they are trying to convey. The idea of reading a collection of elegies, for example, would feel to me like trudging through lines of gravestones. Tidiness could transform the poems into granite memorials rather than explorations of loss and sorrow.

Thankfully, we have *Lily is Leaving*, Leslie Fried's first poetry collection. The book displays an authentic and generous submersion into grief, personal history, shared tragedy and longing.

Fried, who is Steven Jesse Bernstein's widow (Bernstein was the [Seattle] poet, punk rock hero and spoken word performer before there was spoken word who died by his own hand thirty years ago this year), began her own arts career as a set designer. For thirty years, she worked in plaster and paint depicting scenery for film and theater. She came to poetry later, after her life with Bernstein, and she took to it with both humility and gusto, taking courses at Hugo House, reaching out to other writers and editors, and going back and back to her verse, recalibrating it.

In *Lily is Leaving*, Fried's eponymous subject, "Lily," is Lillian, her mother, to whom the book is dedicated. But the collection is not a series of elegies to her mother; the poems merge different grief pools, mingling her mother's death with the loss of her partner, the dissolution of families, the holocaust's destruction, and the isolation the speaker feels in later life.

Throughout the poems, tragedies emerge in scant Beckett-like landscapes, often empty except for a hut or train or field. In "Dune Shack," for example, a "great ball of sun pasted to the window" shapes the background for two lovers. In "Existential Texas," "sooty careless clouds drift across Texas/like God's ink blotter" and in "Travail," a tiny chicken coop is a home where, in the end, the "door is closed for now/to the fields beyond." The simple objects serve as set designs. They are layered into the poems and their flatness serves as a backstop that promises depth of a world beyond. From a playhouse in a vacant lot, to a hayloft, to levees in New Orleans and Warsaw during the Second World War, to an unnamed border town and into a residence hotel on Airport Way South in Seattle, Fried anchors the scenes into places that become palpable as objects to fixate on in the midst of disorienting loss.

In "Special Collections," Fried's speaker is organizing her belongings into an archive. (As Bernstein's heir, the poet did study library science to prepare Bernstein's papers, recordings and ephemera for Special Collections at the University of Washington.) In the poem, the objects arise from diverging losses and they transcend physicality until the speaker is shelving despair and longing: "I thought I would die/I didn't die/shelf" and "lost boys/lost boys I loved/shelf." The "shelf" becomes a repetition throughout the poem, often serving as the only word on the last line of a tercet. "Shelf" is like a flat of scenery rolled upright onto a stage. On the poetic line as well, it carves horizontally through the mind. Within Fried's craft, grief can't be pinned down and the tension of the poem lives within futile attempts to make shelves, to collect and categorize what won't stay fixed.

Leslie Fried

In "Why Children," a magnificent lyric set in couplets as one rolling sentence that moves between love and rage, the poem conjures vulnerability and ferocity in a grief-music that resonates with the craving to tell the truth. "To have children is to know hard love," Fried writes, and the poem sings of the duty of a parent "to carry a great stone/ tenderly without a horse." You get the sense that our speaker and those she has loved, have carried burdens without help, without solace and, in the end, pulling it off was "a trick of the trail." Whether it is the journey, the place one finds herself in or the craft of holding and expressing grief, the hard love that one carries is tenderly and tragically felt in these poems. In "Playhouse in a Vacant Lot," Fried reaches out to those she's lost, all crammed in a hut together:

> To all the beloveds in this hut
> I am indebted
> you pet and pinch and drift along
> this world made of paper
> this map of kin where the names have changed.

While grief mingles its subjects, surfacing the unexpected, Leslie Fried shapes poems that merge and honor artifacts of loss and the disorienting love with which we handle them. ◧

This review first appeared in Raven Chronicles Press, June 17, 2021 and is used here with permission. www.ravenchronicles.org

REVIEW

Jean Anderson

A Review of Ann Chandonnet's *Baby Abe: A Lullaby for Lincoln*, Circles, an imprint of Cirque Press, Anchorage, AK, 2021

A Balm for a Troubled Age

At a time when our country veers as close to dissolution and civil combat as we've come since the Civil War, Ann Chandonnet has a new book that feels like a balm for this troubled age. *Baby Abe: A Lullaby for Lincoln* (Cirque Press, 2021) examines the infancy and young childhood of our nation's most beloved President, "Honest Abe."

The book is difficult to categorize. At heart, it's a storybook, its text a poetic history of the first decades of existence for a then very young United States, set on a sparsely settled edge of our vast frontier. As biography, it presents a period not often considered in Lincoln's life,

the years from birth to age three, intended for readers age five to twelve. Each page of its central text stands alone as a small prose-poem-like vignette, sometimes with engrained rhymes and always full of vivid details. Chandonnet invites readers to enter fascinating historic territory, as in this excerpt:

> April offered dandelions: spring tonic.
> Kettle steamed on the trivet.
> Rye `n Injun rose on the hearth.
> On his stomach
> Little Abe blinked at the restless flames,
> strained to lift his heavy head.
> Hungry, always hungry.
> Sooty kettle, sparks and ashes,
> dirt floor, corn-husk bed.
>
> Nancy dared
> to bathe Baby before the fire,
> rubbed him with goose grease.
> He stretched his knobby limbs.
> "Spider child!"
> marveled Nancy re-wrapping his sinewy length.
> "My fine foal, my colt."

Baby Abe quickly becomes many-tiered, existing on its most obvious plane as a storybook told in the familiar, slightly strange lilting American English slang of its time. *Rye `n Injun*, for example, was a bread made of half rye flour and half *Injun*, a common term for cornmeal, which was introduced to early settlers by Native Americans, as Chandonnet tells us in the *Glossary*. It was popular because rye was easier to grow than wheat, making the bread cheaper to bake than a loaf made solely of wheat flour. Like this sustaining food, the book becomes a treasure house of historic exploration for curious children, whether they're reading it alone, pondering events and foods and sometimes challenging or difficult words, or being read aloud to by an adult at bedtime. *Baby Abe* never talks down to its readers. Abe's newborn brother dies shortly after birth. We hear the scraping and moaning sounds made by a *coffle* of slaves chained together, driven in a line down a narrow path near the family's first cabin close to the Old Cumberland Trail. I can imagine this book tattered and dog-eared, a beloved tome clutched to a small chest or tucked under a pillow in youthful devotion, as one's very own introduction to *real* American history and its truths.

The book is suffused with hard truths. Though never overtly political, it feels grounded in our nation's core values. Hard work is ever-present, as is danger and the potential for catastrophic failure, like a corn crop failing, or wolves howling in the surrounding woods, or poisonous weeds eaten by a family cow that poisons its milk and kills you, as actually happened to Lincoln's beloved mother when he was nine years old. She'd probably by then barely reached her thirties. We learn this in the *End Notes*. In this sense, the book seems perfectly suited to readers experiencing a global pandemic. Death hovers over its pages as a part of daily life.

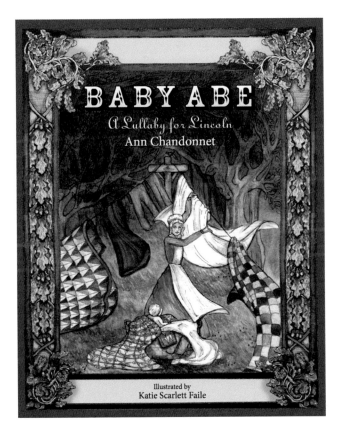

But there's joy too. *Baby Abe* challenges its readers with tidbits of everyday events, paired with depictions of lively doings, in and around backwoods *Kaintuck*. I think the section of Chandonnet's *End Notes* ending the book enchanted me most of all its fine parts. For instance, another quote: *"The term "Kaintuck" was used to describe the state as well as rowdy boatmen who floated merchandise (including wheat and coal) down the Ohio and Mississippi from areas embracing the Ohio River Valley. More than 10,000 Kaintucks walked home from delivering goods to Nashville, TN, in 1810 alone."* She continues: *"The 500-mile journey, on foot, took about 35 days…The roots of the term are unclear, but it seems to derive from an Iroquoian term meaning "(on) the meadow or (on) the prairie"* [...

or it possibly comes from]…*a Shawnee word, Kanta Aki, meaning 'The Land of Those Who Became Our Fathers.'"*

Are you hooked yet? In *"A Brief Abe Chronology"* in the *End Notes* section, we learn that Abe was named for his grandfather, Captain Abraham Lincoln, who was ambushed and killed by Indians in 1786, when Abe's father Thomas was eight years old. Tom escaped with the aid of an older brother, but was abandoned by his widowed stepmother, becoming *"a wandering labor boy."* He apprenticed as a carpenter in the shop of a future relative-by-marriage, Joseph Hanks, and was also taught by slaves on his Uncle Isaac's Tennessee plantation, learning to support himself with the skills of a carpenter, mechanic and farmer.

Anti-slavery sentiments must have started early for Abe's father; by 1788, ten-year-old Tom was in Elizabethtown listening to a talk by an Emancipationist. In 1806, at about 28 years of age, Tom married Abe's mother, Nancy Hanks, whom he'd known for years, and in 1808, with Abe's older sister Sarah, still an infant, the couple followed antislavery pastor William Downs to settle in an existing cabin at Knob Creek Farm near Hodgenville, Kentucky on the Old Cumberland Trail. Abe was born here on February 12, 1809. All these details also appear in the book's *End Notes*.

Chandonnet is a poet, journalist, longtime book reviewer, culinary historian, wife for decades to a fellow writer, and mother; she lived for 34 years in Alaska, on another edge of our nation's still vast frontier, and now lives close to Lincoln's former home sites. Her work has won many honors, and she's authored numerous books — of poetry and American history, as well as our nation's food history. She clearly did her research for this one, working on it for ten years, she says, and adding that it's her favorite so far.

Early on, she tells readers in the text, Abe's mother Nancy glimpsed not just her son's clear intelligence and precociousness, but the terrifying looming fate of her second child. While he was still *"a tall toddler in short skirts,"* Nan noted his *"wizard eyes."*

It seemed that in Abe's age-old stare
roiled blue smoke, gray smoke
dying campfires,
ranks of spare men
stumbling forward in mired cloaks.
Nan imagined scattered gunshots and muffled cries.
To dismiss such trying thoughts,
she shook her head, hard.

Still her brow twisted in knots.
…What could these dire images mean?

There's deep tragedy here, by every national or personal metric. But *Baby Abe* manages to offer plenty of plain old fun as well. Chandonnet's *Glossary* holds many amusing items like its definition of *Britches Beans*: "*Beans dried in the pod; each pod looks like a pant leg.*" One section gives instructions for building a cabin from an empty half-pint milk carton, well-washed and dried, plus Graham crackers and pretzel rods (as logs, of course: the thicker the better) held together with peanut butter, and with roof shingles made of Wheat Thins or Triscuit crackers "*slightly overlapping.*" Another strength of the book is its striking visual form. The text's accompanying illustrations, colored sketches by Katie Scarlett Faile, are flat-out gorgeous, adding a fairytale-like dimension to the book, a distinct and somehow feminine-feeling style, which at times contrasts slightly with Chandonnet's often gritty historic *End Notes*. But Faile's lovely sketches are mostly an asset, lending the text a delicate, sharp beauty nicely attuned to the imaginative, quietly courageous personality of Abe's mother, Nancy Hanks Lincoln, who in many ways is this multilayered book's actual protagonist, or heroine.

Ann Chandonnet

Though *Baby Abe* is described on its cover as a storybook for children (and their teachers), I dare *any* book-loving adult to avoid falling in love with the thing. It has the feel of an instant classic, like the man Abraham Lincoln himself. Lincoln's too-short but boldly triumphant life was marked by deep character and unerring compassion, as

well as humility and profound humanity. All this perhaps links directly to Abe's love of language, which was central to his being — as his famous speeches attest, as well as the fondly recorded jokes and witticisms. He deeply understood, and felt, the power of words. From childhood on, Lincoln loved books, reading by firelight as he grew taller, which is related in every biography — including this one, where even as a toddler he works to mark his own careful babyish A in the dirt of the cabin's clearing with a stick. I think he'd be pleased, even enchanted, by the characters in Chandonnet's "lullaby." This generative and generous book invites readers of any age or nation to ponder a time when people were every bit as deeply divided as we are now on this globe, but with no such poisonous meme as the notion of "alternative facts" to hobble us.

Baby Abe is an American history source book perfectly suited to our times. It's also a paean to the importance of decency, dignity and truth for a nation and its leaders. Americans bestowed the fond nickname "Honest Abe" on their martyred president for good reason. Truth lovers prevailed then and may, with hard effort, do so again. ◼

INTERVIEW

Alex J. Tunney

"It's beautiful. It's stupid. It's not practical, but I loved it.": An Interview with Matt Caprioli

August 2021

Matt Caprioli's writing has appeared *Cirque Literary Journal*, *Opossum Literary Magazine*, *Newtown Literary*, *Mr. Beller's Neighborhood* and *Understory* as well as the anthologies *Best Gay Stories 2017* and *Worn in New York* (which led him to tell his story on Netflix's adaptation, "Worn Stories"). He currently teaches writing at Lehman College in New York.

His recently published memoir, *One Headlight*, begins with a mother and son braving a turbulent drive through an Alaskan snowstorm in a Mustang with one headlight. It's an apt metaphor for the relationship he had with his late mother, Abby, something he explores while also shedding light to an experience of Alaska beyond its cold, yet picturesque landscapes.

As it turns out, Matt and I have a friend in common, a fellow Alaskan ex-pat, in New York City. This lends credence to what Caprioli describes as Anchorage's small-town feel, something which we discuss in our interview, alongside the state's literary character, how the memoir came to be, and what new projects Matt is working on.

Alex J. Tunney: You have a great line early in the book: "This is a theme with Alaska: what first appears inhospitable can become nourishing; middling expectations will be outshined by the unbelievable reality." And it had me thinking about the stories that certain areas tell. I'm a Long Islander, where we have *The Great Gatsby* and stories about suburbia. Can you expand on what you feel the literary character of Alaska is?

Matt Caprioli: That's a good question. I say it's a good question, because it seems obvious on the surface, it should be about the wilderness and wildlife and making your own in the great unknown, from everything from Jon Krakauer, most recently, and then all the way back to Jack London and John Muir, the naturalist. Historically, as you know, Long Island is tied to *The Great Gatsby*. Alaska is tied to those three authors.

They're all white and male and straight. Which is interesting, because most of the people who live in Alaska are not necessarily white, male, or straight. And I love contributing to this expanding notion of Alaska, especially with an urban environment, where most of the people live—I think Anchorage is home to half of the state's population, or approximately. So it's interesting that not much literature about Anchorage itself and more urban environments hasn't yet been created.

One exception is the anthology by Martha Amore and Lucian Childs, *Building Fires In The Snow*. That collection is amazing, because you have Black trans writers, you have Alaskan Native writers, you have people like me, there's a lot of Latino writers in that collection. So I'm glad that as of—at least—2014, the notion of what Alaskan literature is, is continually expanding.

Tunney: What I liked about reading the book is my notions of Alaska were tied to those wilderness narratives, and it was nice to get a glimpse of one person's understanding and depiction of the people of Alaska. That leads me into my next question. A mutual friend of ours describes Alaska as a big place that can often feel like a small town. Does that feel like an accurate description?

Caprioli: Yes, I think that is definitely accurate. Every time I go back, my fiancé and the other friends I bring are kind of amazed how everyone seems to know each other. So yeah, that definitely strikes a chord, especially in the queer community. I think we all have at least heard of each other.

But every time I go back, I realize more and more how weird it is. For Anchorage, the nearest city of a similar population is Seattle, and that's 1100 miles away or so. It's so isolated, and growing up there, you don't quite realize how isolated you are. And the nice thing is, I think that encourages a sort of resilience and self-reliance. The downside is it encourages perhaps too much self-reliance. I think I can do everything by myself and the idea of people helping me is just very foreign to me. I can't generalize to say that's like an Alaskan thing, but there is a sort of weariness to the

degree that you can trust people.

One of the best essays I've ever read about contemporary, urban Alaska is called "Out in the Great Alone" by Brian Phillips. It's part of his collection, *Impossible Owls*. The first essay in that collection is him traveling to Anchorage to observe the Iditarod. So he participates in the travel for a little bit and observes a lot of Alaskans. He has this one line about when you meet an Alaskan, when you talk to them, they respond with bright, wide eyes. And they're like, "Who are you?" This great force of consciousness.

There's a little anxiety with meeting people when you're from Alaska. Whereas when you come to New York, or even on the East Coast, there's this sort of social facility that I don't think a lot of people in Alaska have. It can be very, very awkward. People can be very awkward. It does have that small, tiny feel.

Tunney: As someone who's written personal essays about their life, one of which has its way towards Netflix, when did you decide that you wanted to write a memoir and what made you decide specifically on a long-form memoir as opposed to an essay collection or something different?

Caprioli: This memoir, *One Headlight*, came out of grief. My mom died in 2017 and I needed to grapple with that. Writing is how I grapple with the world and find some stability and meaning. So my response, the day she died, I started writing in a journal. And I've been journaling since I was like 10, it's just a part of who I am. I eventually wrote the whole book in a journal from September 19, 2019, until the day before Christmas.

There's something about writing by hand that is super important to me, I can almost feel closer to the people when I write by hand and you have to think things through at a slower pace. So you absorb the past a little more powerfully when you write by hand from when you type. I don't think there was a conscious choice to write this memoir, I would have written it if no one read it. I really wrote it out of necessity to remember my mom and come to grips with our fairly complex relationship.

And initially, I wrote weird short stories, I wrote a play, I wrote some poem where Abby interrupted the 2016 election and became a surprise candidate. So instead of Trump energy, who is very aggressive and mean, you get someone who is incredibly kind and compassionate.

It was an awful poem. It took me two years to find some emotional stability to be able to write this book.

I remember coming up to the second-year anniversary of her death, I kept on thinking about how I plan to have kids and would I put my children and some of the situations I was in? Then I thought about the opening chapter which is about a mother and a son driving in one of the worst snowstorms to ever hit Alaska in a shitty old Mustang. I was thinking about that and how I would not put a child in that situation; I would have called a friend, I would have gotten a hotel, I would have parked in a parking garage for the night. There's so many alternatives to choosing to take your child through a blizzard in that unstable car, but then I just started thinking about all the other times she's driven and how important driving was. When you're driving with your loved one, you're in this enclosed space, it's quiet. You have a lot of intimate revelations in a car. And that led to the tsunami of images of the two of us driving. And I think in 90 minutes, maybe less, I had an outline of the whole memoir. And it was all based on this one headlight. Because this one headlight became the symbol of our relationship. It's beautiful. It's stupid. It's not practical, but I loved it. And I would do all of it again.

I wrote it because I wanted to and I didn't think I would find a publisher—a debut memoir from anyone, especially someone like me—I'm no one, they are so impossible to sell. This is actually the second memoir I wrote, because I studied memoir in grad school, and the first memoir was about sex work. I was a sex worker for about a year in 2012. I thought that would surely sell because sex sells. It didn't sell. And for a while, I was like, "What?" Now I look back and I'm like, "Okay, you were a baby writer, you didn't know what was happening," and it was not that good. This is all to say that when you write something without any hope of publication, I feel like the final product will always be better. There are many people who can just use that I'm sure, but that's kind of my personal belief at the moment.

Tunney: Speaking of driving, a central metaphor in the book, there's a forward momentum in *One Headlight*. But I wouldn't describe it as a straightforward memoir. Some chapters don't focus on periods of time, they focus on topics. You call into question your own memories and sometimes you revisit a period of time. Did this structure come out of the journaling that you did? Or out of a poetic sense as opposed to straightforward, A-to-Z storytelling?

Caprioli: I think I pursued the emotional truth more so than the chronological truth. I'm happy that once I got the outline of that one headlight, I knew it would have to, as we say, have that forward momentum. And it is chronological, but within each chapter it goes kind of all over the place. Time, in a memoir, can be almost fictionalized or you can slice it up and reach a better truth.

I think I didn't think about the structure so much because of that M.F.A. program. I studied a lot of memoirs, especially grief memoirs, memoirs that were, like this one, written in about three or four months in response to the loss of the most important person in your life. I studied *The Year of Magical Thinking* by Joan Didion and *The Light of the World* by Elizabeth Alexander. I think Richard Blanco, his memoir, *The Prince of Los Cocuyos*, was really powerful and inspirational to me. It's about a mother and a grandmother and it's chronological about his boyhood in Miami, but he allows himself this poetic freedom to kind of meander toward the truth and incorporate these memories that seem to have no relationship or no urgency to the present topic at hand.

Matt Caprioli

There's this one chapter, as far as following chronology, that surprised me. It was where I talked about the last drive Abby and I took together and at one point, I described how she vomited and was super sick and the fact of her dying was kind of undeniable at that moment. So I talked about her having this awful vomiting scene and then I somehow go into the time when someone else threw up in my car. It was the ex-girlfriend of my first boyfriend. I go from something that's really dramatic to something kind of lighthearted and ridiculous. I go from my mom throwing up because of stage 4 cancer, to driving my ex's girlfriend, who just realized that her boyfriend was gay, and driving her home and she starts vomiting in my car. I remember thinking, "Why is that memory there?" It can be seen as disrespectful or irrelevant, irreverent. But to me, it just seems necessary. I don't know why. I think Abby would have liked the contrast between the drama and the humor; we were always crying one moment, laughing the next.

Tunney: In the memoir, there are a few moments where you talk about the memoir itself. What made you want to include the creation of the memoir within the book?

Caprioli: That's something I picked up during an M.F.A. program. I didn't think about any of this consciously, but I definitely needed the structure of the M.F.A. program to realize what you can do in the genre. But the idea of using memory itself and the willingness of memory as a generative tool is really fascinating. When you ask yourself, "Why can't I remember something?" there can be a reason for that lack of memory or a dim, shadowy memory. Pursuing why you don't remember something can be really fascinating and revealing.

I also find it liberating to talk about the meta-narrative or how something is created. I like that honesty. I think I was inspired by Dave Eggers's *A Heartbreaking Work of Staggering Genius*. The third page or something is a block text, single space, telling you how much he is making from this book. He says, "You know, I got a $40,000 deal, that might seem like a lot, but you have to think about the promotional expense, the agent cut…" and he constantly interrogates himself as to whether he is being honest. And being honest about the meta-narrative, I think, is part of that quest for veracity. There's another wonderful thing where he imagines that he is being interviewed by an MTV reporter. And this is the early 90s. MTV is at its height. So there's this question of fame, and whether he is producing this heartbreaking work of staggering genius in order to get fame or does he want to do something larger than this almost narcissistic tendency to write. So I think that's partially why I reference the behind the scenes, as a part of a quest for more veracity.

I remembered something else I thought of cutting. It was about writing in Florida. I was just thinking about class, and how I am now, in this social world, where a lot of my friends will go on these fancy vacations that are totally normal to them. But it's very foreign to me and I feel a little unease at all times when I'm on one of their vacations. But, you know, I'm part of that very privileged world now and I kind of wish I was able to bring Abby and Victoria, my grandmother, into that world. I think that was important to include the up-to-a moment, honest depiction of how I think about these two very important figures in my life.

Tunney: I got the sense that it was important to include that because you were trying to capture this relationship that you ended up producing this tribute to, and that tribute was an important part of the relationship that you also wanted to capture. For me, it made a kind of emotional sense to include that both as a reader and as somebody who writes nonfiction themselves.

I'm going to ask the annoying writer question now: After this, do you have any other projects that you're starting, or are you resurrecting the initial memoir? What's next on the horizon?

Caprioli: I'm always trying to do like 20 projects at once. I've tried to order that and one way to order that is ask yourself: if I die in a year, what needs to exist before I die? So that adds to my urgency. But I also don't want to be totally morbid.

After this memoir, which was so intense—I cried so much, I want to reward myself and just kind of go down another path, a lighter path, perhaps. This was more of a serious drama and now I kind of want a comedy. I'm working on a fun novel and usually I've only written literary fiction. It's fun to go in this other direction. It's a satire about vampires who kill vampire authors. And it gets a little complicated— they're also in a book club—it's so ridiculous, but I'm having a lot of fun. I'm also finding that characters that initially seemed really archetypal, or even stereotypical, in the second or third draft, gain a little more nuance.

I'm doing a screenplay, which is also a little more lighthearted. The screenplay is called Sally May. It's about a young gay Columbia [University] student who learns that his father is kind of a mafia billionaire, which means his need-based aid at Columbia is revoked. So now he needs to find a way to make a shit-ton of money. He turns to sex work and he turns to drag. And his drag name is named after the student loan company, Sally May.

I'm also doing a biography about Robert Rauschenberg and Jasper Johns. Johns was gay and he lived with Robert Rauschenberg from 1954 to 1961. Over those six years,

they happened to create their most famous work. And they had a really unique creative partnership. They would literally assign each other things to do. Robert would be like, "Hey, Jasper, I think you should paint the U.S. flag or something." And Jasper Johns would give him an assignment. So the story hasn't really been told, I think, largely because of homophobia. They hinted at their relationship, but they never really talked about it openly. I think now, in 2021, they can, there's a lot more acceptance of their relationship. I've been working on that, that's more of an academic thing.

There's always a lot of stuff to do. ◪

This interview first appeared in Pine Hills Review, *August 20, 2021 and is used here with permission. www.pinehillsreview.com*

REVIEW

Monica Devine

A Review of Gretchen Brinck's *The Fox Boy: A Social Worker in the Alaska Bush 1968-1970*, Cirque Press, Anchorage, AK, 2021

A Story of Bethel Past

The Fox Boy is a sensitive portrayal of the Yup'ik Eskimo people of Southwest Alaska, their struggles and triumphs living with White outsiders (teachers, priests, store owners) who brought monumental changes, both bad and good, to their traditional way of life. In her role as a social worker, Gretchen Brinck squarely faces her own failed expectations and works tirelessly for favorable outcomes in families besieged with alcohol abuse. She calls out prejudice and failed government programs and fights for the rights of children to be adopted within their own cultures. As an outsider working in a culture that is not her own, her rendering is not Pollyannaish, rather a sincere telling of the pitfalls and bureaucratic tangling when faced with the nearly impossible task of doing what's best for kids. I closed this book thinking Ms. Brinck is a woman who chose her profession because she truly cares about people. She fights for Native children, depicting the importance of placing adoptees with Yup'ik over White families.

Gretchen Brinck

These situations are complex, for this book is equally about the dire need to protect children from abuse. "No innocent child should be beaten, chained with the dogs, and left to starve." This line stayed with me for a long time afterward, and I predict others will be similarly moved. Social workers understand the need for culturally intact families, but at the same time have an obligation to protect children from familial harm.

Sandra Kleven, a social worker and the publisher of *The Fox Boy*, writes a compelling forward to the book, delineating how the Yup'ik culture was severely disrupted by contact with the Western world. Without genetic adaptation to alcohol, the Yup'ik people have no defense and alcohol dependence remains a chronic problem in many villages today. She, too, worked diligently in village communities where loss of hope has led to a

suicide epidemic among adolescents. "I will always be an outsider," she writes. "… still, my growth of soul is tied to village Alaska tundra."

The Fox Boy is a harsh, yet tender account of one woman's fight to right wrongs, while simultaneously dealing with the pain of her own distressed marriage in the absence of family support. The writing is universal; we can all easily empathize, but it is also up-close and personal. *Fox Boy* was submitted for consideration for the National Book Award. A compelling read, indeed. ◪

FEATURE

Publication of Karen Tschannen's Apportioning the Light, *in 2018, kicked off Cirque Press, bringing us to the light. Early in 2017, Karen was the featured poet at a public reading. That night, her poetry had a strong impact on me, so I asked her "Do you have enough for a book-length collection?" She told me she thought she probably did. We worked for a year to bring it together, me a little clumsy and her endlessly patient. This interview celebrates our first Cirque Press book and Karen Tschannen's role in the creation of a press that has now published more than twenty-books— poetry and prose.*

—*Sandy Kleven, publisher*

Cynthia Steele

An Interview with Poet Karen Tschannen

even in the stiff night of winter
you will find bulbs like infant fists
—Karen Tschannen, "Episteme"

We are in Karen Tschannen's cozy condo on Muldoon Road, where I've been many times on the porch, surrounded by a rolling grass lawn, for lunches and tea, where the moose come to the edge of the woods to show off their young. The recently-replaced floor shines, thanks to her kids. Both Sandra Kleven and I, separately and together, have long been drawn to Karen's published stories, two of which she's published in *Cirque*, in addition to her poetry and the stories she tells around roast beef sandwiches. We love to hear her read aloud. Karen's joined the evenings of Poetry Parley and other local book releases at the Writer's Block Bookstore & Cafe, and elsewhere, serving as Featured Poet. But, she reads for us at lunches where we are rapt with attention.

Relatability is one of her draws. Her poem "Writer's Block" expresses the frustrations of looking for a journal to write in and for a sharp pencil among the "bone pile" of writings. She asks about the desk, "How many words leaked into its corners, abandoned or lost?" She surely bears the scribbler's plight at the keyboard. "The curser curses me. I curse it."

But when I read her poems, I recall her taking command of the stage at The Writer's Block. I see Monica, Eric, Toby, Lucky, Tonja, and so many others taking their turn at the mic. Myself included. All of us with our own occasional, often hidden cases of personal writer's block.

Karen serves me crisp, thin, caramelized Biscoff cookies with tea.

"Tell me," she says, "what prompted this whole thing?"

"We wanted to do a feature about you because you have another story appearing in this issue of *Cirque*, and a book already, the first Cirque Press book: *Apportioning the Light*."

"Oh, then, my San Francisco story? 'SF Avenues.'"

Yes, of course, she's right. But there are many reasons. I've scribbled all over my copy *Apportioning the Light*. I've read through it again, marking pages. There are poems that Sandra has alluded to, and stories that I want to know about. So, I sip my tea and listen.

Whole Crayoned Histories

In a photo, Karen's father, relaxed-jawed, looks up at the photographer atop the roof of a building. His dark, shiny hair is flipped up. He wears a three-piece suit with a pocket kerchief. Next to him, her much smaller mother crosses ankles in a dark floral dress and pin curls.

"My father, Enrique, was visiting in SF with his Peruvian diplomat father. Mother was in her late teens. She wanted to get her degree—to be a head librarian somewhere. But, she fell for my father right off the bat. One of nine children, my mother was the eldest."

In the poem "Bridge Album Bread Forever," she describes a Japanese garden scene complete with arched bridge over water:

Where the lovers and three small children spill bread
To calico carp swimming under-over-under it forever

The image skillfully freezes the moments of entrancement in a lovely, young family.

I explain that I'm intrigued by the three girls who appear in her poems.

Karen points to a photograph near the kitchen table.

"Well, so my three, the three of us—me, my middle sister, Carla, and my elder sister, Margaret. I'm the youngest." I nod and she continues. "We're all one year apart, plural; you know, literally November, November, November."

In another poem, she tells of the resonance of her father's absence.

She explains: "My father left my mother when I was three months old. She had one in each arm, and one by the hand. It was during the Depression."

black and white

in the photo the father
I do not remember
sits by my mother on the seawall

in the photo the sky
above their heads is white
and featureless

the father I do not remember
has a strong face and he smiles easily
into the camera

I think my father's eyes look knowing
and I read whole crayoned histories
into his look

my mother in white
looks out past the camera
in this picture she believes she is happy

the ocean behind them
appears calm and remarkable
in tones of gray

In many photos, they're on the sea wall in San Francisco at the beach. But this photo was taken on a rooftop.

During the war, her mother remarried. Forrest Haines served as a machinist for the war effort in the shipyards. She felt close to him as a young child. She describes, through the voice of a child, the wartime lights flashing danger in the street and daddy, Forrest, going to work:

> and daddy put on his hat and got his lunchbox
> And mamma got his paper off the porch and he
> said *lock the doors* and went and got on the streetcar
> to go to work at the shipyard where he makes metal
>   things
> so he dint have to go to france and shoot strangers
>   with guns

This child's voice creates the space to talk about fear and uncertainty, security, and war—topics that sometimes seem clearer in the eyes of children.

Forrest, 4F from an eye injury, provided some fatherly qualities. "Forrest was union. That affected our lives quite a bit. That business of bvieweing union, you know, they're forever on strike. Jesus—couldn't pay our bills because we were on strike. It was a bad thing. But, you know, we'll work; we're labor all the way down. True and true. I still will not cross a picket line of any kind. I don't care who it's for or against. Isn't that funny? I mean, that's a way of being."

In her poem "Moving Inland," Karen describes the time period when they "moved to another daddy." Going from the city to the country was frightening for her as a young girl because the noise, now infrequent, was startling, and the wildlife more prevalent.

> bluebottle flies
> raged on distant ceilings
> in every cobwebbed corner
> on every blistered sill
> and mother wouldn't go
> down to the cellar
> said *it isn't safe*
> said *it's chuckfull of*
> *black widow spiders* said
> *one-bite-pfffft-dead-just-like-that!*
> …
>
> I lay wide-eyed in the dark
> listening hard to the floorboards
> for any sound of strain

> gauging exact distances
> to every open window
> to every closed door

From the beach to the valley, they moved with Forrest, who was a good father when the girls were younger.

"We'd had that feeling of not ever being quite sure where your feet were going to stand the next day."

Back in San Francisco, years later, Karen, 11, accompanied Margaret to the police where Margaret told them Forrest had swatted them with a rubber hose. "Anytime he lost patience with us and we weren't minding well enough. [Each time after that,] Mother had to go to the police department to collect that rubber hose to do laundry." Margaret moved in with an aunt and uncle, then quickly married a man a decade older and had nine children.

Karen Tschannen
photo by Cynthia Steele

This postwar period brought many changes.

"After the war, they closed down all the programs where people couldn't raise the rent. We no longer had a three-bedroom house with a dining room, a living room, a kitchen, and a garage. We moved into a little apartment. There was only one bedroom, but there was a pull-down Murphy bed that came down in the middle of a big dining area. That's where my mother and my stepfather slept. Sister Carla and I slept in the only little bedroom."

Karen's mother and Forrest soon divorced.

The Sea Salt Smell of Love

All of the girls married young. Karen said she "kept with her older sister's follies and married at 16, while still in high school, in Reno, Nevada, but annulled almost a year later on grounds of a false filing (age)."

Looking back at the photo, I tell her, "I recall that in one poem, you encourage a sister to leave her husband."

Karen explains, "Carla married at 16, had an older, alcoholic husband, a disabled Korean War veteran; [married him] as he was being discharged from the hospital…

"Carla and older sister, Margaret, were with a hospitality group visiting soldiers…That's where they met. Within the year they were pregnant and married after mother drove them through a snowstorm over the Sierras to Reno, Nevada, where the laws were leaner than California.

"[Carla] was a good mother.

"She kept having children but after they moved to Dunsmuir, California…He had some serious issues caused by drinking and a gun." I interjected, "It sounds like you wanted to help her."

"That's really it. I was just cautious. She wouldn't leave him."

Karen proceeds to read the poem: "Instructions to My Sister in Mount Shasta" (quoted here in part):

Go down off the mountain to the city.
Leave the doors unbarred.
Leave bleached wash graying on the line.
Bring away only your diary and these instructions.
…

At three bridges before the city
You will find toll gates closed and barred
With lights the color of danger.
Do not retreat!

Go down instead under the water.
Men have tunneled there in the dark
For decades without harm.
You will not hear the weight of the tide
Nor can you stray too far
If you follow these instructions.
…

Karen explains the landmarks and details: "All of

these elements have an actual physical reality to them. The dust will cover your eyes. It's long and hot. It was whole stretches of just a few houses and a gas station, you know, here and there. And the tunnel under the water business is not a thing of the imagination. There actually is a tunnel across the Bay from Oakland to San Francisco. Anyway, I just took those pieces of geography. So, there's actually a kind of roadmap."

I inquire about the poem about her other sister.

"My other sister, Margaret, had 10 children, nine of whom lived."

The poem for Margaret is called "Saying Grace," where Margaret doesn't stop at thanking God:

My sister Margaret, with folded hands,
presides over peppered peas and potatoes,
beef brisket cooling in its pink juices.

And once again engages the Lord.
gives thanks for the table's bounty,
for the blessings of many children.

for a regular—though meager—paycheck,
a strong roof. She opens her hands, beseeching,
adds, "but there are days I can go on only by

loving what is certain, the sea salt smell of love,
a child at my breast." She demands better jobs,
kinder neighbors. The recession of boils.

A faithful husband.

The words and phrases, succinct, like a quick prayer said by a busy mother. When Margaret was in her 50's, she fell in love with a married minister. Most of her children were grown. He divorced his wife, married Margaret, and suffered for it, losing his pulpit. He took work as a mailman, instead.

"We all loved John so much. He was magnetic," Karen explained. But, after marrying Margaret, he strayed again with their housekeeper who was the church pianist, and the housekeeper got pregnant. He divorced Margaret and married her. Of all of the men in her life, this was the true love of her life."

"Brokenhearted, Margaret finished doing what she always wanted to do. She went to Bible college and became a Methodist minister. There you go," Karen says.

Her sister, Margaret, died at 61.

Karen often cared for her family members, like Margaret and their mother for months at a time in their times of need.

"Mother and I ended up living together for a while. But Mother did marry again later, a Jewish man who, years later, died in his sleep."

"I am glad that Mother managed out of that whole thing to have a nice house in San Francisco, right on Fulton Avenue on the way to the beach. Very nice district—all the row houses just up against each other. A property line, literally a sheet of paper between them. She had a nice single life for years. [And a busy as a member of the Workman's Circle, St. Thomas the Apostle Church, Friends of the Library, the de Young Museum, the American Civil Liberties Union, and the League of Women's Voters.] For that period of time, my mother's life was the epitome of the way I wanted my life to go. I would live in a nice house and no husband." Karen later followed in her mother's footsteps in the American Civil Liberties Union and the League of Women's Voters.

"But," she added, "I did marry. I had my Martin."

Karen Tschannen (right) and her sisters

Tarpaper Brick and Good Cognac

Karen met Martin in San Francisco when they were in their 20s. He worked for Bosch, a German Corporation. He spoke German, French, and Swiss-German.

"Martin is from Switzerland from a very large family. I guess, he was my sweetie; he was my guy. I always said no one would ever love me like that; no one has.

"Married for 27 years. 1960 to 1987. I didn't realize it when we were going together, the reason he didn't drink. He'd go out to all the bars and everything with me. He was 'on the wagon' when we first met. Anyway, we finally cut a deal and he never drank outside the house.

"Of course, you know, he liked the good stuff. And after a while we could afford it. He was drinking nothing but the best cognac. We had collection of cognac. I had cognac glasses there, the little ones. We had a big, beautiful one that he loved. We both loved the same music. We just had a passion for the same music, which is a big deal. It's a big binding thing.

"We used to have arguments over who was the best violinists and who has the best violin, you know? Well, I think the Guarneri has it. And I used to tell him, well, it's because I'm a woman and my hearing is pitched differently. We'd have conversations like this."

Coming to Alaska from California, was a struggle. "We owed everybody but their cousin, and we had no jobs. I had a new baby when we arrived in January 1961. That was it. I went to work. The following week, still nursing our son. I went to work at FAA as secretary to two department heads with the bigwigs up in the top of the Post Office Building."

"We got by and lived in this terrible little place. It was really, really small with tarpaper brick on the outside. It was a cut-up house that had four tenants. We had a little itsy-bitsy bedroom, living room, kitchen, and bathroom. I mean, it wasn't much bigger than the bathroom in this place."

Karen went from that place to one that would have a grand piano.

"Oh, Martin worked for IBM. He became the specialist for Alaska for computer science. He was just, I guess, a natural. He made decent money. We paid our bills off, and I worked, too.

"And it wasn't even a baby grand. I got this parlor size grand. It's somewhat bigger than a baby. Shiny, shiny, white. All it needed was a candelabra on the doggone thing, and I don't know if Martin was drunk when he did it, but he overheard me talking with the girlfriends who were over for drinks and yacking about when we're young, what our dreams were like. What you we really wanted to do. The two things I wanted to do was take ballet and piano lessons, which I didn't get either. I got to sit in on those type things a couple of times, but that was it. I'd have these crazy dreams. When I was a kid, I would sometimes sit by the window overlooking our street in San Francisco. When mother wasn't home, everybody's off at work, I'd be home from school. I would put a chair by the window, put the record player on Chopin real loud, so they could see me playing this beautiful music. And, I pretended, on a white, shiny, grand piano.

"Well, Martin, I guess, must've overheard that because the next thing you know, it was shipped from Japan to San Diego, from San Diego to Anchorage. And he gifted me with a shiny, white parlor grand. Our grand."

Mad Men

Some parts of Karen's life don't appear in her poetry, but they're too good to pass up.

"The wives, we were all one big—well, IBM is a family organization. It was a big deal that I worked outside of the home when I had kids.

"They sent out these beautiful printed cards sayings that they've invited us to a coffee at the home of such and such. And, it was almost impossible to find it; it was way out there. It was that area: Bayshore. It was all new.

"They had just swept out all the trees and everything. It was a brand-new subdivision. They had moved in, and they were welcoming all the wives. Only wives. There were no females, except for maybe the few secretaries in the place. The wives of the technicians and the specialists. So, it was kind of like a command performance. I'm looking at Martin; Martin's looking at me. He knows what's going through in my mind. He says, 'You have to go.' I said, 'It's a work day for me. I'm not going to take off a day without pay.' But, you had to go to this tea; you had to, though, didn't you? 'Well,' he said, and we both knew how the world worked by then.

"I said, 'Okay, I'll do that.' I was a little bit late, but I got there. She greeted me. She said, 'I've been waiting to meet you.' She said, 'Come in, dear, and sit by me. I want to hear all about it. I understand you *Work*.' That was my introduction. She said, 'What do you *do?*' I mean, she's got like a tone of wonderment. You know, what would a young woman like you *do?* I mean I was a secretary. Looking back, it felt like I was in an episode of Mad Men—my favorite show to this day. I'd be in a rage and laughing at the same time through that whole series because I lived that life. I worked for the White Alice Communications contract for the government.

"You know, I lived that life. Amazing. I ended up being an operations coordinator on the White Alice System. Does that sound impressive? Sure, until the sector manager I'd been filling in for came back from his temporary assignment to the Middle East. He said that I could stop attending planning meetings because I wasn't needed anymore. He wasn't my boss at the time; he was like a step between being my boss and the real boss of the department. The whole thing turned into this monster of him hitting on me regularly.

"The men rated you by number. Who would be the one you most wanted to sleep with tomorrow? You know, that type thing. 'You're a number one,' they said."

Aftershocks Distant People Do Not Feel

Karen and Martin had a son and daughter and worked for IBM; then he retired early, getting a golden parachute. Then, he died suddenly of a massive heart attack at 53.

In the poem "Short Story," Karen likens her husband, Martin, to a "hero in a Hemingway story." She describes the shock she still feels about his death:

> As such things go
> I've been assured
> It was a good death
> but I know its red explosion
> moved the ground half a world
> away. Even now after all this time
> sensitive seismographs still
> measure aftershocks distant people
> do not feel.

That was my grief. The loss of surety of love. I mean, deep, deep appreciation, admiration and love. Even when we were fighting, it was there."

Friendly Territory

In 1969, Karen and Martin both met Paul, the man who would later become her partner through mutual loss.

"He was my neighbor's husband. His wife became my very best friend; we were just as thick as thieves. She and Martin died six months apart. We were kind of a foursome as friends. She died of breast cancer. They had seven kids. They moved in when the last one was still a babe in arms, and he was a lieutenant colonel in the Army.

"Martin died 1987. And she died in 1988. Mother

died in 1986. My dog died in the '87. The 80s were rough."

"Yes, they were. They certainly were," I said.

"They just fell like dominoes."

Karen writes to her sister of numerous shared losses in her poem "Letzte Lieder (last song)":

Our mother—yours and mine. Our best friends.
Our best friends' children. Our husbands.
Our sister's children. And then our sister. (We sang
For All the Saints!) If possession is nine-tenths
of the law of grief, is that final fraction saved
for the loss of grief itself?

Still, the poem ends with positivity, on a note of encouragement: "Be well. Breathe."

I asked Karen if she'd ever written about Paul, 91, her tall, handsome trapper.

She says her poem "Two-Part Invention for Winter" does ask if there is "a formula for the reinvention of love."

But, she says, she's only written specifically about Paul "once. 'Course some people thought it was awfully racy, and it was. I guess it was.

The poem, 'Sleepless in Spenard,' ends like this":

sweetheart, I say,
I know the sharp geography of my life alarms you,
trapper trapped dreaming someone else's dream,
but this room, this bed, this warm flesh here
is friendly territory and it's safe for you to stay

The poem is alluring throughout, tastefully so. Perhaps stopping a bit short of e e cummings' style. Still, it's just as satisfying. I particularly like the lines "complacent city girl testing the fine bones / of your feet with my toe." It's so tangible and fly-on-the-wall.

The Hard Choice to Love My Life

Perhaps being bound in threes with her sisters put Karen in a position of finding her niche in a poetic sense as well, because, she'd become bound to two other ladies whose paired photos and poems are on her office wall: Nancy McCleery and Joanne Townsend.

"Nancy was my teacher, and Joanne was my friend and was close to Nancy McCleery, and we became a threesome, you know, the way that happens, the comfortable, three, something, everything. I took a couple of classes from Joanne, and I took a couple classes from

Nancy McCleery, Karen Tschannen, Martin Tschannen and Jim Heynen

Nancy McCleery and we were all friends by that time. I was writing poetry with Joanne in the nineties, I guess it was."

Karen's always written, but her poetry grew by leaps and bounds in this group of poets.

"I always wrote. I had stories when I was a kid. I wrote a few short stories when I was 20. I went through three years of college, a lot of it was lit stuff. I was very good at writing papers. I sounded just like the library books. But, no matter what I did or said, it was with an academic gut. All formal writing. It's cold."

Technical writing seems so far removed from Karen's poetry; for example, her passionate "Episteme":

Oh, I have seen a wild upland iris
take deep into its purple throat
the long tongue of the sun
                    and surely
you too have noticed the lily
offering day after day without shame
her naked shoulders to the heat?

She'd always had a passion for writing, but she was suddenly surrounded by poets.

"I met Sandra [Kleven] against that doggone railing right there on the patio when Joanne Townsend came to town. [Townsend served as Alaska State Poet Laureate officially from 1988-1994 until the appointment of Tom Sexton.] I introduced her to Joanne, or did Joanne introduce me to Sandra? I have forgotten. All I know is our friendship only happened because Joanne Townsend was visiting from her New Mexico home.

"Yes, Joanne was the featured poet at the Hugi-Lewis Studio [for Poetry Parley]. That's where we were. She made the arrangements for that reading. Sandra invited her, and I happened to be her house hostess at the time. Sandra said, 'Joanne's on your wall in the other room, along with Nancy McCleery.' Tom Sexton was my first teacher of poetry around that time."

It was at that particular Poetry Parley that I met Karen's erstwhile daughter, Linda (Paul's daughter). Karen, Linda, Sandy, and I had food at Jens' after the Hugi-Lewis Studio reading.

Suffering the Pale Flesh of the Sea

A few of Karen's holiday letters are published in *Apportioning the Light* because she always writes in a deeply poetic voice, even when writing of ordinary things. In "Dear Friends," she speaks of those topics we put on pause for the holiday season and, instead, emphasizes how we choose to celebrate:

> We don't write of war or of the vacant
> stare of hunger. Or of boats lost at sea. The death
> of sons. Or anything to do with borders
> on the other side of the world. *Look* we say
> without irony. *Look, this is the month of bargains*
> *You don't tell me of your grief, I won't tell you mine*
> And we are left listening to the silences between
>   words

Karen also lost her son, Martin "Christoph" in 2011, who had no children, when he was 50. Her daughter, a Rottweiler breeder and dog trainer, "has her dogs, her man, and no kids."

"They were the light of my life. Whereas she is still the light of my life and, my strength at 84."

Karen explained how her beliefs as a child have changed in later life through her losses.

"I've been a Unitarian since the early 1960's. Unitarians are all to themselves. I mean, we make it up as we go along. We have, uh, we have many, many, differing opinions about many, many things, but, apparently, we do

agree pretty well. I'm not gonna use the word politically as it's not where I'm going, but it's related. It's the way we see the world. And as the world ought to be, to be a good person's world to live in."

She wrote her poem "tree" for the Unitarians:

> clothed in cloudlight
> we arrive singing
> in the orchard at dusk
> dancing among the fallen fruit
> carrying our godpots…

"What it is—it's non-God related. There are a number of people who are fallen away—Catholics—who are there, who don't have any problem with God and still talk to him. I don't talk to him, anymore. I gave up on him. I said, well, what a useless thing that would be, so, no, I don't talk to God anymore.

"But sometimes I feel sad that I don't have the surety of my, not just the religion, not the rules and regulations and the belief systems of my childhood church. I miss very much the beauty: the ceremonial beauty is so emotional. Of course, it's so emotional because I grew up in it.

"I remember a lot of Latin phrases and hymns, like *Panis Angelicus* [she sings a bit], but I don't know anything about Latin. My sister did. The Anchorage Cathedral put on Schubert's Mass in G some years ago. And they literally put on the whole mass with the vestments, everything about it. I went to church. It was fabulous. It was a beautiful thing. Who was the orchestra leader for that one? It was so moving. I was gone in tears. I miss the sureties of being Catholic—the formal catechism and litanies."

Karen explains the idea of her story "Wednesday." "Well, you read my short story. I mean, that's the one that was before this one coming out. It was very sarcastic, and it also was ironic, and it had an awful lot of the belief systems stuff going on."

I'll quote a bit of the superb "Wednesday" here, which appeared in the first issue of *Alaska Quarterly Review* in 1982 and many years ago in the pages of *Cirque*, where it was nominated for a Pushcart. This short passage explains the remoteness beneath the butcher's eyelids:

> This remoteness stems from a time of plaster saints when the butcher and the Church were inextricably joined in a brotherhood of ritual. The visible manifestation of this joining was the parish calendar, Courtesy of Daugherty's Butcher Shop & Grocery, and its seal was the simple outline of a fish. Each

Friday—and on Wednesday during the atonements of Lent—in response to this spare, attenuated symbol, we suffered the pale flesh of the sea and called it fasting.

She combines place, religion, symbol, tradition, into fluid writing where the reader feels so present.

Karen's "SF Avenues," that appears in this issue of *Cirque*, has the same immediacy.

She, hopefully, will be appearing at upcoming readings and continuing to share her work with us. She is truly a finely crafted talent and continues to delight us with her poetry, warmth, and wit. ◪

Karen Tschannen

SF Avenues

Clinton Edwards lived in an area of rectangles defined on the south by a stripe of fog-glistened park and on the north by a rock-bastioned bay lined with obsolete forts, divided east to west and then again north to south in long streets which, in submission to some long-dead engineer's passion for order, were christened in secular equations of alphabet and number. After the streets of shops and churches, past the main arterial carrying traffic from the downtown district, the ordinary residential blocks bore identifications of regimented nicety—Anza Street progressed to Balboa Street and Balboa Street logically to Cabrillo. The following wide street parallel to the park was named inexplicably Fulton Boulevard, Mr. Fulton perhaps too grand a personage to have submitted to common drill. On the other side of the park the alphabet continued, moving from Irving to Judah to Kirkham, all the way to Vicente where the Great Highway and sand dunes terminated the march to the sea. But this area was outside of Clinton Edwards' concern and he did not often think of it.

Clinton Edwards was a duly examined and certified pharmacist, having graduated at the neatly bracketed midpoint in his class standing nine years prior to this damp summer and moving directly into his father's long-established corner drugstore. His parents seized this opportunity to display their devotion to son and city by moving to Florida. Promptly each quarter Clinton mailed a certified check in partial payment on the good will and deed.

Clinton married his college sweetheart the same day he graduated and still loved her, though the nature of this love

had undergone a transformation, the significance of which he did not yet comprehend. They made love in exact proportion to his stated needs though she could be inventive when the long hours of his occupation caused his energies to flag. He was still flattered by their pairing and somewhat in awe of her bold good looks. The planes and angles of her long body may have been called boney on another woman, but she had the stunning grace and tentative gravity of those tall women whose flesh seems burdenless. He had assumed marriage, home, children would weight her substance and spirit into an acceptable nameless solidity. The magnanimity of his acceptance would be the cement of their lives when the juices of their early years thinned and dried. But the children had not come, and Joan spoke less often of the new modes of creative parenting and more of the new requirements for a graduate degree in Fine Arts.

At breakfast on Monday Joan announced "I really *must* take another course from Dr. Gerstenfeld. Ethics was *so* exciting. I don't need any more philosophy credits, but I can use them in the elective count. I've never been so challenged by a professor before. Now *that* is what going back to school is really all *about!*"

She had never completely left it, even in the early days of their marriage. "Keeping her hand in," she called it, taking at least one class each semester.

"He has *such* a *fine* mind," she said.

Clinton once imagined he loved her best when she spoke with such intensity and interest, her neat hands passionately involved with the shaping of her words.

"It is *sad* that someone so young with his background and intellect should be so *cynical,*" she added.

Briefly annoyed, and impatient to get on with his day, Clinton shot back "I believe it was T.S. Eliot who said of somebody that he had a mind so fine an idea couldn't violate it." It was one of those bits of esoterica that clung perversely to memory from a required Modern Literature course in the years of youthful impatience with non-productive studies. Somehow, by denying the value of the mind his wife had risen above, he had denied her the height of her perch.

Really Clinton," she countered, it's not like you to be so horrid. She rose with him, reaching to brush invisible crumbs from his tie. Anyway, I don't believe Eliot meant that in the *pejorative* sense at all. I believe he truly felt James—I believe it *was* Henry James he was speaking of—he felt James had no *need* to *impose* ideas on his work, that they just arose *naturally* as part of the woof and warp--of the very *fabric* of his work."

Her arguments on such subjects took on an italicized character, as if they were part debate, part formal explication or thesis defense. This swiftness of response, the surprising retention of academic phrasing and cadences had impressed him in his university years but now seemed only a clever trick out of place over poached eggs on Eighth Avenue. Their social circle was heavily freighted with academic dilettantes, museum docents, and part-time chamber musicians who spoke this peculiarly emphasized prose.

Ed Daugherty's wife, Margaret, had returned to college too, but she took night classes in tax tips and was active in the League of Women Voters. Not exactly his cup of tea but at least useful. Joan was bored by Margaret ("She has a total lack of sensitivity—no *depth!*") and repelled by Ed Daugherty ("That is a man of *repressed violence*—I can *sense* these things. Some fine day we are going to hear on the six o'clock news that he took his *meat cleaver* to the *whole family!*") But Ed was a hard worker and an effective member of the Richmond District Merchants Association. And Margaret did play a mean hand of bridge. Now that is what he would call a fine mind. Body's not too bad either, even after five kids. Generous. Not a lot of class, but generous looking.

Clinton depended on Joan to arrange the many necessary details of daily living, the evening comforts and entertainments that added variety to each decently regulated workday. She saw him off each morning precisely at 8:45 a.m., sustaining him first with one egg, it's white poached beyond reproach, it's yellow eye discreetly filmed, four ounces of Minute Maid Orange Juice and one English muffin divided carefully with a fork to preserve, toasted, its mouth-rasping texture. He carried a lunch packed with taste and imagination in a charcoal Samsonite briefcase for the three-block walk to his pharmacy where the day would progress in pleasing segments of predictable activity, filling prescriptions, checking stock. On the rare evening Joan had not arranged some social activity, he returned after dinner to his business and helped Godwin Likely, his afternoon man, close the store and tally the day's transactions, taking some pleasure in the neat columns of figures and the sorting of invoices. There was an ordered rightness to his days and a pleasing piquancy in his nights that made him believe himself generally fortunate to be living in this time and this place, between wars and national economic

crises, between defunct forts and the Golden Gate Park.

Late in the morning of Monday details—mopping the tiled floor, straightening the comic books on the magazine rack, preparing the standing maintenance prescriptions—Mrs. Donatti arrived puffing and blowing, shifting her bulk from one stout leg to the other, talking to Clinton before the door was fully open. Behind her was a girl of perhaps sixteen or seventeen with hair the color of Joan's but long and loose to her waist. Her skin was soft, full looking, like newly ripened fruit. She carried a shopping bag full of packages. A skirt of dark wool serge fell in loose folds to an unfashionable length.

Mrs. Donatti was energetic and vocal. The girl's name was Assunta and two weeks before she had come from Sicily by way of Lugano to live on Anza Street with the Donatti's. The relationship was distant but definite. She had accompanied Mrs. Donatti on her rounds to Daugherty's Butcher Shop and Grocers, Dutch Mill Bakery, and Woolworths, at last arriving at Edward's Pharmacy and Gifts to be displayed and the relationship verified. She had been imported to help Mrs. Donatti in a house grown too large with the loss of her sons to their marriage beds and the sudden dual onset of glaucoma and phlebitis in her husband of 42 years.

"So, now we have a daughter to bring us help and joy in our old age," she confided to Clinton in her loud and angry voice. "It is daughters you should have. From sons you get only grief. In pain you bring them into this world, they dirty their clothes and steal whiskey and shame their mothers with bad women. And on the feast days they go to the house of their wife's family to break a mother's heart," she finished with some satisfaction. Like Assunta, she had come from Sicily as a girl. She lived all her married life on Anza Street and yet, through some subterranean linkage of ethnic motherhood, could be placed by ear a continent away in Brooklyn Heights. She took enormous pride in her errant sons.

"Assunta, this is Mr. Edwards. He makes the medicine for your poor uncle. He is a very clever man who has gone to the university. Say good morning." Mrs. Donatti moved off to browse among the support hose and magazines.

The girl's voice was soft and Clinton heard only his name. Her mouth, on the last syllable, displayed its fulness on each side of a center cleft like the plumped gathering of an apricot. She inclined her head in a movement of bestowal at variance with a small gesture of genuflection. The string bag burdened with bloodstained packages from Daugherty's bumped the grey-tiled floor. A long baguette, only partially concealed in its wrapper, shifted with a small rustling sound.

She showed him Mrs. Donatti's list and asked if he could show her to the correct shelves. As she gathered each article, she laid it on the counter and asked in a soft accented voice if the item and the pronunciation of its naming matched the symbols on the list. Of a few she asked their purpose. Items of personal health or of feminine hygiene seemed to cause her no embarrassment. When she needed nothing more, Clinton felt pressed to extend the exchange, to hear the soft syllables from her mouth.

"Your English is very good. Did you learn it at school?" It had that quality of search, of syntax assembled carefully and mortared, brief hesitancies giving each word a peculiar weight, an elusive importance which stirred in him some sense of urgency.

"Yes, in the school of the Sisters." The cold fluorescents overhead mottled the flesh of her bare arms. "A small time."

The Day It Happened   *Tami Phelps*

As if this were too insignificant a return for his praise, she continued, "And in the house of Herr Doctor in Lugano where he have only the German and the English. I have only the English. I have not the German."

She added this last with a lift of her shoulders, like an explanation, then stood mute and patient so that he was struck with the impression she had spread among all the small purchases on the counter before him the whole of her young life to weigh and price.

In the days of his college excesses, he had once journeyed through the heat-worn hills of Mexico encountering again and again black-garbed women weighted to the brown earth, secured with a stillness even in movement that was like waiting yet not waiting, accepting of the sun, of the weight of child on hip, of endless brown hills. He had been relieved in some vague but unquestioned manner to return to his cool patterned avenues.

"No German. Well. That's fine." He said laconically. "Just fine!" He could think of nothing else to say. There was a barrier deeper than language and at this moment he wanted more than he had wanted any small adventure to do battle with this barrier, to defeat it, to change the stillness to…to what? He had a sudden image of her moving flatfooted and carefully as language in pantomime with the shadowy yet correct figure of the German doctor.

He busied himself with entering the Donatti charge in his ledger, not watching them leave.

The image of the girl intruded on his days and possessed his nights. He was subject to swiftly changing moods which left him uneasy and vaguely confused. The lines of his existence had subtly shifted so that his perception of sane and ordinary things would sometimes startle him. Walking to work one Friday, out of the corner of his eye he saw the glass bulb of the VFW's red gumball machine that had stood passively in front of Mansard's French Laundry and Dry Cleaners for years suddenly swell as he passed, and with an undecipherable shrug, the brightly colored gumballs rioted in wild agitation. His left hand flew up to shield his face, but when he let it fall, the machine was the same as always, the colors supporting each other in rest behind the curved glass.

And on Tuesday, returning from the bank, the stucco surface of his pharmacy down the street was not its own restrained and practical buff but appeared to quake in the afternoon light, only tentatively constrained by the grey cement lines of the sidewalk—and moral grace?

Joan remarked more than once about his preoccupation. "Are things going badly at the store?" she asked pointedly one Monday at breakfast.

"Of course not," he answered, defensive. "What gives you such an idea?"

"Oh, this and that." She tapped the napkin covering his knees with one manicured nail. "And mostly *that*," she added with significance.

"Fiscal year inventory time. It's a pain. Sorry if I've been one." He felt contrite and annoyed at the same time.

"You used to enjoy inventory, Love, back when I used to help you. Before Goody came to work for us you *particularly* enjoyed the backroom inventory." Her palm rested warm on his knee, tightened briefly, the nail tapping once, a question mark.

It was true. In the early days of their marriage when money was tight, Joan often helped in the store. But he was glad those days were over, and his business and home life could be neatly segregated and organized. Joan now helped only during Christmas season when the store was full and the neighborhood kids pinched anything not nailed down. She had a knack for swift and artistic giftwrapping. Her many competencies never ceased to amaze him.

"Yes. Well, I'd better get on with it. Wouldn't do to be late, would it," he said, picking up his briefcase.

"Are you sure there's no problem at the store?" Joan insisted. "This is no time for financial problems." She did look worried, her eyes shadowed underneath. He had to shake off this silliness. A man his age.

"No time is the right time. And the answer is, all is well," he said lightly, kissing the air close to her forehead. "But I'd better get on with it or it soon won't be." Today Mrs. Donatti or Assunta would be in to pick up old man Donatti's prescriptions. The girl had come alone the last time.

"Clinton, you probably just need to relax. Why don't I call Ed and Margaret and see if they'll make a foursome here tonight? You always enjoy a few good rubbers of bridge."

Oddly, an evening of bridge held little appeal. But Joan was so obviously trying to please. He felt like a heel. "Sure, but not before eight. I won't be home much before seven. Goody comes in at two so that'll give me about five hours on the inventory." He forestalled comment with a decisive kiss. He did not want to be late opening the store.

When he turned the corner, he could see the girl down the long line of the street standing at the shop door. She stood still and patient, her weight centered over one hip, hands gathered beneath her breasts, her head bowed under a shawl of hair in a timeless attitude of waiting women. He lengthened his stride and the briefcase banged his knee once, the sudden pain strangely comforting. Then he stood facing her, his heart bounding as though from sudden exertion.

"I am sorry to keep you waiting. Have you been waiting long?" He fumbled his key into the lock and held the door open for her to pass in front of him. She gave off a scent like broken fruit, perhaps figs, their centers soft and thickly seeded. The door closed with a pneumatic sigh, the plastic sign flapping its open message at him. The light from the Timex display case threw her shadow across him like a torch. The wall clock registered 8:55.

"Why, it's early! His surprise accused her as if the confusion of five minutes of his life had caused some irreparable harm. This increment of confused time seemed to contain the full weight of her power over him. He had always prided himself on the accuracy of his internal clock. He checked his own watch in disbelief. It confirmed the magnitude of the error.

"I'll get the lights," he said, "then see what you need, moving abruptly into the store's main aisle. She moved at the same time, soundlessly.

"Excuse me," he said, touching her shoulder as he moved past feeling clumsy. The dimness suddenly felt oppressed, the shadows distorting the familiar space.

"Scusa," she replied softly, "I come only for the medicine of my uncle. I have not the list."

You have not the German. You have not the list. You have only this timeless weight and silence. And the smell of broken figs.

"Yes. Excuse me. Let me get the lights," he repeated. Under the fluorescent tubes, the lines of shelves and the two short aisles down the center were neatly defined, displaying the accoutrements of reality—mouth washes next to denture cremes, aspirin abutting cold tablets, hair spray and the shampoos facing the deodorants. The supplier was late delivering the shaving crème and the empty space on the stand directly in front of the drug counter vaguely disturbed him. The girl disturbed him. At thirty four he was a duly registered pharmacist with an ideal wife and a business of his own, his life sanely charted with reasonable allowances made for contingencies. This foreign woman—no, girl—had no place in it. An affair with Margaret Daugherty, outrageous as the thought may be, was infinitely more plausible, more within reason. And, therefore, more within the possibility of control. He busied himself with prescriptions.

"How is your uncle today?" he asked, too conscious of the silence.

"He has the pain. Here." She bent slightly and patted te calf of one leg. "It is very big." She held small reddened hands apart to indicate an ominous swelling. "Again, the doctor comes. Tomorrow."

The doctor has the English. The doctor has not the German. The doctor will take your uncle to the hospital and he will not come home again. Your aunt will go to live with her married sons, one at a time, and you will go away from these long streets bounded neatly by the park and the forts and I will make love to my wife at night and open my store on time each day.

"Here you are. I have only given you half the amount of medicine for the swelling of his legs. The doctor may want to make some change. The charge slip is in the bag. I'll put it on your aunt's account." He had nothing left to say to her. And she would leave.

"You are a kind man Mr. Edwards," she said in her soft voice. She bowed her head to him in the gesture that seemed both bestowing and submissive. "Gratze. Thank you." The smell of fruit hung in the air when she was gone.

That's me all right, support your local child molester!

Clinton shook his head to clear it and entered the Donatti charge with satisfying neatness in the Accounts Receivable ledger.

An evening of bridge with the Daughtery's was usually viewed by Clinton as one of life's small bonuses. The game was bounded by numerous but non-complex rules and conventions, the cards divided nicely into four even hands and four even suits. The two couples had played often enough to understand the other's bid responses and opening gambits and were well matched. They took the game seriously enough to avoid table talk during play but were not out for blood. True, Ed did approach the making of a difficult bid with distracting

ferocity that seemed excessive for a game, but Clinton saw this more as mannerism than passion. An evening of bridge was just what he needed. He was pleased with his considerate and efficient wife. Tonight, Joan was exceptionally warm toward Margaret, asking after the children with a display of concern.

"Oh, they're all well for a change, other than the usual assortment of scrapes and bruises," Margaret replied complacently. "But we can't stay too late. I have to be up early to finish Meggin's first communion dress."

Ed snorted. "It's all a bunch of silly nonsense," he grumbled in his heavy voice. He turned to Clinton. "The women go in for this charade, dressing the kids up like a bunch of infant brides. They have no idea what's going on but they like the fuss and bother." *They* apparently applied equally to the mothers and the daughters. "If you ask me it's all just a Roman gimmick!"

Clinton glanced at Joan, expecting to meet the usual patronizing smile that accompanied any mention of organized religion.

Instead, she turned her winning smile on Ed, and tapped his wrist lightly with her feathered hand of cards. "Oh, come on, Ed, you know you get a big kick out of it too." The two women sat smiling their conspirators' smiles at Ed until his frown relented and he barked his short laugh. Joan rose, patting Margaret's shoulder. "Come give me a hand with the drinks and goodies, Margaret."

Linking arms, the women went off to the kitchen, laughing as though they were privy to some huge joke. Clinton was touched by his wife's sudden show of warmth towards Margaret. He felt a pang of guilt for causing her worry. The pharmacy was fine, in fact in recent months showing a quite comfortable margin. She was a good wife. All a man could ask for. He was a fool. An inexcusable fool.

Ed was talking to him. "Sorry, Ed, my head was in the shop, so to speak. What did you say?"

"I said you've met the Donatti's new girl." It sounded like an accusation. But that was just the way Ed talked.

"Yeah. Seems like a nice enough kid," he answered carefully.

"Old lady Donatti better get her married off quick. She's ripe for it, young as she is." Ed's eyes under veined lids had a knowing look.

"Ed, she's little more than a kid. Give her a break. She's right off the boat, too. Hardly the swinging type." Clinton wasn't sure if it was Ed he was addressing or himself.

The women returned with trays. "Is that Assunta you're talking about?" Balancing drinks, Margaret placed a rim-crusted glass on Clinton's coaster. "I borrowed her to keep the two youngest last week. She is really quite a good worker, every level headed it seems to me. The kids like her, which is half the battle. And she certainly has more patience than I do. A born mother. These salty dogs are grand, Joan!" Still standing, she took a long drink from her glass, finishing with a quick lick at the salt. Under the overhead light she suddenly looked every one of her 39 years.

"Rode hard and put away wet," thought Clinton, momentarily both repelled and touched.

Joan ruffled the cards and dealt them with negligent neatness. "If that's the little dark girl going by every morning with the string shopping bag, *somebody* ought to take her in *hand*. My *God,* all she needs is a *shawl!* After a quick appraisal of her fanned cards, she said, "It's one spade to you Margaret.

There was no dark figure waiting at the corner when Clinton turned down Eighth Avenue on Tuesday. The streets were empty of traffic and the morning overcast drained them of color, blurring the lines and edges of joining structures. The formlessness of the scene vaguely depressed him.

He heard the phone as he let himself in.

"Edwards Pharmacy," he answered, shaking out of his jacket.

"The shop is open. Good. I will come now. For the new medicine." The voice, disembodied and thinned by the line, had a strange effect. It was a voice from a shawled figure standing in shadow. It had no reference, no identity except that suggested by the shawl.

"Yes," he said. There was nothing else to say. The girl hung up. She appeared in the store five minutes later and gravely handed Clinton a prescription in the neat hieroglyphics of the doctor.

"Uncle Donatti does not make the water. This is to help make the water. If there is not enough water, the doctor say he must go to the hospital. Please, I must go fast. My aunt cries and can do nothing."

He realized he was standing there staring at her lips as they filled and flattened with the urgency of her speech. She had stopped speaking.

"Yes. Well. Of course. I'm very sorry your uncle is not better." He gave her the few pills and busied himself with the ledger, willing himself not to watch her as she walked to the door.

On Sunday, Joan had tickets for a recital at the DeYoung Museum. A reception for the guest artist was to follow. Between rubbers of bridge on Monday, she had urged Margaret and Ed to go with them, exclaiming over the talents of the young man. "He's a professor of music at the university. He is going to premier one of his own works, 'American Sonata.' Should be quite a treat. He's really quite good." But Meggin's first communion would not permit.

"Besides, Margaret's probably right, you know," Joan said to Clinton as they went up the broad steps to the museum. "The open-air band concert is more their speed, what with that rambunctious brood. We ought to bring a lunch and try it ourselves sometime. Soon."

Clinton found it quite a reach imagining Joan with her long nylon-slick legs sprawled on the grass picking grass out of potato salad on paper plates, assaulted by the shrieks of rampaging kids and the brassy park band.

"If they won't go with us, then we'll just have to join *them.*" She said firmly and tucked her arm through his, holding it against the side of her breast in an intimate gesture.

After the performance, in a reflex of gratitude for Joan's obvious concern, he praised the performance with a fervor he didn't feel. They stood drinking warm champagne from shallow plastic stemware in a small reception area, an alcove off a large corridor containing objects of startling shape and dubious purpose. This was Joan's world, as the pharmacy and the avenues were his. He tried for a mental picture of Margaret Daugherty, full thighs straining her bright print dress, poised on one of the thin gilt chairs in the recital hall. But the incongruous image shattered and was replaced by a dark shawled figure, before it too disintegrated in the sound of his wife's school voice.

"Oh Clinton. The program was *ordinary*. The progressions were little more than variations on one-four-five-one. The resolutions were totally expected and not at all fresh. A few twists in the rhythm, but on the whole, it was all so *obvious*, completely *lacking* in any *subtlety*. The sonata was a step *backwards*. I mean, it's been *done!*" Her free hand paused in its description and she gave Clinton her glass. "We might as well have gone to hear the park band. Be a love and get me something more."

When he returned, Joan was across the room talking intently to a man with a boney forehead and a hooked nose that gave him a predatory look. As he watched, Joan's hands ceased shaping the air and paused, palms upward in a curiously beseeching movement. The man bared his teeth in a smile and then nodded in Clinton's direction. Joan's cheeks were flushed as she turned to him. He crossed the small room in a few steps, holding her glass out and smiling his introduction smile. He felt mild surprise at his lack of anger. He knew before she said the name that this was the one and only Dr. Gerstenfeld.

Once out of the boundary of trees, they maneuvered across the Fulton Boulevard traffic to the safety of their own streets. Joan leaned against him as she dislodged a piece of tanbark from her shoe. As he stood against her negligible weight, he managed lightly enough he thought, "That was some little tete-a-tete back there with your friend the good doctor. Anything brilliant enough to repeat?"

She stepped back and looked at him, her eyes widening, blue smudges more noticeable in the newly bright sun. He was conscious of their heights, of the striking picture he was so often told they made.

"Clinton! My god, are you actually *jealous*? Of *him*? She put her head to one side and laughed a laugh that was almost singing.

The unfamiliar spike of rage that curved his shoulders inward towards his wife tightened his voice. "And I suppose you are not having an affair with this fine doctor of the fine mind?" The acid edged his voice, a voice strange to him.

The accusation cut off the laughter. "No, I am not." She paused, a small knowing smile curving her mouth. But I do know who is…and who was. He's *hardly* my type. And I'm certainly not *his*. She laughed again, her hands diminishing the stature of the doctor as much as her words. "He goes in for mature,

rather fleshy blonds. You know, the full-hipped variety who are appropriately appreciated and in no position to cause problems. His sex life is really no concern of mine. After all, it doesn't seem to interfere with his instruction and may even improve his disposition. And our grades." She shrugged. "He stimulates my *mind*, Clinton, my *mind* and nothing else. *You* are what stimulates my *else*, Love, only *you*. And then only when you are not fretting about business, it seems. Are things really going that badly? You can tell me. Even if the timing is a bit awkward just now," she added.

"Joan, I've told you. Things are fine at the store. Anyway, even so, why would it be any different now than some other time?" She had said something like this a week or so back, hadn't she?

"Darling, I wanted to wait until after my appointment tomorrow. But I'm sure now. In a little more than seven moths you and I will be responsible for part of the new generation. Of course, I'm planning on *natural* childbirth so we'll both have to attend classes…"

Her hands gathered life from the air and kneaded it into a tangible shape defined by words and set in motion on the avenues where he was born and raised and where he lived his days with this woman who would give added substance and weight to his world and he no longer heard the words but saw clearly the shape of them.

"Oh Clinton, you should *see* your face!" Joan put a cool palm on each side of his head and laughed again, into his face. "Don't you believe me? I was just trying to get Dr. Gerstenfeld to let me take the second semester credits on the directed study plan for when I can't go to class any longer. You are so silly. Here we stand carrying on in the street like a couple of peasants. Let's go home."

She tucked her arm possessively in his and continued to plan and describe the new limits of their life as they approached Cabrillo Street. She would continue with school as long as she was able. She wanted to complete her masters. After the baby, her schooling would depend upon getting *proper* but *reasonable* help.

"I was thinking of the Donatti girl. I've heard she's quite capable. Did you know that she was a nursemaid for some doctor in Switzerland? What do you think, darling?"

Balboa Street was just ahead. Yes. The Donatti girl. That young girl with the shawl. With the sick uncle. "Yes. Not a bad idea. I don't see why not. Margaret recommends her highly and we all know what a mother Margaret is. I'll speak to Mrs. Donatti when the time is right. Not just now."

He knew the details would be worked out to their mutual satisfaction.

The overcast had burned away, and the numbered avenues and alphabetized streets were sharply defined in a diminishing grid pattern. He inhaled deeply, smelling without awareness the pungent eucalyptus trees bordering the park behind him, feeling his chest expand, make space for the certainty of their future.

In bed that night, Joan said into his back, her words muffled, "By the way, darling, I don't think I told you. Dr. Fine Mind is not really a doctor. He never quite *completed* his thesis. The doctor business is just a matter of courtesy." ◪

REVIEW

Paul Haeder

A Review of Fred Rosenblum's *Tramping Solo*, Formite Press, 2021

We Are Never Alone After War — Ghosts

The sorrow of war inside a soldier's heart was in a strange way similar to the sorrow of love. It was a kind of nostalgia, like the immense sadness of a world at dusk. It was a darkness, a missing, a pain which could send one soaring back into the past. The sorrow of the battlefield could not normally be pinpointed to one particular event, or even one person. If you focused on any one event it would soon become a tearing pain.

—Bao Ninh, *The Sorrow of War: A Novel of North Vietnam*

Right off the bat, Fred Rosenblum pounds the fibers and ink of his poetry collection, *Tramping Solo*, as if to announce that insidious and inglorious war — America's War Against Vietnam — can possibly be kept bottled up and locked away in a moment of time.

However, we soon see how time never really heals all wounds. We see a young man tumble through grief and self-effacement as he directs haphazardly his own walkabout. The young Rosenblum is a self-indulgent, bawdy seeker of spiritual reckoning.

He does that as a leatherneck, jumping trains, kipping in every manner of place. The swill of booze and the snake breath of pot and other drugs fuel his journey. This is not a sociological bunch of mutterings, or apologia.

Like all good personal poets, Rosenblum pushes pain aside and captures the vigorous and vain moments encompassing a swath of time in his role of a wondering Vietnam veteran. Tramping.

In the poem that serves as point, "Inspired by a Former Foe," Rosenblum flails the reader with a one-two punch which ends up telegraphing the rest of the book's 34 poems:

> A disturbed young man,
> I hadn't yet begun
> to realized what I'd
> been through when I
> hastened-off to Sitka
> in the spring of 1970,
> attempting to rid myself
> of everything I knew
> would malign me.

Rosenblum was "in country" in 1968 as a Marine. He exited the gashed and poisonous womb of the Vietnam War and pushed himself out of — like a bad birth — the wrecking crew which is the uniformed services (sic) and into the quintessential summer of love, 1969.

The aimlessness was not as misdirected and accidental as one might expect, even with the Kerouac invocations; and even though the concept of "tramping" and, in Fred's case, rough sleeping under overpasses, in the woods, in cabins, on fishing boats, in the back of canneries and in flop houses and other abodes in and around San Francisco and all the way to Sitka, appears to be haphazard.

There is existential meaning in this apparent trippy trauma-affixing journey from the grunt, to a killer, into archetypical witness of horror, and finally through to his discharge into a country deep in systemic spasms around that illegal war (police action, they called it). The supposed anti-colonial USA was the occupier, then with ecocide and napalm, it came like a festering comet into Vietnam when the French colonialists were defeated in 1954.

There are many oddball rites of passage Fred captures in this evolution from naïve recruit through to combat Marine and back to a casualty of an uncaring government, and a chaotic citizenry, his rucksack of demons and traumas foisted on a journey through the Pacific Northwest. Coming of age was shunted, stunted and arrested, but this book of poems is an ode to breaking loose into the slipstream of jumping trains and itinerant work.

Lots of psychedelics, pot and booze to stay the night sweats and Kinescope of the first televised war.

You will not be tasting the burnt flesh of a "war portrayed as a terrible ordeal, a version of hell," because these poems represent a catharsis and baptism of the vet/writer who is wondering as well as seeking supplication in nightmares from a Jack London story.

Beat-bopping poems like "The Blue Cue" flay the reader with Hells Angels, drugging, knives and 9 mm's, black leather chaps and Harleys. It's Rosenblum there, playing pool, and he hits this poem with four- and five- word lines. It's Bukowski and *Howl* all rammed into a fluid scene in this solo tramp's life:

> The worn leather lattice
> of empty pockets refusing
> to hold the strokes
> of the sober and sloppy
> drunk, some of whom,
> in that savage crew,
> preyed on fish — chum
> like the toughs who'd
> come in to play these mean,
> badass, motherfuckers —
> all of them monsters
> and maestros of the masse
> — homicidal, and pushers
> of grade A junk.

Fred Rosenblum

We are seeing the post-traumatic stress disordered brain of a Marine war veteran pulling in the American life he discovers as the very essence of those first heavy literary tendrils set down by the classic interloper into Turtle Island, D.H. Lawrence: "The essential American soul is hard, isolate, stoic, and a killer. It has never yet melted."

Yet, again, the poetry collection as a whole is more than the "gangs of Frisco" or the hard-scrabble mental angst of a fellow tramping from California to Alaska throwing nets into sea and gutting its bounty. It is the work of a man who carries his pain as a young purple heart toting war veteran who'd rather smash brain cells into drugging and depravity than explore Nietzsche or Bly. The "character" in these poems is a young man T-boned by the very society he supposedly went to Indochina to protect — in the killing spree of brown people, mostly farmers — this society's decadent and demonic way of life.

He might agree with Nietzsche when he said, "The individual has always had to struggle to keep from being overwhelmed by the tribe. If you try it, you will be lonely often, and sometimes frightened. But no price is too high to pay for the privilege of owning yourself."

One sometimes has to read between the lines, between the pronouncements, as evidenced in many of Rosenblum's poems but spritely etched in this one, "Bouncing Around":

> I was quasi-seditious
> pandered myself
> with an "Off the Pig" sign
> for a ride through Soledad —
> ate from the bags
> of roaches and shake,
> bouncing on a torn mattress
> in the back of an old,
> rusty panel truck, a
> '51 Chevy stuffed
> full of long hairs
> & someone's mangy,
> spaced-out, funky mutt
> — pulled over
> on the industry fringes
> of Oakland and Berkeley,
> hassled by the heat
> just off the old Bay Bridge,
> where Zappa-like
> freak at the wheel
> could barely stay in his land
> for the wind.

The poem ends in May 1970. Oh, I was 13, with an older sister who lived in Ketchikan. She was a traveler throughout Canada all the way down to LA where she tried her hand

as a go-go dancer. She was with one Vietnam vet after another, and I remember some of those dudes.

We were just back from overseas, in Tucson. Vietnam vets showed me how to tune up my Bultaco. Vets with blackbirds (speed) and Columbian gold. One guy, Damien, was in a wheelchair, but his upper body was as big as Hercules'. He had his souped-up van rigged so he could drive the hell out of it as a paraplegic of war.

Good poems bring one back to some common ground — motorcycles, drugs, screaming with coyotes, older guys showing me some of the ropes. Rosenblum provides some of those gems in this collection.

Yet, now, I feel a monk's words imbued in some of Rosenblum's art, in this collection: Thich Nhat Hanh, *The Miracle of Mindfulness: An Introduction to the Practice of Meditation*:

> My actions are my only true belongings. I cannot escape the consequences of my actions. My actions are the ground upon which I stand.

The one poem I'd ask Rosenblum to serve up if he had been on my Spokane radio show would have had to have been, "Many Rivers to Remind Me." This is the tour d' force, his homage to the hitchhiking, from Santa Cruz to Skagit.

Those rivers, man, as Heraclitus, said 2,500 years ago, dog the soul: "No man ever steps in the same river twice, for it's not the same river and he's not the same man." Fred juxtaposes the trip up Highway 1 with scrambling fugues and nightmares of Vietnam.

> Up on the rainy day
> railway tracks in Kelso,
> on the daylight side of the 5 pm
> still warm, gravel ballast,
> and up from a camp
> of hammered tramps — the Cowlitz,
> like a tributary of the Perfume, roiling,
> and where I watched the familiar
> and the unfamiliar faces
> of mortal men hoisted
> onto a cargo floor, heard
> that it was still slick with
> the viscera of another mother's son
> two hills over — one more LZ in Quang Tri

cut-out of the bamboo cordilleran
machete monkey jungle —

Later in the book, near the end, another tributary poem, "In the Zen of the River." Here, he meets his soon-to-be girlfriend (and later, his wife): It was around that time/I was shanghaied by a/redheaded woman, stolen/into her heart and made/ to explain my situation/ before she'd accept/ a wild hairy beast from the forest/ into her house.

Here's the blue collar kid who grew up in Southern California in the 1950s and '60s, A bus driver for a father, and both parents were Freemasons. "Baloney and American cheese," and then the black and white TV-fed life of a typical USA family.

He was 19 when he was there for the TET Offensive, another lie of the Westmoreland and LBJ kind. Rosenblum crouched in jungles for 13 months, and he was part of a security detail for convoys running supplies into "the ruins of Hue City."

Ahh, I was in Hue in 1994, and I was on that Perfume River, too, with a Dragoon boat captain, and that image is below. Our lives could have been interlaced, me 18 when the fall of Saigon sputtered on TV, and now, the fall of Afghanistan, Rosenblum eight years my senior. April 29, 1975 the Armed Forces Radio played "White Christmas" as a code to begin Operation Frequent Wind, the ultimate evac of American Civilians and Vietnamese refugees by helicopter.

What a shit show, and some 26 years later, "Never another Vietnam" heralds in yet another human debacle by the flagging empire that is this un-United States of America, AKA US of Amnesia (à la Gore Vidal).

For the former Marine, that is, for the poet, he ends his book with a bio declaring, "In 2011, following a 36-year odyssey in Alaska and the Northwest, Fred returned to his hometown of San Diego, CA with his wife and muse of too many years, where they now enjoy a very therapeutic existence 'in the warm California Sun.'"

But like many of the ex-soldiers I have counseled over the years as a teacher and social worker, especially homeless combat vets, they taste this acridity of all that wrongdoing, the hell, the killing, and inhumanity. It's "Still Smoldering After All these Years," the last poem declaring the fire of

war ebbing:

> And I asked myself in that apropos
> moment of recovery—
>
> How many years more will the embers of war
> smolder as such, inside me.

This book is worthy of reflection, sort of a time capsule in a guy's walkabout and quest for something outside himself.

Emblematic of Rosenblum's collection, "On the Bum in '72," says it all about the forces of his every man's existence:

> I'm a Scottish-Irish
> Hungarian-Cherokee
> Polack-Jew,
> who went off to war,
> back in the day
> when they weren't calling us heroes
> anymore.

Simply, he is a man, burnt by the verdant rice paddies and jungle, captured in the flash of napalm, held frozen in the boom of mortar fire. ◪

Market Musician   *Jack Broom*

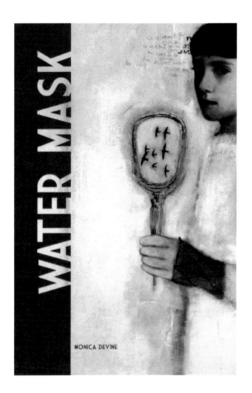

REVIEW

Kerry Dean Feldman

A Review of Monica Devine's *Water Mask* University of Alaska Press, 2019

Reading *Water Mask* reminds you why you read. Monica Devine's essays are extraordinary glimpses of an Alaska few people can even imagine. She also writes about the desert land of New Mexico where she dialogues with the mystical beauty that inspired Georgia O'Keeffe, and other places that forged her awareness.

Devine hurls her entire being into living, into her writing, and her work as a speech therapist, often in remote Alaska villages. She sees deeply into the hearts, minds, wisdom, humor, and survival challenges of Native men, women, and children because they trust her, know her, hunt and gather with her, share with her their *muktuk*, caribou stew, seal oil, and rotten fish heads that were buried underground. She's not an intruding, prodding stranger. She's like family. She adjusts her professional speech

therapy toolkit to their cultures rather than demand that they conform to Western ways, and learns from them.

Each sentence of these life stories offers unexpected insights which awaken a reader to one's own life. As she writes, "How do sudden bursts of memory and imagination burn through the banality of an uneventful day?" Devine adheres in these stunning essays to the Zen master's advice which she quotes, "Speak nothing unless it is an improvement on the silence." For her, this means write nothing unless it is an improvement in some way, no matter how small, on being. The world to which she takes you—her world—is more holistic and contemplative than any writer I've read. "Nothing is missing when you feel a part of everything," she notes.

I had to pause for a day or two after each chapter to allow her honesty about life and death (a clubbed fish, her own father's), sink in, take me to the tearful deaths I have endured. Then I opened another chapter, dug into another adventure, traveled with her on a sub-arctic frozen river that is too-quickly thawing, flew in a small plane through treacherous clouds with a young pilot from the Lower 48 who asks *her* if she "knows the way" to a village. This long-legged woman, writer, mom, wife, daughter (originally from Michigan), is not (like Margaret Atwood also claims) a "feminist" writer. She's simply an amazing writer and artist, open to how life comes—a remote cabin she and her husband built threatened by a surging river, a -40f winter day that challenges breathing, or when "A bluebird spoons up a lilting song from the crooked branch of a juniper." The book title comes from a Jim Harrison poem.

Read Monica Devine, then go for a walk outside. Everything will seem different:

Fireweed shoots of deep fuchsia point their tips toward the sky. Light is chasing every leaf, stem, and seed, doing an illustrious job of pulling up life by its britches with or without my well-intentioned efforts. ◪

Monica Devine

CONTRIBUTORS

Jean Anderson is the author of two collections of short stories, most recently *Human Being Songs: Northern Stories* (University of Alaska Press, 2017) and *In Extremis* (Plover Press, 1989). She co-edited the regional anthology *Inroads: Alaska's Twenty-Seven Fellowship Writers* (Alaska Association for the Arts, distributed by University of Alaska Press, 1988). She's lived in Fairbanks since 1966 and was a founding staff member and early editor of the UAF journal *Permafrost*. She's received several awards for her fiction and is assembling another collection of stories focusing in part on relationships between Alaskans and Siberians. Some of her work has appeared in *Cirque*.

John Argetsinger: I am a retired social worker who worked for over a decade in Seattle, Washington serving the poor. I have begun cataloging some of the events I encountered in my line of work while allowing the subjects to be anonymous such as changing names and so on. I am of Inupiaq descent and my father is from Juneau, Alaska. I come from a mixed-race background. I am an autodidact and engage in all art forms from paintings to photography. I am also a sound engineer and graphic designer. I now reside in Anchorage. I was raised in Kotzebue, Anchorage and Juneau. Thank you for the opportunity to share my work with you.

A native of Seattle, **Gabrielle Baalke** is a first-year PhD in theology at the University of Nottingham, examining allegory, apology, and conversion narrative in CS Lewis' *The Pilgrim's Regress*. She received her MA in English (Nottingham 2018) with a focus on place-names. Research interests also include literary onomastics and naming, medieval expressions of faith, the Middle-English Romance, and the poetry of T.S. Eliot.

John Baalke holds an MFA from Seattle Pacific University, currently resides in the Peak District, UK, and has previously published poems in *Stoneboat, Cirque, Hummingbird*, and other journals.

Thomas Bacon lives in Sitka, Alaska, a small island community in the Tongass Forest. His work has appeared in *San Pedro River Review, borrowed solace, The Tiger Moth Review* and *Tidal Echoes*. He is a previous contributor to *Cirque Journal*.

Christianne Balk's most recent book is *The Holding Hours* (University of Washington Press). She loves broken music, the rhythms of everyday street talk, and open water swimming. Previous books include *Bindweed* (Walt Whitman Award, American Academy of Poets) and *Desiring Flight* (Verna Emery Prize, Purdue University Press). Honors include fellowships/grants from Artist Trust, Hedgebrook, The Ingraham Merrill Foundation, The Seattle Arts Commission, and the Strousse Award from *Prairie Schooner*. Her work has appeared in *Harper's, Cirque*, Poemoftheweek. org, *Atlantic Monthly, Nimrod, Terrain*, and other mags.

Gabrielle Barnett is a writer based in southcentral Alaska. Her work has appeared in *Cirque Journal, Alaska Women Speak*, and the anthology *Building Fires in the Snow*.

Rachel Barton is poet, editor, and writing coach. She is a member of the *Calyx* Editorial Collective, reads for *Cloudbank Magazine* and for the *Timberline Review*, and edits her own *Willawaw Journal*. Her most recent poems are published or forthcoming in *The Main Street Rag, the Oregon English Journal*, and *Sin Fronteras*. Find her chapbooks, *Out of the Woods* and *Happiness Comes* on her website, rachelbartonwriter.com.

Sue Biggs is an emerging Alaskan photographer whose work has been selected for many Alaskan juried shows including Rarified Light, All-Alaska Biennial, and Alaska Positive. She has been published in *Alaska Magazine* and *Cirque Literary Journal*. Over the last few years, her photos have been in galleries from Juneau to New York. She has been a participant in the Pacific Northwest Drawers exhibit and Artworks

Northwest Biennial. Her work primarily features portraiture and street photography, but during the isolation because of Covid, she has been exploring textures in her beautiful Kenai Peninsula in South-central Alaska.

Jennifer Bisbing is an award-winning book editor and photographer originally from the Midwest, now living in Missoula. Raised by a renowned forensic scientist, Bisbing's murder mystery *Under the Pines* reveals childhood memories of trips to the crime lab. And in her forthcoming poetry chapbook *Sticky Menus*, villains still linger as she rummages through the high desert of Idaho and mountains of Montana. She currently writes for *Montana Quarterly*, edits for several publishers, and has poems published in several literary journals. Find her online at jenniferbisbing.com

Kristina Boratino was born and raised in the Pacific Northwest, where her wanderlust soul is quenched daily by surrounding beauty. Kristina has been published in *Cirque Literary Journal, Sonder Midwest Magazine, Compassion International Magazine, Route 7 Review*, and more. She resides in Edmonds, Washington with her two children.

Pacific Northwest native **Gretchen Brinck**, MSW, left Seattle at 14 when her family moved to California. After earning a 1964 BA in Creative Writing, Spanish and Religious Studies at Stanford, she worked in a Kansas mental hospital, then, was a VISTA Volunteer in the South. Later, she earned a Master's Degree in Social Work at Syracuse University, where she met and married "Brigham." They shared adventures in the Alaska Bush and had three children but divorced when their youngest was four months old. Returning to California, Brinck held bilingual social work positions until retiring in 2010. Her true crime book *The Boy Next Door* came out in 1999, and her short fiction appeared in obscure publications until she discovered *Cirque Journal*, which published several of her Alaska-focused essays. *The Fox Boy* recounts her Alaska child welfare work and her encounters with abuse, injustices against Alaska Natives, controversial adoptions, and the tragic Gabriel Fox disappearance. Now retired, Brinck lives in the Southwest with her long-time male partner, a paraplegic Viet Nam era veteran, who plays original, melodic guitar when she is writing.

Jack Broom is a Seattle native who retired in 2016 after 39 years as a reporter and editor at *The Seattle Times*. He earned a bachelor's degree from Western Washington University in 1974. His work in photography began in the 1970s as a reporter/photographer for *The Wenatchee World*, where he worked before being hired as a reporter at *The Seattle Times* in 1977. In recent years, his photographs have won awards at state-fair competitions in Washington and have been featured in previous issues of *Cirque*. He is currently President of the Puget Sound Camera Club, an affiliate of the Northwest Council of Camera Clubs.

Mark Burke's work has appeared or is forthcoming in the *North American Review, Beloit Poetry Journal, Sugar House Review, Nimrod International Journal* and others. His work has recently been nominated for a Pushcart prize. See: markanthonyburkesongsandpoems.com

Matt Caprioli is a tenure-track Lecturer in Professional Writing at Lehman College, City University of New York. He teaches courses in creative nonfiction, English composition and literature, queer literature, and professional communication. As a journalist, he has contributed to dozens of media outlets, including *The Anchorage Daily News, The Anchorage Press, Bushwick Daily, The Paris Review Daily, HuffPost,* and *The Red Hook Star-Revue*, where he was the Arts Editor. He has also written forewords for the classics imprint of Shakespeare & Co., summaries of business books for SuperSummary, served as a mentor in the publishing program at Columbia University, and ghostwritten two business books for c-suite executives. He is the author of the memoir, *One Headlight: an Alaskan Memoir* (Cirque Press; 2021), and has published fiction, poetry, and creative nonfiction in several anthologies and literary journals, including *Epiphany Literary Journal, Brevity, Best Gay Stories, Chicken Soup for the Soul, Understory, Newtown Literary,* and *Worn in New York,* which was adapted in episode four of the Netflix docuseries *Worn Stories,* written by Emily Spivack and produced by Jenji Kohan and Morgan Neville. He lives in Astoria, Queens with his partner, Adam, and is rebuilding a house on Lazy Mountain, Alaska.

Dale Champlin, an Oregon poet with an MFA in fine art, has poems published in *Willawaw, Visions International, San Pedro River Review, catheXis, The Opiate, Pif, Timberline Review* and elsewhere. Her first collection, *The Barbie Diaries,* was published in 2019. Three collections, *Leda, Isadora,* and *Andromina, A Stranger in America* are forthcoming. *Callie Comes of Age,* Dale's second full-length collection, was published with Cirque Press in 2021. Ever since her daughter married a bull rider, Dale's been writing cowboy poems. Memories of her early days hiking in the Black Hills of South Dakota, the bleachers at Pendleton Roundup, and summers camping at Lake Billie Chinook imbue her poetry with the scents of juniper and sage.

A native of Massachusetts, poet and food historian **Ann Chandonnet** retired to Lake St. Louis, MO. In 1965 Chandonnet, flew from graduate school in Wisconsin to Alaska to teach English at Kodiak High School. She fell in love with the state and returned with her husband Fernand and baby son Yves in 1973, remaining until 2006. For two years she was the weekly children's reviewer for the *Anchorage Daily News.* This was part of her preparation for writing her own children's books. Chandonnet's children's books include *Chief Stephen's Parky: A Year in the Life of an Athabascan Girl* (set among the Athabascans of the greater Anchorage area during the 1898 gold rush) and *Baby Abe: A Lullaby for Lincoln* (Cirque Press, 2021).

Nancy Christopherson's poems have appeared in *Helen Literary Magazine, Peregrine Journal, Raven Chronicles, Third Wednesday, Verseweavers* and *Xanadu,* among others, as well as various regional, national and international anthologies. Author of *The Leaf,* she lives and writes in eastern Oregon. Visit www.nancychristophersonpoetry.com

Nard Claar, nardclaar.com, nardclaar@gmail.com, promotes non-profits who value the environment, arts, and sustainable community. An avid cyclist, skier, and 2D and 3D artist. His work is currently exhibited in Colorado at 45 Degree Gallery, Old Colorado City, Academy Art & Frame, Colorado Springs, Manitou Art Center, Manitou Springs, and Stone, Bones, & Wood, Green Mt. Falls, as well as at Stephan Fine Arts in Anchorage, AK, Attic Gallery in Camas, WA, and the Encaustic Art Institute in Santa Fe, NM.

Janet Clemens is an Anchorage resident whose creative pursuits through photography and acrylic painting are often inspired by wildlife, landscapes, and colors.

Mark Crimmins's first book, a psychogeographical memoir, *Sydneyside Reflections,* was published in Australia on 10 June 2020. His fiction was nominated for 2015 and 2019 Pushcart Prizes, a 2015 Best of the Net Award, and a 2015 Silver Pen Authors Association Write Well Award. His short stories have been published in *Confrontation, Prick of the Spindle, Eclectica, Cortland Review, Tampa Review, Columbia, Queen's Quarterly, Apalachee Review, Pif Magazine, Del Sol Review,* and *Chicago Quarterly Review.* His flash fictions have been published in *Eunoia Review, Flash Frontier, Portland Review, Gravel, Eastlit, Restless Magazine, Atticus Review, Apocrypha & Abstractions, Dogzplot, Spelk, Long Exposure, Chaleur, Pure Slush,* and *Flash: The International Short-Short Story Magazine.*

Writer/artist **Monica Devine** is the author of *Water Mask,* a collection of reflective stories set in Alaska that touch on family, memory, perception, place, and culture. She is a Pushcart Prize nominee, a first-place winner of the Alaska State Poetry Contest, and her piece *On The Edge of Ice*

won first place in creative nonfiction with *New Letters journal.* She has authored five children's books and is published in four anthologies. See her essays, photographs and figurative ceramic work on her website Image Sculpture Verse at monicadevine.com.

Jennifer Dorner's poetry has appeared in *Chicago Quarterly Review, Clackamas Literary Review, Cloudbank, Sugar House Review, Timberline Review, The Inflectionist Review,* and other journals. In 2019, Dorner received 1st Place in the Oregon Poetry Association's spring contest, as well as 1st Place in the Willamette Writer's Kay Snow Award for Poetry. In 2020, she was long-listed for *Palette Poetry's* Sappho prize. Dorner received her MFA from Pacific University in January, 2020. She lives in Portland, Oregon.

Gene Ervine was privileged to grow up playing in the woods. He imagined the books he read, acting them out among the cedars and alders. Then at Western Washington State College, the Imagist Poets captured his attention along with Ferlinghetti, Gary Snyder and Kenneth Rexroth's translations of Asian poems he found in the campus bookstore. Since then, he tries to write clear and vivid poems. He lives in Anchorage where the spring mornings are brilliant, so crisp with bright snow and blue shadows.

Amelia Díaz Ettinger is a "Mexi-Rican" born in México but raised in Puerto Rico. As a BIPOC poet and writer, she has two full-length poetry books published: *Learning to Love a Western Sky* by Airlie Press, and a bilingual poetry book, *Speaking at a Time /Hablando a la Vez* by Redbat Press. A historical/environmental poetry chapbook, *Fossils in a Red Flag* is being released by Finishing Line Press, in 2021. Her poetry and short stories have appeared in literary journals and anthologies. Her short story "A Girl Like Me," won honorable mention this year by *Ice Colony.* Presently, Amelia Díaz Ettinger is working on an MFA in creative writing at Eastern Oregon University in La Grande Oregon.

Helena Fagan lives and writes poetry, memoir and young adult fiction in Juneau, Alaska and Cape Meares, Oregon. Her work is inspired by gratitude, the beauty of the places she lives, and by her mother's survival of the Holocaust. She most recently won the first Hoffman Center Poetry Contest for Poets of the North Oregon Coast and was a finalist for the Sally Albiso Poetry Book Award.

Kerry Dean Feldman is Professor Emeritus of Anthropology at the University of Alaska Anchorage, and co-founder of the Alaska Anthropological Association. His publications are found in British, Canadian, and U.S. books/ journals. Five Star/Cengage (Maine) will publish his Frontier Historical novel *Alice's Trading Post: A Novel of the West,* in January 2022. Cirque Press published *Drunk on Love: Twelve Stories to Savor Responsibly,* in 2019.

Chase Ferree (he/him) is a teacher in Seattle, WA. Originally from North Carolina, he's also lived in Missouri and Massachusetts. His poems have appeared or are forthcoming in *Emerge Literary Journal, Peripheries Journal, Juke Joint, Horse Egg Literary,* and elsewhere.

Leslie Fried turned to poetry after thirty years as a scenic artist in theater and film, and a muralist working in paint and plaster. Her writing reflects her love of imagery as a means for addressing difficult subjects. She draws on the themes of nature, death, love, family and history to weave her emotional tapestries. Her book *Lily Is Leaving: Poems by Leslie A. Fried,* was published by Cirque Press in 2021. Ms. Fried is Curator of the Alaska Jewish Museum in Anchorage. She has two sons, Daniel and Julien, and a granddaughter Sacha.

Brigitte Goetze lives in Western Oregon. A retired biologist and goat farmer, she now divides her time between writing and fiber work. She finds inspiration for both endeavors in nature as well as stories and patterns handed down from generation to generation. Yet, she always spins her own yarns. Links to her most recent publications can be found at: brigittegoetzewriter.com

A child of the Azores and Europe, **Paul Haeder** ended up in Arizona, in the Chiricahua Mountains as a newspaper reporter in Bisbee. He followed that avocation to Washington, Oregon, Mexico, Vietnam, Central America. He's widely published as a nonfiction writer, storyteller and poet. His collection of short stories, *Wide Open Eyes: Surfacing From Vietnam,* was published by Cirque Press in 2020. He's got novels under his belt, and lots of narratives from south of the USA border ready for unpacking. His penchant for social and environmental justice takes him places most people fear to travel. He's been a college teacher, social worker, homeless veteran advocate, faculty union organizer. He lives on the edge of the Pacific, in Oregon, with a wife, snake and cat. He was guest editor of the last *Cirque* (#22), with the special theme of Land Ethic/Sustainability as a highlight. He was recently appointed Projects Editor to *Cirque Journal.*

Jim Hanlen has published over 70 poems. He has poems printed recently in *Rattle, Cirque, Earth's Daughters* and *13 Chairs.* He retired from teaching in Washington and lives in Anchorage, Alaska.

Annekatherine Hansen: I grew up near the rugged Baltic Sea beaches in North East Germany. I funneled my creativity for eight years while attending Waldemar Kraemer's drawing and painting classes at Konservatorium Art School in Rostock, Germany. I also studied and received an Engineering degree and worked in Germany and Australia. I learned to interpret aerial photos and create all types of maps. In 2010 I moved to Alaska. In several workshops, I learned skills to sculpture, photograph, photo transfer, mixed media, paint and mosaic. Further self-studies and life changes led to my recent artwork.

Jennifer Healey is a high school teacher in Portland, Oregon. She has lived in just about every state that makes up the North Pacific Rim and is the granddaughter of Ketchikan pioneers. She has only recently publicly admitted to being a poet and hopes to publish her latest work, *Obituary: A Memoir,* before her next full trip around the sun.

Sarah Isto is a lifetime Alaskan and retired doctor living in Juneau. She is author of two non-fiction Alaska books. Her poetry has appeared in various journals including *Timberline Review, Tidal Echoes, Penwood Review, Minerva Rising, Gold Man Review* and *Cirque.*

Among **Brenda Jaeger**'s publications are: *Cirque; The Salal Review; Calyx, Written Arts*/King County Arts Commission; *Calapooya Collage 16; Fishtrap Anthology; Whole Notes; Lynx; Northwest Magazine/The Oregonian; Cowlitz County Advocate; Musher Monthly/Bethel;* and *8th Annual Collection of Haiku/WPA.* Her poetry readings include: Portland Poetry Festival Series, Quartersaw Gallery, Portland, OR; It's About Time Reading Series, Other Voices Bookstore, Seattle, WA; News from the Writing Life, Looking Glass Bookstore, Portland, OR; Fishtrap Gathering, Fellow Readings, Wallawa Lake; Walla Walla Children's Poetry Festival Presenter; and the *Calyx* 15th Birthday Party Reading at Conant & Conant's, OR.

Marc Janssen lives in a house with a wife who likes him and a cat who loathes him. Regardless of that turmoil, his poetry can be found scattered around the world in places like *Penumbra, Slant, Cirque Journal, Off the Coast* and *Poetry Salzburg.* Janssen also coordinates the Salem Poetry Project, is a Pushcart and Oregon Poet Laureate nominee. Cirque Press published his poetry collection *November Reconsidered* in July 2021.

Eric Gordon Johnson was born in Fairbanks and raised in Anchorage, Alaska. He earned an MFA in Creating Writing and Literary Arts in poetry at the University of Alaska, Anchorage. He won an honorable mention for a short story in University of Alaska, Anchorage and *Anchorage Daily News* writing contest. He published poems and a short story in *Cirque Literary Journal.* He also published a memoir in *Anchorage Remembers* published by 49 Writers. He is currently working on a novella.

Jill Johnson splits her time between Alaska and Eastern Oregon. Feels lucky.

Penny Johnson: I have lived in Washington since Mount Helens blew up & adventure did not stop there. I have degrees from The Evergreen State College & Goddard College. I have published in many small press journals & been a finalist for the Joan Swift Prize/*Poetry Northwest.*

Marilyn Johnston is an Oregon writer and filmmaker. Her poetry has been published in *Calyx, Natural Bridge, Poetica,* and *The War, Literature and the Arts Journal,* among others. She received a fellowship from Oregon Literary Arts and won the Donna J. Stone National Literary Award for Poetry, as well as a Robert Penn Warren writing competition award. Her poetry collection, *Before Igniting,* was published in 2020 (Rippling Brook Press). She is a creative writing instructor in the Artists in the Schools Program, primarily working with incarcerated youth.

Jan Jung lives in Bellingham, Washington with her husband. She enjoys walking in the woods, choral singing, photography, and visiting with her three children and five grandchildren. She has worked as a mental health counselor and an elementary/special education teacher for many years. Jan has a passion for capturing images that might otherwise go unnoticed. Her photos have appeared in *Cottage Magazine, Cirque,* and in the children's book, *Bridges Cloud.*

Jason Leslie: I live in Seward, Alaska with my wife and daughter in a small downtown home overlooking Resurrection Bay. I create highly colorful geometric landscape paintings in my home studio. My art can be seen in Rez Art in Seward and Dos Manos Gallery in Anchorage. I believe being an artist is more than just making art; it's supporting a culture and community of art making and appreciation. From working to bring artists into schools, to leading community mural projects, to serving on the Seward Arts Council, I strive to connect and inspire people via the power of visual arts.

Carol Levin lives in Seattle and is the author of three full collections: *An Undercurrent of Jitters* (MoonPath Press), *Confident Music Would Fly Us to Paradise* (MoonPath Press), and *Stunned By the Velocity* (Pecan Grove Press); also chapbooks, *Red Rooms and Others* (Pecan Grove Press) and *Sea Lions Sing Scat* (Finishing Line Press.) Her work's been widely published in journals, anthologies print, and online, in Russia, UK, New Zealand, Germany. As the US. Literary Manager of the former Art Theatre of Puget Sound, she, along with two Russians, translated Chekhov's four major plays. She's an Editorial Assistant at *Crab Creek Review.*

Julie Lloyd is a lifelong Oregon resident and a digital artist. She uses common objects and pressed plant life to create art enhanced by computer. Her work has been seen at Las Laguna art Gallery, Light Space & Time, *Eris and Eros, The Closed Eye Open,* and *Cirque Journal.* Julie has been creating art for over 20 years, and she credits her background in classical dance as inspiration, as well as her career in healthcare and the souls who have crossed her path.

Doug Margeson is a former newspaper reporter from Seattle, Washington. In his career as a newspaperman, Margeson won 184 regional and 28 national journalism awards; 212 in all. His first novel, *Gazing at the Distant Lights,* was published by W&B Books in November, 2019. Margeson's fiction short stories have been published in *The Chaffin Journal, The MacGuffin, 580 Split, Straylight, Worcester Review, The Homestead Review, SNReview, Soundings East* and *New Millennium Writings* magazines. His creative nonfiction has been published in *The Palo Alto Review* and *The Santa Clara Review.* His story "Gold Star Buckle" was nominated for the 2011 Pushcart Prize. His story "Barton's Pipe" was chosen for the anthology *Best Indie Lit New England, Vol. 2,* 2015. He has written two feature film screenplays and was a contributing screenwriter writer for a made-for-TV movie for Central Independent Television, London. Margeson has taught as a guest lecturer at the University of Washington and for the Pacific Northwest Writers Conference, the Washington Journalism Educators Association and the Washington Press Association. He served on the boards of directors of the Washington Press Association and the Western Washington Chapter of the Society of Professional Journalists, Sigma Delta Chi. In 1983, he was presented the press association's Superior Performance Award for his work with the state's student press. Margeson is a graduate of the University of Washington and served in the Marine Corps during the Vietnam War. He lives in Woodinville, Washington.

Joe McAvoy's essays, short stories, sport pieces, satire and poetry have appeared in *Catamaran, The Opiate, Timberline Review, The Sport Digest, Speculative Grammarian* and other literary journals and magazines in the US. He lives in Portland, Oregon, with his wife, Kyle, and English Lab, Rosie.

Frances McCue is an American poet, writer, and teacher. She has published four books of poetry and two books of prose. Her poetry collection *The Bled* (2010) received the 2011 Washington State Book Award and the 2011 Grub Street National Book prize. Three of her other books, *Mary Randlett Portraits* (2014), *Timber Curtain* (2017), and *The Car That Brought You Here Still Runs* (2014) were all finalists for the Washington State Book Award. In 1996, McCue cofounded Richard Hugo House, a literary organization in Seattle, where she served as the founding director for the organization's first decade. During that time, she researched Richard Hugo and the Pacific Northwest towns that inspired his poems. McCue is a professor at the University of Washington. http://www.francesmccue.com/

John McKay is pleased to be back in the pages of *Cirque*, though discouraged that our ability to engage in civil public discourse on issues that divide us has not dramatically improved in the 17 years since he wrote the poem appearing in this issue. In his law practice, he continues to represent journalists and others involved in First Amendment issues. He snacks constantly to ensure he has not lost his sense of taste to Covid. He is grateful to have survived the plague thus far, and for the love and inspiration that flows from family and friends.

Intrepid world traveler **Karla Linn Merrifield** has had 900+ poems appear in dozens of journals and anthologies, with 14 books to her credit. Following her 2018 *Psyche's Scroll* (Poetry Box Select) is the newly released full-length book *Athabaskan Fractal: Poems of the Far North* from Cirque Press. She is currently at work on a poetry collection, *My Body the Guitar*, inspired by famous guitarists and their guitars; the book is slated to be published in December 2021 by Before Your Quiet Eyes Publications Holograph Series (Rochester, NY).

James R. Merrill is a former high school and university-level writing instructor with an MFA in Writing & Poetics from Naropa Institute of Boulder, Colorado. He hails from the San Francisco East Bay community of Lafayette; and his cultural influences lean heavily on the Berkeley free-speech, anti-war movement. He taught literacy in Los Angeles for the Labor Immigrant Assistance Program, in China and at University of Colorado. He retired from Chemawa Indian School in 2014, and currently teaches "Self-Expressive Writing 1 & 2" using his own *Writing Manual: You're a Genius All the Time* in Salem, Oregon. He has published two volumes of poetry, *Blues Fall Down Like Rain* and *The Lust of Experience*.

Thomas Mitchell: I received my MA in English, Creative Writing from California State University, Sacramento, where I worked and studied with the poet, Dennis Schmitz. I studied with Richard Hugo and Madeline De Frees at the University of Montana where I completed my MFA in Creative Writing. My poems have appeared in numerous journals including *The New England Review, New Letters, California Quarterly, The New Orleans Review, Quarterly West*, and *The Chariton review*. My two collections of poetry, *The Way Summer Ends* (2016) and *Caribou* (2018) were published by Lost Horse Press. My new collection, *Where We Arrive*, is scheduled for release in the Spring of 2021. I was recently selected as the recipient of the 2020 *Cloudbank* Poetry Award.

Daniela Naomi Molnar is an artist, poet, and writer working with the mediums of language, image, paint, pigment, and place. She is also a wilderness guide, educator, and eternal student. She founded the Art + Ecology program at the Pacific Northwest College of Art and is a backcountry guide and founding Board member of Signal Fire. She can be found in Portland, Oregon, on public wildlands, or at www. danielamolnar.com / Instagram: @daniela_naomi_molnar

Rebecca Morse: Fairbanks, Alaska has been my home for over 30 years. Recently retired from a career in teaching and administration, nothing suits me better than to gaze out over the Alaska Range, read by the fire, fish in remote streams, visit with friends and neighbors, and immerse myself in all that Alaska offers. *Cirque Journal* has published some poetry of mine in the past. This is my first submission of nonfiction.

Susan Morse moved to the Willamette Valley in 2016 and is currently a member of the Oregon Poetry Association, as well as the Mid Valley Poetry Society. She frequently participates in readings through the Salem Poetry Project. *In the Hush*, her first chapbook, was published in 2019 by Finishing Line Press.

Anne Carse Nolting has published three Young Adult novels. Her nonfiction articles appear in periodicals; 2003 and 2005 Holt Language Arts textbooks, and *Measuring Up To The New Jersey State Standards in English*. Anne has participated in Alaska Sisters in Crime "Authors In the Schools" program. Presentations include YWCA Alaska Women Speak at the Anchorage Museum of History and Art, Young Writer's Conferences, and Literacy Festival for high school students. Anne presently lives in Vermont.

Al Nyhart: I received an MFA from the University of Montana and has been a painting contractor for over 40 years. My first book of poems, *The Man Himself*, was published by Main Street Rag Publishing Company in 2019.

Mary Odden has lived and worked in rural Alaskan places as a wildfire and aviation dispatcher, teen counselor, writing teacher, small newspaper owner/editor. Her work has appeared in journals and magazines, including *The Georgia Review, Alaska Quarterly Review*, and *Alaska Magazine* (November 2020). Odden's book of memoir/essays, *Mostly Water: Reflections Rural and North*, was published in June 2020 by Boreal Books/Red Hen Press. Odden received a Rasmuson Foundation Individual Artist Award in 2015, and an Alaska Literary Award from the Alaska Arts and Culture Foundation in 2020.

Monica O'Keefe is an Alaskan artist who paints both distant vistas and close-up views of the natural world. She is motivated by patterns of color and texture found outdoors, and intrigued by variations in scale from tiny to vast. She studies her surroundings while outdoors, and takes many reference photos for use in varying degrees of detail and accuracy for her acrylic paintings. Her work is influenced by her thoughts about mountains, clouds, sky, water, snow, wildflowers, birds, lichen, rocks, and other subjects of interest. Her paintings range from fairly realistic to whimsical to more abstract compositions.

Barbara Parchim lives on a small farm in southwest Oregon. Retired from social work she volunteered for several years at a wildlife rehabilitation and education facility. She enjoys gardening and wilderness hiking. Her poems have appeared (or are forthcoming) in *Ariel Chart, Isacoustic, The Jefferson Journal, Turtle Island Quarterly, Windfall*, and *Trouvaille Review*. Her first chapbook *What Remains* has been selected by Flowstone Press and will be published in October 2021.

Tami Phelps is an Alaskan mix-media artist using cold wax, oil, photography, assemblage, and fiber. Her work has exhibited in national and international exhibits and is included in the permanent collections of the Anchorage Museum at Rasmuson Center, and the Museum of Encaustic Art in Santa Fe, NM. She is a regularly invited Artist-in-Residence at McKinley Chalet Resort, Denali National Park, Alaska. She grew up in Anchorage, Alaska, where she works in her studio loft. Online at www.tamiphelps.com

Native New Yorker and long-time Seattleite **Diane Ray** hung up her shingle as a psychologist after 40 + years in behalf of if-not-now-when, expanded dedicated writing time. Her covid era work appears in: *Cirque, Canary, Sisyphus, What Rough Beast, Poems in the Afterglow*, and the anthologies *Voices Israel, Sheltering in Place*, and *Civilization in Crisis*.

Unexpected covid era consolations: a personal relationship with every neighborhood flower, bush, and tree with Ray suddenly a born-again gardener; her older daughter's family's pinch-me-is-this-real relocation nearby; exhilarating zooms to New York for primo ballet, Limon modern, and African dance classes.

Michael Eden Reynolds is a Canadian poet and mental health counsellor who, for 25 years, has made his home in the traditional territory of the Kwanlin Dün First Nation, and the Ta'an Kwäch'än Council, in Yukon. Michael's book, *Slant Room*, was published in 2009 by Porcupine's Quill. He has been anthologized in *Best Canadian Poetry*, and was awarded the Ralph Gustafson Prize, and the John Haines Award.

Richard Roberts' poem was submitted by his son Mark Roberts for his late father, Richard Roberts, who was born in Montana and lived there his entire life. When he passed away in 2007, he left behind a large volume of poetry. His poems have not been published nor submitted elsewhere. Richard was always a poet. He published an early anthology of his poems in 1944 while he was in his 20's and in later years his work appeared in *The Educational Forum, Christian Science Monitor*, and *High Country News*. He resided during the last three decades of his life in a log house that he built off the grid near Superior, MT.

Zack Rogow is the author, editor, or translator of more than twenty books or plays. His ninth book of poems, *Irreverent Litanies*, was issued by Regal House Publishing. He is also writing a series of plays about authors. The most recent of these, *Colette Uncensored*, had its first staged reading at the Kennedy Center in Washington, DC, and ran in London, San Francisco, and Portland. His blog, Advice for Writers, features more than 250 posts on topics of interest to writers. He serves as a contributing editor of *Catamaran Literary Reader*. **www.zackrogow.com**

Fred Rosenblum currently lives in San Diego with his wife of 48 years where they can typically be found tending to their community garden plot when they're not facetiming with their granddaughter in Boulder, CO. Fred's the author of four, largely autobiographical, collections of poetry and numerous individual pieces appearing in publications throughout the US and Canada.

Joel Savishinsky is a retired professor of anthropology and gerontology. He has studied human adaptations in the Canadian Arctic, Turkey, the Caribbean, the US, England and India. His books include *The Trail of the Hare: Environment and Stress in an Arctic Community*, and *Breaking The Watch: The Meanings of Retirement in America*, which won the Gerontological Society's annual book award. His poetry and essays have appeared in *The American Journal of Poetry, Atlanta Review, Blood and Thunder, California Quarterly, Cirque, From Whispers to Roars, The New York Times, Poetry Quarterly*, and *Windfall*. He lives in Seattle, helping to raise five grandchildren and as much political trouble as he can.

Tamara Sellman lives in the Pacific Northwest. Her hybrid collection, *Intention Tremor* was released by MoonPath Press in January 2021. Her most recent work has appeared, or is forthcoming, in *Burning House, Gargoyle, Conclave, The Coil*, and *Hunnybee*. Her work has been nominated twice for the Pushcart Prize and has earned other awards. She works as a sleep educator, healthcare writer, and MS advocate/columnist. In her spare time, she's an avid kitchen gardener.

Tom Sexton spends his days walking his Irish Terrier, Murphy, writing poetry, and making breakfast for his wife. Many years ago, he began the Creative Writing program at the University of Alaska, Anchorage and was the English Department Chair for many years. He is proud to say Mike Burwell was his student. His poetry collection *Cummiskey Alley: New and Selected Lowell Poems* was published in 2020 by Loom Press. *Snowy Egret Rising* from Chester Creek Press is coming out in 2022.

Ali J. Shaw has Rocky Mountain air in her blood, Alaskan mist on her face, and Pacific Northwest dirt on her boots. Her nonfiction has been featured in *The Manifest-Station, r.k.v.r.y., Hippocampus Magazine, Calyx,*

and the Get Nervous reading series, among others. Ali is an editor, a new mother to three children, and a doughnut aficionado. You can read more of her work at **www.ali-shaw.com**

Deborah Chava Singer is originally from California where she began sharing her photography publicly as a member of the creative writing and performance group, Queer Players. She now resides in Washington state. Her photography has been published in *Molecule Magazine, Harmony Magazine, Up the Staircase Quarterly, City Works Journal, Blue Mesa Review, Cirque*, and *Off the Coast* and included in shows in Oregon, Washington and beyond. In 2019 her photography series, "Trees," was displayed at the Olympic Mills Commerce Center (Portland, OR) and her first solo exhibition, "Road Stories" was at the Auburn City Hall Gallery (Auburn, WA). www.latenightawake.com

Merna Dyer Skinner's current and forthcoming poems appear in *The Baltimore Review, Rust + Moth, Caustic Frolic, Quartet, The Ekphrastic Review, Sulphur Surrealist Jungle* among other journals, and three anthologies. Her chapbook, *A Brief History of Two Aprons*, was published by Finishing Line Press (2016). Merna holds an MA in Communication Studies from Emerson College. She's lived in six U.S. states, and traveled to five continents.

Cheryl Stadig grew up meandering the woods, fields, and waterways of Maine before moving to Alaska where she continued these exploits in the environs of Teller, Anchorage, Ketchikan, and Prince of Wales Island (POW). These explorations, as well as the everyday adventures entailed in raising two sons on POW, are her major creative influences. Her work has been published in *Cirque, Inside Passages*, and other publications. She currently splits her time between Maine and New Hampshire.

Kathleen Stancik is a Northwest poet whose work has appeared in *Cirque, Windfall, Ekphrastic Journal, Twenty-Fourth, WA129+3 Digital Chapbook*, and others. She was a featured poet at the Inland Poetry Prowl in 2017 and was awarded the Tom Pier Prize by the Yakima Coffeehouse Poets in 2018. She enjoys reading, walking in the woods with her dog, and watching life unfold in her back yard.

Cynthia Lee Steele, a published poet and nonfiction writer and award-winning photographer, is an associate editor for *Cirque: A Literary Journal of the North Pacific Ri*m, and an occasional reader for Poetry Parlay. She has also, for a decade, read plays for the Valdez Last Frontier Theatre Conference.

Richard Stokes is a 50 year Juneau resident. He writes both prose and poetry. His work usually reflects his love of nature, his aging, and his boyhood in the sharply defined black-white world of rural Georgia in the 1940-50's. He graduated from Emory in Atlanta in 1961.

Doug Stone lives in Western Oregon. He has written three collections of poetry, *The Season of Distress and Clarity, The Moon's Soul Shimmering on the Water*, and *Sitting in Powell's Watching Burnside Dissolve in Rain*.

Sheary Clough Suiter grew up in Eugene, Oregon, then lived in Alaska for 35 years before her relocation to Colorado. Her encaustic fine art is represented in Anchorage, Alaska by Stephan Fine Art, in Camas, Washington by the Attic Gallery, in Santa Fe, New Mexico by the Encaustic Art Institute, in Green Mountain Falls, Colorado by Stones, Bones, & Wood Gallery, and in Old Colorado City, Colorado by 45 Degree Gallery. When she's not on the back-roads of America traveling and painting with her artist partner Nard Claar, Suiter teaches at Bemis School of Art, Colorado Springs Fine Art Center at Colorado College, and works from her studio in Colorado Springs. Online at www.sheary.me

Mark Thalman is the author of *The Peasant Dance, Catching the Limit*, and *Stronger Than the Current*. His poetry has appeared in *CutBank, Paterson Literary Review, Pedestal Magazine*, and *Valparaiso Poetry Review*, among others. Thalman received his MFA in Creative Writing from the University of Oregon, and he retired after 35 years from teaching

English and Creative Writing in the public schools. Thalman is a lifelong Oregonian and lives in Forest Grove. Further information can be found at markthalman.com

Russell Thayer's work will soon appear in *Evening Street Review, The Phoenix*, and *Close to the Bone*. It has appeared in *Hawaii Pacific Review, Potato Soup Journal, Pulp Modern*, and *Tough*. He received his BA in English from the University of Washington and worked for decades at large printing companies. He has cooked a lot of meals, watched a lot of French films, and currently lives in Missoula, Montana, with his wife of thirty-five years.

Jim Thiele worked as a photographer for a biological text book company for several years before moving to Alaska in 1974. He has worked for The Alaska Department of Fish and Game and the University of Alaska as a biologist. He is a recently retired financial advisor. His photographs have been seen in several publications, including *Alaska Magazine, Alaska Geographic*, and *Cirque*. He lives in Anchorage with his wife Susan. Taking photos forces him to stop and really see the world.

Gary Thomas is an amateur photographer living in Pacific Northwest.

Hamish Todd: A fan of writing since a teenager, I started two newspapers: *The Pioneer Square Independent & The Vashon Ticket* which ran for nearly 8 years and had a readership of 10,000. It grew and grew, a real writer's forum. In 1993 I read my poetry with Xavier Cavazos and Allen Ginsberg at The Act Theatre in Seattle. Some colleagues and I went and performed at The National Poetry Slam in San Francisco. We won the first round but went home disappointed. I've been writing poetry (and some prose) and reading out ever since.

Karen A. Tschannen: Some of her words have appeared in *Alaska Quarterly Review, Ice-Floe, PNW Poets and Artists Calendar(s), North of Eden* (Loose Affiliation Press), *The Sky's Own Light* (Minotaur Press), *Crosscurrents North, Cirque*, and other publications. She has been nominated for the Pushcart Prize, and her full-length poetry collection *Apportioning the Light*, was published by Cirque Press in March 2018.

Alex J. Tunney, contributing editor to *Pine Hills Review*, is a writer somewhere in downstate New York. His writing has been published in the *Lambda Literary Review, The Rumpus, The Billfold, The Inquisitive Eater, First Person Scholar* and *Complete Sentence*. You can keep up with them on Instagram at @axelturner.

Lucy Tyrrell sums her interests as nature, adventure (mushing and canoeing), and creativity (writing, sketching, photography, quilting). After 16 years in Alaska, where she worked as research administrator and science communicator for Denali National Park and Preserve, she traded a big mountain (Denali) for a big lake (Superior) when she moved to Bayfield, Wisconsin. She holds a PhD in botany and ecology from the University of Wisconsin-Madison. Lucy has published poems in a variety of journals and anthologies. She has published one chapbook *I Fly with Feathered Forelimbs* (2020), co-edits *Ariel Anthology*, and is Bayfield Poet Laureate 2020-2021.

Seward Soundboard (Cirque Press, 2020) is **Sean Ulman's** debut. He is working on a novel about senior citizens who start an ice cream truck business. He teaches writing in Seward. see www.seanulman.com & IG @sewardsoundboard

John Van Dreal is a published writer, musician, and an award-winning artist, with work featured in a number of notable collections. A jack of many trades and a master of some, he uses his creative vision and straightforward style of prose and poetry to explore both the darker and lighter sides of human behavior. He has spent three decades observing and adoring quirky people at their best and worst amid the backdrop of Salem, one of Oregon's most interesting towns. He lives with his wife, dog, and one cat. He is currently writing a novel.

A recipient of fellowships from Artist Trust and the Jack Straw Cultural Center, **Jeanine Walker** has published poems in *New Ohio Review, Prairie Schooner, Third Coast*, and other journals, and has a full-length collection forthcoming from Groundhog Poetry Press. She teaches poetry to children and adults in Seattle, WA, where she's lived since 2009.

Anne Ward-Masterson was born and raised in NH. She received her MLIS and worked as both a public and special collections librarian. After marrying into the military, she traveled just enough to know she wants to see more of the world.

Margo Waring has made Juneau her home for five decades, drawing inspiration from the community and its natural environment. Margo's poetry has appeared previously in *Cirque* and in other publications. Her poetry collection *Growing Older in this Place: A Life in Alaska's Rainforest* will be published by Cirque Press in 2022.

Alan Weltzien, a newly retired English professor in Montana, grew up in Puget Sound country and returns to Camano Island for part of every summer. He's published a couple of chapbooks and ten books, which include a memoir, *A Father and an Island* (Lewis-Clark Press, 2008), and three poetry collections, most recently *Rembrandt in the Stairwell* (FootHills Publishing, 2016). His most recently published poem, "Earth Day 2018," appears in the anthology, *Civilization in Crisis* (FootHills Publishing, 2021).

Matt Witt is a writer and photographer in Talent, Oregon. His photography and blog may be seen at MattWittPhotography.com. He has been Artist in Residence at Crater Lake National Park, Absaroka-Beartooth Wilderness Foundation, John Day Fossil Beds National Monument, Cascade-Siskiyou National Monument, Mesa Refuge, and PLAYA at Summer Lake, Oregon.

Tonja Woelber has lived in Alaska for forty winters, loving the mountains in all weathers. She is a member of Ten Poets in Anchorage.

Christian Woodard guides hunting, river and mountain trips with an emphasis on human accountability to land. His writing on similar topics can be found in *Gray's Sporting Journal, Artemis, Plough Quarterly*, and others.

Sandra Yannone published her debut collection *Boats for Women* in 2019 and will publish *The Glass Studio* in 2022 with Salmon Poetry. Her poems and reviews have appeared in print and online journals including *Sweet, Ploughshares, Poetry Ireland Review, Prairie Schooner, Impossible Archetype, The Blue Nib, Live Encounters, Women's Review of Books*, and *Lambda Literary Review* and have been nominated for the Best of the Net and Pushcart Prizes. She currently hosts Cultivating Voices LIVE Poetry on Facebook via Zoom on Sundays. Visit her at www.sandrayannone.com

In A Sunflower   Jack Broom

HOW TO SUBMIT TO CIRQUE

Cirque, published in Anchorage, Alaska, is a regional journal created to share the best writing in the region with the rest of the world. *Cirque* submissions are not restricted to a "regional" theme or setting.

Cirque invites emerging and established writers living in the North Pacific Rim—Alaska, Washington, Oregon, Idaho, Montana, Hawaii, Yukon Territory, Alberta, British Columbia and Chukotka—to submit short stories, poems, creative nonfiction, translations, plays, reviews of first books, interviews, photographs, and artwork for *Cirque's* next issue.

Issue #24—Submission Deadline closed September 21, 2021

Issue #25—Submission Deadline: March 21, 2022

SUBMISSION GUIDELINES

-- *Poems:* 5 poems MAX
-- *Fiction, Nonfiction, Plays:* 12 pages MAX (double spaced).
-- *Artwork and Photography:* 10 images MAX accepted in JPEG or TIFF format, sent as email attachments. Please send images in the highest resolution possible; images will likely be between 2 and 10mb each. If you do not submit full-size photo files at time of submission, we will respond with an email reminder. No undersize images or thumbnails will be eligible for publication.
-- *Bio:* 100 words MAX.
-- *Contact Info:* Make sure to keep your contact email current and be sure that it is one that you check regularly. If your contact information changes, make sure to inform us at *Cirque*. To ensure that replies from *Cirque* bypass your spam filter and go to your inbox, add *Cirque* to your address book.

-- Submit to https://cirque.submittable.com
-- Replies average two to three months after deadlines, and we don't mind you checking with us about your submissions.
-- *Cirque* requires no payment or submission fees. However, *Cirque* is published by an independent press staffed by volunteers. Your donations keep Cirque Press going. You will find donation buttons on Submittable and you can also support us via Paypal to cirquejournal@gmail.com.

Thanks for your poetry, prose, images and financial support.